SHOP AND LABORATORY INSTRUCTOR'S HANDBOOK

A Guide to Improving Instruction

Albert J. Pautler, Jr.

Allyn and Bacon, Inc.
Boston, London, Sydney

Previous edition published under the title *Teaching Shop and Laboratory Subjects*. Copyright © 1971 by Allyn and Bacon, Inc.

Library of Congress Cataloging in Publication Data

Pautler, Albert J
    Shop and laboratory instructor's handbook.

    First published in 1971 under title: Teaching shop and laboratory subjects.
    Bibliography: p.
    1.   Manual training—Methods and manuals.   I.   Title.
TT168.P38 1977   607'.1   77–9092
ISBN 0–205–05841–8

To: Margaret Pautler (October 22, 1900–   ),
*mother, teacher, friend, who always had or made
time when advice, assistance, or help was needed,
with great respect for the dignity of all people.*

Albert Pautler, Sr. (May 21, 1904–   ),
*father, teacher, friend, who always had the time
to teach those skills that he so well possessed
with an honest dignity for all work and workers.*

/

CONTENTS

PREFACE

This book should prove useful to shop and laboratory teachers in all service areas of vocational education and serve as a ready reference to both experienced and inexperienced teachers.

The first part of the book deals with the preparations a teacher should make before classes actually begin. Such things as objectives of education, school policies and services, and shop organization and management are covered. An in-depth discussion of lesson planning makes up Part II, which deals with not only organization of teaching materials, but also what should be taught. The third part covers the presentation aspect of teaching including first day procedures, the teaching-learning situation, and aids and methods of instruction. Part IV deals with both the theoretical and practical sides of evaluation and grading. Each chapter is followed by a listing of source materials that may be helpful to the reader.

The author would like to thank the many pre-service and in-service teachers with whom he had the opportunity to work in past years, including those at the State University of New York at Buffalo, Rutgers—The State University of New Jersey, and McGill University in Montreal. Special thanks are extended to Dr. Carl Schaefer, professor in the Department of Vocational-Technical Education, Rutgers University, for his encouragement and advice in the preparation of the original manuscript and his interest and support for this revision.

Special thanks must be extended to those vocational school administrators who provided and allowed for the use of the forms and materials included in this book: Mr. Edward Nicholson, principal, Oswego County Occupational Education Center, Mexico, New York; Mr. Donald Springle, superintendent, Camden County Vocational Technical Schools, Sicklerville, New Jersey; Dr. J. Henry Zanzalari, superintendent, Middlesex County Vocational and Technical Schools, East Brunswick, New Jersey; Dr. Donald Dayer, Director of Occupational Education, Board of Cooperative Educational Services, Erie County, New York.

Thanks also go to Dr. N. C. Alexander of Clemson University; Dr. James Sullivan of Southern Illinois University; Dr. William Wolansky of Iowa State University; Dr. Doyle Stewart of Lehigh University; Dr. John Cummings, Dr. Benjamin V. P. Verdile and Dr. Myron Corman of Rutgers—The State University of New Jersey for taking the time and interest to comment on a survey conducted before this revision was started.

The author would also like to thank Barbara Furmick, Patti Goralski, and Dr. Gerald Thomas for their assistance in the preparation of the original manuscript.

And finally, to you, the user. I hope that the book is of real value to you throughout your years in the teaching profession. Some twenty years of teaching experience have gone into the preparation of this book. My hope is that this time will benefit both you and your students.

Albert J. Pautler, Jr.

ACKNOWLEDGMENTS

Acknowledgment is gratefully made to Dr. William Wenzel, Assistant Commissioner of Education, Division of Vocational Education, New Jersey Department of Education, for permission to reprint the Hunterdon County Student Vocational Profile;

to Dr. Donald Dayer, Director of Occupational Education, Board of Cooperative Educational Service, Erie County, for the Equipment Specification Summary, Application for Occupational Education, Student Disciplinary Report, Interim Report to Parents, and Cosmetology Record;

to Donald Springle, Superintendent of Camden County Vocational and Technical Schools, for Day School High School Programs, Post-Secondary Programs, Progress Chart—Architectural Drafting, Progress Chart—Plumbing and Heating, and Student Progress Chart—Carpentry;

to Edward E. Nicholson, Principal, Oswego County Board of Cooperative Educational Services, for the Employability Profile, Heavy Equipment Operation Profile, Heavy Equipment Repair, and Dental Receptionist and Laboratory Assistant Profile;

to Dr. J. Henry Zanzalari, Superintendent, Middlesex County Vocational and Technical High Schools, for the Emergency Card; Pupil's Daily Program, Attendance Card, Student Receipt, Tardy Admission Slip, Shop Attendance Report, Time Lost Sheet, Permission to Visit Guidance Counselor, Visitor's Pass, Field Trip Permit, Report of Misconduct, Interview Request, Production Work, Bake Shop—Production Work, Standard Supply List, Safety Form, Accident Report Form, Instruction Sheet for Shop Substitutes, Shop Teacher Substitute Report, Lesson Plan, Applicant Blank, Report Card, Progress Chart, Student Appraisal Sheet, and Classroom Instructions for Substitutes.

PREPARATION

Part I

1

THE
TEACHING
ASSIGNMENT

GOALS FOR EDUCATION

As early as 1918, educators realized the importance of viewing the student as an individual. At this time, the Commission of the Reorganization of Secondary Education, established in 1913 by the National Education Association, issued a statement entitled *Cardinal Principles of Secondary Education*. The statement identified the following seven aims or principles of secondary education.

1. Sound health, knowledge, and habits.
2. Command of the fundamental processes (reading, writing, arithmetical computation, and oral and written expression).
3. Worthy home membership.
4. Education for a vocation.
5. Education for good citizenship.

6. Worthy use of leisure.
7. Ethical character.[1]

These aims are still important today. When asked what he taught, one teacher always replied, "Students." His responsibility was always to the student first and to subject matter second. The impact of the teacher-pupil relationship will be a much longer lasting one than that of the subject matter. The teacher should always remember that schools exist for students and not for teachers, principals, and guidance counselors.

If it were not for students, teachers and administrators would not be employed. Many experienced teachers have soured to the point of feeling sorry for themselves and developing the attitude that they are doing students a great favor by teaching. When a teacher feels this, he should get out of teaching before his negative attitude is conveyed to his students.

The National Education Association Commission on Educational Policies identifies the following *Ten Imperative Needs of Youth*.

1. All youth need to develop salable skills and those understandings and attitudes that make the worker an intelligent and productive participant in the economic life. To this end, most youth need supervised work experience as well as education in the skills and knowledge of their occupations.

2. All youth need to develop and maintain good health and physical fitness.

3. All youth need to understand the rights and duties of the citizen of a democratic society, and to be diligent and competent in the performance of their obligations as members of the community and citizens of the state and nation.

4. All youth need to understand the significance of the family for the individual and society and the conditions conducive to successful family life.

5. All youth need to know how to purchase and use goods and services intelligently, understanding both the values received by the consumer and the economic consequences of their acts.

6. All youth need to understand the methods of science, the influence of science on human life, and the main scientific facts concerning the nature of the world and of man.

7. All youth need opportunities to develop their capacities to appreciate beauty in literature, art, music, and nature.

1. Commission of the Reorganization of Secondary Education, *Cardinal Principles of Secondary Education* (Washington, D.C.: U.S. Office of Education, 1918), p. 10.

5

8. All youth need to be able to use their leisure time well and to budget it wisely, balancing activities that yield satisfactions to the individual with those that are socially useful.

9. All youth need to develop respect for other persons, to grow in their insight into ethical values and principles, and to be able to live and work cooperatively with others.

10. All youth need to grow in their ability to think rationally, to express their thoughts clearly, and to read and listen with understanding.[2]

If fulfilled, these needs would satisfy not only the objectives of vocational education but also the ultimate goal of most educational programs which is the development of a worthwhile citizen who can function in a democratic society.

A publication by the University of the State of New York entitled *Goals for Elementary, Secondary and Continuing Education in New York State* will serve as an example of state-level goals or objectives:[3]

The goal statements below reflect desirable conditions necessary for one to reach maximum fulfillment. *Achievement of the goals is not necessarily the responsibility of the school. Many also fall within the purview of the individual, the family, religious institutions, and the community at large.* The educational outcomes which follow each goal statement do indicate more directly what the responsibilities of the school are in attempting to achieve the goals. *They are not presented in any order of priority since they are all important as expressions of our aspirations for a fully educated person.* Differing priorities, reflecting regional differences, may well be determined at local district levels.

There are, however, three goals listed below as separate goals that are so pervasive they could just as well be considered part of every goal. These are the goals labeled "Basic Skills," "Knowledge," and "Values." Development of basic skills is essential to the accomplishment of the other goals and is generally agreed to be a primary responsibility of the school. Similarly, the achievement of each goal requires the acquisition of relevant knowledge, which also is promoted by instruction. Although value education may be treated as a separate "subject," values and the process of making value choices can be taught in connection with any goal. Indeed, it is virtually impossible to avoid value considera-

2. Educational Policies Commission, *Education for All American Youth.* (Washington, D.C.: National Education Association, 1944), pp. 225–226.
3. The University of the State of New York, *Goals for Elementary, Secondary and Continuing Education in New York State* (Albany, N.Y.: State Education Department, 1974), pp. 5–8.

tions in the presentation of any subject. Even the decision to be "value free" is itself a value. The school, therefore, cannot and should not avoid dealing with values. Recognizing this fact, the school should try to be as conscious as possible of the values it does communicate.

The educational outcomes that are the particular responsibility of the school are listed with each goal.

GOAL 1: MASTERY OF THE BASIC SKILLS OF COMMUNICATION AND REASONING ESSENTIAL TO LIVE A FULL AND PRODUCTIVE LIFE

    a. Communication skills (e.g., reading, writing, speaking, listening, and viewing)
    b. Computational operations (e.g., mathematical conceptualization, problem-solving, data collection)
    c. The logical process of thinking creatively, critically, and constructively in problem solving, planning, evaluation, analysis, research, etc.

GOAL 2: ABILITY TO SUSTAIN LIFETIME LEARNING IN ORDER TO ADAPT TO THE NEW DEMANDS, OPPORTUNITIES, AND VALUES OF A CHANGING WORLD

    a. Knowledge of contemporary society
    b. Knowledge of alternative futures
    c. Learning skills
    d. Personal planning skills
    e. Problem defining and solving skills

GOAL 3: ABILITY TO MAINTAIN ONE'S MENTAL, PHYSICAL, AND EMOTIONAL HEALTH

    a. Knowledge of good health habits and the conditions necessary for physical and emotional well-being
    b. Knowledge of the physical and health problems caused by drug addiction and other personally harmful activities

    c.   Knowledge of sound community health practices
    d.   Understanding body processes and functions
    e.   Development of physical fitness
    f.   Knowledge of safety principles and practices

*GOAL 4: UNDERSTANDING OF HUMAN
RELATIONS—RESPECT FOR AND ABILITY
TO RELATE TO OTHER PEOPLE IN OUR
OWN AND OTHER NATIONS—INCLUDING
THOSE OF DIFFERENT SEX, ORIGINS,
CULTURES, AND ASPIRATIONS*

    a.   Respect for and knowledge of other social, cultural, and ethnic groups
    b.   Understanding one's relationship to his natural, economic, and social environment
    c.   Respect for the community of man
    d.   Understanding of home and family relationships and involvement in the home, community and society in general

*GOAL 5: COMPETENCE IN THE PROCESSES
OF DEVELOPING VALUES—PARTICULARLY
THE FORMATION OF SPIRITUAL, ETHICAL,
RELIGIOUS, AND MORAL VALUES WHICH
ARE ESSENTIAL TO INDIVIDUAL DIGNITY
AND A HUMANE CIVILIZATION*

    a.   Knowledge of the diversity of values
    b.   Skill in making value-based choices
    c.   Commitment to one's own values and acceptance of diversity of values in society

*GOAL 6: KNOWLEDGE OF THE
HUMANITIES, SOCIAL SCIENCES, AND
NATURAL SCIENCES AT A LEVEL REQUIRED
TO PARTICIPATE IN AN EVER MORE
COMPLEX WORLD*

    a.   Knowledge of the basic methods of inquiry in each field
    b.   Interdisciplinary efforts to focus knowledge on problems

THE TEACHING ASSIGNMENT

8

*GOAL 7: OCCUPATIONAL COMPETENCE
NECESSARY TO SECURE EMPLOYMENT
COMMENSURATE WITH ABILITY AND
ASPIRATION AND TO PERFORM WORK
IN A MANNER THAT IS GRATIFYING TO
THE INDIVIDUAL AND TO THOSE SERVED*

    a. Developing work skills and habits
    b. Developing awareness of work opportunities
    c. Occupation selection
    d. Occupational training and retraining

*GOAL 8: KNOWLEDGE AND APPRECIATION
OF OUR CULTURE AND CAPACITY FOR
CREATIVITY, RECREATION, AND
SELF-RENEWAL*

    a. Knowledge of major art, musical, literary and drama forms
    b. Appreciation of the diversity of mankind's historic and cultural heritage
    c. Appreciation of beauty
    d. Development of individual creative talents
    e. Wise use of leisure time
    f. Promotion of increased use of and appreciation for community resources (museums, historic sites, performing arts groups, etc.) that reflect our cultural heritage and achievements

*GOAL 9: UNDERSTANDING THE
PROCESSES OF EFFECTIVE CITIZENSHIP
IN ORDER TO PARTICIPATE IN AND
CONTRIBUTE TO THE GOVERNMENT
OF OUR SOCIETY*

    a. Knowledge about political, economic, and legal systems with an emphasis on democratic institutions and on the global interdependence of these systems
    b. Knowledge of the American political process at national, State, and local levels
    c. Knowledge about taxation and fiscal policy
    d. Acquisition of citizenship skills:
        1. Decision making

PREPARATION

2. Group participation
3. Leadership and "followership"

*GOAL 10: KNOWLEDGE OF THE
ENVIRONMENT AND THE RELATIONSHIP
BETWEEN ONE'S OWN ACTS AND THE
QUALITY OF THE ENVIRONMENT*

a. Awareness of one's relationship to the environment
b. Preservation and wise use of resources
c. Understanding the effects on the environment of man's activities and values—lifestyles, technology, population growth, energy utilization, etc.

Goal number 7 listed above would be of special concern to vocational educators in New York State; however, each of the ten listed goals have implications for all educators. It would be a good idea to get a copy of the current goals or educational objectives of your state, province, or county so you could consider those that might be more appropriate to your needs. However, if you are unable to do this, I doubt whether they would vary much from those listed for New York State.

PHILOSOPHY OF VOCATIONAL EDUCATION

The phrase *occupational education* refers to an educational program specially designed to prepare the learner for employment upon completion of the program. It is used here to mean all the service areas associated with vocational education, including industrial arts, technical education, trade and industrial education, home economics education, as well as agricultural and health-related occupations. Industrial arts education was in the past considered part of general education but, with changes in federal funding and legislation, can be considered a significant component of a comprehensive vocational education program.

Evans defines vocational education as follows:

In its broadest sense vocational education is that part of education which makes an individual more employable in one group of occupations than in another. It may be differentiated from general education, which is of almost equal value regardless of the occupation which is to be followed.[4]

4. Rupert N. Evans, *Foundations of Vocational Education*. (Columbus, Ohio: Merrill, 1971), p. 1.

A New York State paper defines occupational education as follows:

> We define occupational education as that part of the educational process which prepares people for occupations requiring less than the baccalaureate degree. However, occupational education in its broadest sense should be seen as an aspect of the total educational process.[5]

The author in a paper dealing with a research project on self-evaluation by local programs defines vocational education as follows:

> The (vocational) education program provides education and training in specific occupational areas, closely following industrial and technical practices in private industry. The *primary purpose* of the program is to make an individual more employable in one group of occupations than in another. Completion of a program should prepare individuals for gainful employment as semi-skilled or skilled workers, technicians, or subprofessionals in recognized occupations and in new and emerging occupations, or to prepare individuals for enrollment in advanced technical programs.[6]

One could continue to cite any number of statements or philosophies dealing with vocational education as well as the service areas involved in the total picture. The reader is urged to obtain the approved definition of vocational education for his or her own situation.

THE STATED OBJECTIVES OF YOUR SCHOOL

Most schools have some general statement of philosophy as well as stated objectives that guide their operation. You might want to ask the principal about the school philosophy and stated objectives that influence the faculty, students, and curriculum of your school. The stated philosophy and objectives should be developed by faculty, student, and community committees working together to provide the best and most meaningful program for the students. When a problem is being evaluated, it should be evaluated in terms of the stated objectives. An agreement and a common effort should be made by all staff members to carry out the stated objectives.

5. Regents of the University of the State of New York, *Occupational Education* (Albany, N.Y.: State Education Department, 1971), p. 6.
6. Albert J. Pautler, "Establishing Measurable Objectives for the Self-evaluation of the Local Vocational Education Program: A Case Study" paper presented at the American Vocational Association Conference in New Orleans, December 10, 1974, p. 7.

11

The following list is an example of one school's statement of the functions of the high school curriculum:

1. To help every student grow up successfully in our society through meeting and carrying out his developmental tasks.
2. To teach the essential understandings, habits, and attitudes necessary for good physical health.
3. To make available to each student a chance to sample a variety of recreational activities and interests and to develop skill in some of them.
4. To provide each student with vocational guidance and that part of occupational education needed for vocational effectiveness in the world of work.
5. To evaluate community provisions for health, recreation, housing, employment, etc., to call attention to needs and lacks in these areas, and to promote community action where needs and lacks exist.
6. To provide in all aspects of school life a living example of the first principle of democratic human relationships—respect for the dignity of the human individual.
7. To teach the skills of democratic group planning and discussion.
8. To teach the skills of reflective thinking and group problem solving.
9. To support the family as an institution by a realistic study of the problems and difficulties confronting the family today. To work with homes, churches, and other agencies on these problems.
10. To develop an understanding of world-wide social problems and a sense of responsible concern for our country's role in world affairs.
11. To develop a sense of responsibility and concern for the welfare of the local community.
12. To study continuously the meaning of democracy, to create awareness of needs for enrichment of that meaning, to protest against violations of the basic democratic faith.
13. To help students begin to formulate values and standards.
14. To help students continue developing needed proficiency in various skill areas—language skills, number skills, consumer skills, etc.

The following two examples taken as before and after situations will illustrate how one vocational school modified its objectives to facilitate self-evaluation. The following were listed as school goals before being modified by the teachers and approved by the board of education.

1. To make optimal use of Craft Advisory Committees and Community Resource Personnel.
2. To promote and distribute information explaining program opportunities and structure.
3. To promote and develop flexibility of program structure and to extend program offerings to all who want them.
4. To develop and coordinate programs of continuous placement and follow-up for all enrollees in occupational programs.
5. To educate youth for immediate and emerging employment opportunities.
6. To encourage youth and adults to seek post-high school education and/or additional occupational training.
7. To provide a continuous program of evaluation of services.

Such statements are of such general nature that the task of evaluation was difficult if not impossible. The administration and staff, with the assistance of a consultant, rewrote the statement, setting the following objectives for their program.

1. Upon completion of an occupational education program, 65 percent of the students will rate the experience satisfying.
2. Upon completion of an occupational education program, 65 percent of the students will indicate that they would tend to take the same program again if they had to make the choice over again.
3. Upon completion of an occupational education program, 60 percent of the students, available for employment or advanced education, will indicate that they plan to enter the area of specialization they prepared for or go on to advanced training/education in their area of specialization.
4. Seventy-five percent of the graduates of any licensed occupation program will pass the appropriate examination.
5. Within six months after graduation, 60 percent of the graduates available for and having sought employment will be employed full-time.
6. Within six months after graduation, 35 percent of the graduates available for and having sought employment in their specialization will be employed full-time in their area of specialization.
7. Within six months after graduation, another 15 percent of the graduates available for and having sought employment in their

specialization will be employed in a full-time position they consider related to their area of specialization.

Many more examples of local vocational goals could be stated at this time. It is important to get a copy of the philosophy and objectives of the school you are planning to teach in or are already employed in. Every teacher should be familiar with those objectives, since they set the tone for the educational program of the school.

In Part II, we will be concerned with determining what to teach. The subject will then be the stated objectives of your particular course, be it mechanics, cosmetology, practical nursing or other specialization. Thus, a concern with the objectives that influence the total school are an important consideration.

Of course, your request to see the stated philosophy and objectives of the school might be met with a blank stare from the principal. It is possible, but not probable, that the school is operating without any clearly written statement of objectives. If this is the case, your request might prompt a committee to develop such a statement. As stated earlier, a statement of this nature should come about as a result of faculty, student, and community involvement. All parties involved should be actively engaged from the start in the development of the philosophy and stated objectives.

THE SCHOOL ADMINISTRATION

Wherever you teach, you will want to become well acquainted with your building administrator. In most cases, he or she will carry the title of principal. The principal can be invaluable in helping teachers see their roles and recognizing individual abilities. He can show teachers how they are a part of the total curriculum and engender a concern on the part of his staff members that extends beyond the scope of each special area and encompasses the broader interests of the school.

A principal is a human being with inherent strengths and weaknesses. Because the principal is in a position of authority, he or she comes under much pressure from forces both within and outside the school. Please remember this in your relationship with him. The principal assumes the responsibility for the quality of the total program in the school. It is, therefore, one of his most important functions to see that the program meets all of the standards required of a total curriculum. In the vocational setting, this means that the program is designed to meet the educational needs, both short and long term, of all the students enrolled. This, in turn, means that students of widely varying interests and abilities should be able to find a satisfying and worthwhile educational experience within the framework of the subject offerings.

The principal may not be well versed in every subject area offered in his school; however, he is expected to see that the offerings do meet the needs of the students and the society in which they will ultimately find employment. This requires that he, as the educational leader of his school, know his students and the community from which they come, in addition to the community into which they will most likely go upon graduation. From these understandings should grow the educational objectives on which the curriculum and its related learning experiences are based. The principal must see to it that the educational objectives of the program are stated in such a way that the outcomes may be objectively and accurately measured.

As teachers evaluate their own progress and come up with suggestions for improvement, the principal can be instrumental in making their innovations work by providing them with assistance in implementing their ideas. It is the principal's responsibility to create a suitable climate in the school to foster the best educational system possible. The teachers can help or hinder the principal in this.

FELLOW STAFF MEMBERS

The relationship established with other staff members is as important as the relationship with the principal. At times during the school year, you, no doubt, will be asked to serve on various committees in the school. These committee assignments will give you the opportunity to interact in a professional relationship with other teachers and administrators. Use caution in the extent to which social relationships develop with administrators. Let the administrator establish the rules and the name of the game. Some teachers have established social relationships that later resulted in school relationship problems. Look on fellow staff members and yourself as members of a team that functions to provide the best educational program possible for the students.

THE STUDENTS

As stated earlier, schools exist for students and not as employment locations for administrators and teachers. You are employed as a teacher because students seek an education.

PREPARATION

The student population of the school will determine the atmosphere that exists in the school. How administrators and faculty treat students will also affect the school's atmosphere.

As a teacher, you have contact with students on a one-to-one basis, in small groups, and in class. Your relationship with students will largely determine your success or failure in the teaching profession. You will function as teacher, counselor, and personal advisor to students in your day-to-day activities.

Always respect the dignity of the individual in your relationship with students. They are human beings first, and your students second. Treat each student as you would like to be treated. Try to be firm, fair, and consistent in your relationship.

You might consider the teacher as a kind of educational coordinator. As the instructional manager of the learning environment, the teacher is responsible for coordinating the three basic functions of teaching: diagnosing, prescribing, and presenting. The students are the center of the learning situation and the teacher's concern is to diagnose, prescribe, and present information based on the ability and interest of every student in his class.

PERSONAL APPEARANCE

No matter what shop or laboratory subject you teach, enter and leave the school just as if you were teaching English, history, or mathematics. Just because you are a shop specialist, it does not mean that you come to work dressed any differently than the principal or related-subjects teachers.

If a shop coat is necessary in your shop, keep it clean and in suitable condition. You are on daily display to your students and fellow faculty members. If you, as the teacher, wear dirty shop clothes, they will follow your lead and take the same privilege.

Many automotive mechanics and machine shop teachers look as if they have their shop coats cleaned yearly; others always appear to have a clean, well-fitting shop coat. In most cases, the students reflect the style established by the teacher.

Maintain a suitable personal appearance and encourage the same from your students. They are preparing for the world of work as well as for life in general. Teach them good work habits as well as good personal habits. Remember you are a teacher, not a plumber, baker, or cosmetologist. You are employed as a teacher first, and as a subject matter specialist second.

SUMMARY

In this chapter, some of the basic educational philosophies and goals have been discussed along with more specific goals and objectives for the vocational education program. Consideration was also given to the philosophy and objectives of the local school program. The basic purpose of this chapter was to point out to the reader the importance of the philosophy and goals or objectives of the educational program, since the curriculum should be based on such statements. Every teacher should ask to see the philosophy statement and the objectives of his school.

Basic material was presented dealing with the administration of the school, fellow staff members, and the students. Brief mention was also made of the importance of personal appearance.

A good source book on the historical background of vocational education is Evans' Foundations of Vocational Education, *which is listed in the Source Materials at the end of this chapter. The Evans book concentrates on basic principles affecting all of human resources development of which occupational education is a fundamental component.*

SOURCE MATERIALS

Barlow, Melvin L. *History of Industrial Education in the United States.* Peoria, Ill.: Bennett, 1967.

Evans, Rupert N. *Foundations of Vocational Education.* Columbus, Ohio: Merrill, 1971.

Leighbody, Gerald B. *Vocational Education in America's Schools.* Chicago: American Technical Society, 1972.

Nystrom, Dennis C. *Occupational and Career Education Legislation.* Indianapolis: Sams and Co., 1973.

Report of a Special Task Force to the Secretary of Health, Education, and Welfare. *Work in America.* Cambridge, Mass.: Massachusetts Institute of Technology Press, 1973.

Venn, Grant. *Man, Education, and Manpower.* Washington, D.C.: American Association of School Administrators, 1970.

Venn, Grant. *Man, Education, and Work.* Washington, D.C.: American Council on Education, 1964.

SHOP
ORGANIZATION AND
MANAGEMENT

The vocational teacher, by the nature of the assignment, will spend the major part of the teaching day in a shop or laboratory. Shop teachers need more organizational and management skills than do English, mathematics, and social studies teachers, not in subject matter, but in facility management and organization. There is a great deal more involved in a shop situation than in an academic classroom.

It would be nice if school districts *required* and *paid* shop teachers to come in a week or two before school started to organize the shop. This, unfortunately, is usually not the case. However, you might still consider spending a week organizing the shop to suit your needs. Being well organized the first day of school will make you more comfortable and certainly better prepared to meet your students.

Many books have been written about shop organization and management and much has been written about designing and planning new voca-

I. To provide programs beginning in grades K–8 that will make youth aware of the world of work and their work role in life.

II. To provide youth starting with grades 7–9 with exploratory and prevocational programs and experiences geared to vocational development tasks.

III. To provide youth in grades 10–12 with work attitudes and job entry skills in broad occupational clusters and/or the foundation for more specialized post-secondary education.

IV. To provide post-secondary youth with specific skills and attitudes for employment.

V. To provide entry skills and job upgrading skills to adults in, or desiring to enter, the labor force.

VI. To increase the accessibility of vocational programs for those populations to be served.

VII. To provide assistance to students in vocational development tasks and provide vocational counseling services, including initial job placement, to populations served by, or to be served by, vocational education.

VIII. To provide persons served by vocational education with skills, attitudes, and competencies compatible with the present and future needs of Georgia's employers.

IX. To provide adequate financing for vocational education and distribute funds in an equitable and effective manner that will provide incentive for expansion and quality.

X. To provide an adequate supply of competent educational personnel to operate vocational programs and to continually upgrade their abilities through inservice programs.

XI. To assist consumers to make wise use of income, improve the home environment and improve the quality of family life.

XII. To contribute to the holding power of educational agencies.

XIII. To provide leadership and consultation to local education agencies in program operations, program planning, and evaluation.

XIV. To interweave vocational education with a total educational system that will educate the whole person.

XV. To improve the public understanding of and attitude toward vocational education.

XVI. To provide for the rapid dissemination of innovations to keep vocational programs up-to-date.

XVII. To increase the meaningful and constructive involvement of local citizens, parents, students, local educators, and employers in the planning, operation, and evaluation of vocational education.

FIGURE 2-1. *Goals for Vocational Education (Georgia)*
Georgia Department of Education 1971

tional-technical facilities. If you are asked to plan a new facility, consult the references listed at the end of this chapter. This chapter is written mainly as a guide to the teacher who will be teaching in a shop someone else designed and organized for teaching.

Ideally, the shop organization as well as the curriculum should be based on the educational philosophy and objectives of the state and school district. The materials that went into the construction of the school as well as the equipment and supplies available for the instructional program should ideally all be based on the philosophical tenets of the educational program. The Goals for Vocational Education in Georgia (Figure 2-1) serve as some direction for the educational program in Georgia. The schools and vocational programs that develop in Georgia should be based on these goals and those of the local school district that will sponsor the vocational education program.

As a new teacher you may be forced to adjust to the philosophy and objectives of the school in which you are employed. In many cases you may be far removed from the ideal situation. However, you, the teacher, are the prime mover for creating the best educational situation with what is available.

THE PHYSICAL FACILITY

One of the most important features of your teaching will be the shop or laboratory. The physical plant, as it is sometimes called, is part of the learning environment, and you should do as much as possible to make it attractive to the students. Ask yourself, "Will students want to work and learn in the shop atmosphere?" The impression left with the student when he enters the shop for the first time is important. This does not mean you should create a home-like atmosphere of comfort, but rather an industrial atmosphere designed for work, as attractive as possible for the particular specialization. Try to create a physical plant that makes students say, "Let's go to work."

Your primary concern should be the safety of the students in your shop. It is your responsibility as teacher to be concerned with the physical well-being and safety of the students in your class. The physical layout of the shop should provide safe work areas, walk zones, and independent study areas. Any experience from industry will be helpful in this area.

Arrange equipment and machines to promote safe walk areas in the shop and a work area around each piece of equipment. Pay special attention to the traffic areas of the shop. Is there sufficient walk space to the tool panel and the storage areas in the shop? Does student movement in the shop cause unsafe working conditions at some of the stations? Is there sufficient work space for each student and for every work station?

Another important physical facility is the instructional area or center. The total shop facility, of course, is used for instructional purposes, but is there an area that can be used for formal lesson presentations? One suitable arrangement would be a small classroom adjoining the shop with glass separating the two. The glass wall between makes it possible for students to be at work in the shop while others are engaged in independent study or research in the classroom. The teacher, while in the shop, is able to see what is going on in the classroom. This is the ideal situation, but you might not be in such a situation. In that case, develop a lecture area within the shop. You need proper seating facilities, a chalkboard, a movie screen, and shades to darken the area for slides and movies. Make the instructional areas as comfortable as possible both for the students and for yourself.

Color can add to the appearance of your shop. Lines painted on the floor can be used to outline safety zones, work areas, and walk zones. Color coding of tools and safety devices on machines and equipment can be a useful control device as well as a safety feature in your shop. If you find yourself in an old shop, the addition of some paint may help improve its general appearance.

Heating, lighting, and ventilation should be a daily concern of every teacher. Make every effort to assure the comfort of your students. Good lighting is necessary both for safety and for the accuracy of the work students are engaged in. A certain amount of fresh air is needed even on the coldest day. Your attention to these small details will help to promote a good teaching-learning situation.

If you are planning a new shop facility, seek expert advice from someone engaged in shop planning activities. New facilities should be designed that are flexible enough to meet the changing needs of a technological society. The most up-to-date shop may be outdated in five or ten years if flexibility of design is not considered during the planning stages. Wide open spaces with movable walls are most appropriate for modern shops. Electrical grids in the floor assure that equipment and machines can be moved. The emerging occupations of tomorrow should be our concern in planning shops for today's schools.

Equipment

The adequacy and safety features of the shop equipment will be a major concern of the teacher. Check out each piece of equipment for proper operation as well as safety before allowing students to operate it. It is your responsibility to maintain the equipment and make sure the proper safety guards or features are operational. Students, likewise, should be instructed to report any damaged equipment immediately to the instructor.

It is the teacher's responsibility to make sure the necessary preventive maintenance is performed on the equipment as stated in the instruction booklet. It is wise to keep a maintenance log book for each piece of equipment. Students can and should be assigned to do the maintenance after receiving proper instruction, but it is the instructor's responsibility to make sure it is properly done.

The teacher is also responsible for equipment repair. If the repairs qualify as a learning experience for the students, they can be done during class time. If not, the instructor can do the repairs after class, or request an outside source to do them. Always remember your major function is instructor, not repairman.

You may want to consider color coding the equipment. This might be as simple as putting red paint on the safety guards and green paint on the control functions. Markings on the floor may be used to indicate the work zone of the machine operator. Allowing no one but the operator in the work zone at any one time tends to keep two students away from any piece of equipment at the same time and is a safety feature.

How the equipment is placed in the shop is important. As a new teacher in an old shop, you may not have much control over equipment location. At least give the layout a fair trial before requesting any major movement of wiring and equipment.

Establish a priority listing of new equipment or replacements needed to keep your shop up to date. Do not be afraid to ask for new equipment, but be able to justify the request.

The equipment specification summary (Figure 2-2) used by the vocational centers operated by the Board of Cooperative Educational Services of the First Supervisory District of Erie County, New York, is an example of the type of justification needed to support a teacher request for new equipment. This is a reasonable type of statement to expect of a teacher requesting equipment for the shop. The justification in terms of the curriculum is particularly important, and the key question is what improvement in the program will result with the new piece of equipment. Note that letters of support are also requested on the form. If you have an active advisory committee in your specialization, request their support in the form of a written endorsement that the equipment is needed to improve the existing program.

BOARD OF COOPERATIVE EDUCATIONAL SERVICES
First Supervisory District, Erie County

EQUIPMENT SPECIFICATION SUMMARY

LOCATION_____ DIVISION_____

EQUIPMENT DESCRIPTION _____

_____

JUSTIFICATION OF NEED IN CURRICULUM: _____

_____

_____

_____

_____

SPECIFICATIONS: (Attach additional sheets if necessary)

_____

_____

_____

_____

_____

GENERAL: Useful Life Expectancy _____ Estimated Cost $_____

            New or Replacement _____ Annual Student Use _____
                                                                    (Total Hours)

            Other _____

SAFETY FEATURES: _____

_____

COMMENTS:_____

_____

Attach any letters, etc. in support of this justification

Initiator _____ Principal_____

Date _____   Date _____

FIGURE 2-2. Equipment Specification Summary

Hand Tools

Students should be instructed to report any unsafe or damaged hand tools to the instructor, but it is the instructor's final responsibility to make sure the tools are in safe operating condition. It is a good idea to have some system of marking or color coding tools to identify in what shop they belong. Some tools of a special nature will be found in only one shop, but others may be common to more than one shop. Color coding or marking is a good tool control device and should be helpful to the smooth operation of the shop.

Hand tool storage can be a problem. Many shops still use tool cribs and, as a student needs a tool, he checks it out of the tool crib. Other shops may have tool cabinets or storage areas that are available to all students. Some form of daily inventory must be used with either system. Each week a different student should be assigned to check the tools at the beginning and again at the end of the class period. Any missing or damaged tools should be reported to the instructor.

If an existing tool crib is used for storage, not much can be done about its location. If tool storage cabinets or wall panels are used, some rearrangement is possible. The tool storage area should be easily accessible to everyone in the shop. However, student traffic in this area should not cause unsafe working conditions.

If there is a tool crib in the shop and you decide to have one student sign out tools, make the experience a learning one. Can you justify having a student spend two or three hours per day in the tool crib? If your answer is yes, at least make sure that the tool crib assignment is rotated on a weekly basis.

The instructor is responsible for the repair or replacement of defective hand tools. A tool inventory at the beginning and end of each school year can be helpful. Each year, order tools to replace those lost or damaged during the past school year.

Depending on the shop you are teaching, students may ask to borrow various hand tools for home use. Before loaning tools, it is wise to check with the principal if any school-wide policy exists dealing with the subject. If you are allowed to loan shop tools on an overnight basis, develop a shop loan slip that the student makes out and signs. It should state what tool he is taking, the date he will return it, and, if damaged or lost, that he will replace it.

MIDDLESEX COUNTY VOCATIONAL AND TECHNICAL HIGH SCHOOLS
STANDARD SUPPLY LIST — SCHOOL YEAR 19

Date_____ School_____ Dept. or Shop _____ Teacher_____

Category_____

Item	Quantity	Description *Give complete description including sizes, types, catalog data, etc.*	Unit Cost	Total

FIGURE 2-3. Standard Supply List

Supplies

The ordering, storage, and inventory of supplies is another task faced by the shop teacher. Most vocational schools require teachers to submit an annual order for their particular shop. In addition, it is usually possible to submit smaller purchase orders during the normal course of the school year. However, it is usually to the best advantage of all parties if the needs for the total school year can be anticipated in advance and ordered on the annual order. The Standard Supply List (Figure 2-3) is a typical form used by schools for ordering shop supplies.

If you maintain a monthly inventory of supplies, it should be easy for you to anticipate the demand for various items. Your inventory sheet actually becomes a "needs" list and makes the preparation of your annual order a less demanding task.

Maintain good security on all your supplies. It is a good idea to keep them under lock and key when you leave the shop. Your policy concerning student use of supplies should be made clear to students early in the school year. Are students allowed to take supplies directly from the storage area? Are they supposed to ask the instructor for supplies? Whatever your decision or policy is in regard to supplies, be consistent in the enforcement of the policy.

Lecture Area

Many times lesson presentations in the shop involve a demonstration on a certain machine or special piece of equipment. At other times, lessons and class discussions are carried on in a more formal setting in a lecture area of the shop. Set up a lecture area in the shop if an attached classroom is not available for your use. The best arrangement is a classroom attached to the shop and divided from it by windows. This allows the teacher to be in the shop but still able to supervise students involved in report writing or research in the classroom.

If your lecture area is in the shop, you can still do a number of things to make it a suitable instructional area.

Adequate seating facilities for all students should be provided. Do not require students to sit on work benches during your lesson and discussion periods. The seating that is provided should be movable and have suitable space for writing. Arrange the seating area so that students will not have to face a window. A seating arrangement in which the window area is to the left or right of the seating area is most favorable. Adequate chalkboard and bulletin board space should be available in the lecture area.

SHOP ORGANIZATION AND MANAGEMENT

You will want to use visual aids from time to time during your presentations. These visual aids may include the use of the overhead projector, filmstrip projector, slide projector, and movie projector. If you plan to use visual aids often, it is reasonable to request that a permanent screen be provided in the lecture area. In addition, window shades or blinds on the windows are needed to darken the shop.

You will need some type of bench or movable cart to put your lecture materials on during the presentation. This bench or cart should be positioned so that it is visible to all the students.

As you start using the lecture area, you will no doubt want to make various modifications. Ask your students for their reactions. Ask them for recommendations that might result in a still better lecture area. After all, you as the instructor see only from one side of the desk; the students observe from the opposite side—the most important side.

SHOP SAFETY

It is essential that you be prepared on the first day of school with a list of safety rules or regulations. Do not allow students to start any shop work whatsoever until after some basic instruction in safety procedure has been given to them.

The list of rules may be general safety regulations that apply to all shops and laboratories in the school and to specific regulations for your shop or laboratory. It is possible that a set of rules of the general type has been developed and is used by all teachers in the school. Find out about your school's shop safety regulations.

No one list of general shop rules will meet the requirements of all schools or all shops. You may want to consider the following rules in developing your own list.

1. Do not run in the shop.
2. Do not throw any object in the shop.
3. Report all accidents, no matter how minor, to the instructor immediately.
4. Always wear the proper eye glasses or shields as required by law and your instructor.
5. Never use a machine without the approval of your instructor.
6. Never ask to operate a piece of equipment on which you have not received instruction.
7. A business-like atmosphere should exist in the shop. Horseplay will not be tolerated.

8. Clean machines after use.
9. Return unused materials to their proper storage areas.
10. Do not make adjustments on machines while they are in operation.
11. Use appropriate safety devices on the machine you are operating.
12. If in doubt about procedure or the operation of any machine, check with your instructor.

In addition to the general shop rules or regulations, you should develop a more specific set of rules for your specialization. It is impossible to list all the rules concerning safe work practices in the school shop. Your shop, the level of students, and the kind of instructional activities that go on will all determine the kinds of safety regulations required for a safe shop. An electronics shop will have one set of regulations and the cosmetology laboratory, another set.

Before any student is allowed to work in class, you should review the safety regulations with the students and make sure that they understand them and agree to follow them.

It is a good idea to ask each student to sign a copy of the shop rules indicating they received instruction on the rules and agree to observe them. You can file these statements and use them in case of violation of shop regulations. The main value of the statement is that you have a written indication that all your students received instruction on the safety regulations.

The forms displayed in Figures 2-4 and 2-5 illustrate two examples from the safety program used in the Middlesex County Vocational and Technical High School. One form pertains to general shop safety and the other to eye protective safety. You may find these forms of value in your own situation. However, check with your building administrator on the safety program recommended by your school district.

A week or so after you review the shop safety regulations you might want to give the students a written test on the safety rules. This has two advantages. First, it provides a review of all the safety regulations. Second, you can file the safety tests as a second indication of instruction in shop safety.

Shop safety is not something you discuss for one day and forget about the rest of the year. Each day you should discuss it in relation to your demonstrations and lessons. Safety is an ongoing subject, and it is your responsibility as a teacher to impress its importance on the students.

In recent years, many states have passed special regulations concerning eye safety protection. Those states that have laws concerning eye safety in schools specify when eyeglass protection must be worn and also what type of glass and glasses should be provided for the students. Your local

---

Middlesex County Vocational and Technical High School
256 Easton Avenue, New Brunswick, N.J.

Safety Program

I_____have received instruction

in the proper care and use of eye protective devices.

_____   _____
        Date   **Sign Here**

FIGURE 2-4.   *Eye Safety*

administrator should have a copy of the state regulation concerning eyeglass safety in your state. It is to your advantage and that of your students to adhere to the state law requirements.

Industry is very concerned with the safety of its employees and spends a great amount of money on accident prevention. You should be able to obtain posters and publications dealing with local industrial safety practices to use in your classes. Display industrial posters in suitable areas of your shop to remind students continually of the importance of industrial and shop safety.

Be sure you understand the school procedure to be followed in the event of accident, injury, or sickness. Every school should have some policy or procedure to be followed in such cases. If you are qualified to administer first aid and do so in an emergency, will you be supported by your local administration? Many schools have a nurse on duty, but precious time may be wasted before the nurse is able to get to the shop. The victim may require immediate care. Shop teachers should have some basic understanding of first aid and what care or treatment, if any, is needed. A statement concerning accidents and injuries should be included in your list of shop rules.

Accident report forms should be available in your school. All accidents, no matter how minor, should be reported immediately. The use of an

Middlesex County Vocational and Technical High School
112 Rues Lane, East Brunswick, N. J. 08816

SAFETY PROGRAM

I _____ have received instruction

in Safety in the _____ pertaining to the use of

tools and equipment. I was also instructed on safe practices while in

the school building and this department.

_____   _____
       Date   Sign Here

FIGURE 2-5. *Shop Safety*

accident report form provides a definite record of the accident and may be useful in the event of liability action against the teacher and school. The teacher should keep one copy and send one copy to the office. If your school does not have a regular accident report form, you should design a form which includes at least the following information.

1. Name of student
2. Date, time, and place of accident
3. Person in charge at time of accident
4. Nature of the injury
5. Cause of the accident
6. How accident could have been avoided
7. Witness to accident

The Accident Report Form (Figure 2-6) is an example of the type of form used in one established school district. However, the best advice is to use the form that is approved for use in your own school district. Whatever form is used, it should be completed as accurately as possible and the names of witnesses listed with care.

SHOP ORGANIZATION AND MANAGEMENT

The Board of Education of the Vocational Schools
in the County of Middlesex

Administrative Offices: 112 Rues Lane, East Brunswick, N. J. 08816

Accident Report Form

School Insurance Yes ☐ No ☐   Date_____

Name of pupil injured _____ Age _____

Address _____

Name of parent or guardian _____

Address _____

Date of accident _____ Hour _____ a. m. _____ p. m. _____

Name of school _____

Where on premises did accident occur? _____

_____

_____

Where taken after accident? _____

_____

Probable length of disability? _____

_____

_____

Nature of injury _____

_____

_____

What was the direct cause and how did accident happen? Describe fully: ____

_____

_____

_____

_____

_____

Has any claim been made? If so, by whom? _____

_____

ALL ACCIDENTS REQUIRING MEDICAL ATTENTION SHOULD BE REPORTED BY TELE-
PHONE IMMEDIATELY TO THE DIRECTOR, USING THIS FORM AS A GUIDE AND THE
FORM SHOULD BE MAILED TO THE DIRECTOR THE SAME DAY THAT ACCIDENT OCCUR-
RED.

FIGURE 2-6. Accident Report

Was accident caused by negligence of injured person? _____

_____ If so, please explain. _____

_____

_____

Was accident due to negligence on part of any other persons? _____

_____ If so, how? _____

_____

_____

What statement, if any, has injured person made? _____

_____

_____

_____

Who was in charge of class or shop where accident occurred? _____

_____

What statement does person in charge make? _____

_____

_____

What medical attention, if any, did injured person receive? _____

_____

_____

_____

By whom treated? _____

Address _____ Telephone _____

Names of witnesses: _____

_____

_____

_____

Signed _____
Principal

FIGURE 2-6 continued

Teacher Liability

A concern of many shop teachers is legal action against them, by a student or his parents, in the event of an accident. Check with your local administrator about board of education policy on teacher liability. The important question is "Are you covered as an individual by a board of education insurance policy, in the event of a legal judgment against you?" If the answer is no, you might want to consider a personal liability insurance contract designed especially for shop teachers.

The subject of teacher liability as a result of accidents in the school or shop is technical and varies from state to state. A book by Denis J. Kigin, entitled *Teacher Liability in School-Shop Accidents* (1973), is probably the best reference for shop and laboratory teachers. Since laws vary among the states no attempt is made in this book to go into detail about teacher liability. It is best to get a written opinion from the school attorney in the district in which you are employed. The State Vocational Association of your state should also be able to provide you with information regarding teacher liability. The American Vocational Association can provide you with information about personal liability insurance should you feel such coverage may be necessary for you in your teaching situation.

The safety of students is a major concern of all teachers and school personnel. It is both a moral and legal responsibility of everyone involved with schools. The teacher must do more than teach safety—he must practice it and see to it that the students do likewise at all times.

First Aid

First aid in the school and shop is another very technical subject that can only be treated in general terms in a book of this nature. To what extent if any can or should a shop teacher administer first aid to a student or another teacher? This question is to a large extent related to teacher liability. The answer to the question is complex and depends on the answers to a number of related questions, such as:

1. To what extent is the teacher trained and qualified to administer first aid?
2. What first aid supplies and equipment are available in the shop or laboratory? The make up of the first aid kit depends on the qualifications of the person expected to use it.

PREPARATION

3. What professional medical care is available? Is a physician or a professional nurse on call or available in an emergency situation?

Each question seems to raise another question before a suitable answer can be given to the first question. The best advice is to follow local policy established by the board of education regarding to what extent first aid can be rendered in any emergency and what qualifications the person administering first aid must have. This information must be obtained from the educational system in which you are employed.

Safety Standards

Certain safety standards are necessary as part of any shop safety program to protect the students as well as the teacher from unsafe conditions. On December 29, 1970, Congress passed a bill which became a significant part of federal labor laws. Public Law 91–596, known as the Williams-Steiger Occupational Safety and Health Act (OSHA) became effective on April 28, 1971. Congress declared the purpose of the Act, and hence the Labor Department's and OSHA's mission, as "to assure so far as possible every working man and woman in the Nation safe and healthful working conditions and to preserve our human resources." The Act requires each employer to provide a workplace free from safety and health hazards and to comply with the standards established by the OSHA.

The OSHA is an example of a Federal Act established to protect workers from unsafe working conditions. The shop or laboratory teacher must be aware of safety standards required for public school shops and comply with these standards. The administrator of your school should be aware of the safety standards required in your state and district. Detailed information about the OSHA can be obtained from the U.S. Department of Labor.

The shop or laboratory teacher has an obligation to inform his students about the OSHA since within a year or two many will be working in private industry. Schools should meet or exceed the standards required by the Act and voluntarily comply with the law.

An article by Wolff in the April, 1976, issue of *School Shop*, entitled "After 5 Years: OSHA and the School Shop," reviews the implications of this legislation from an educational point of view. The best and safest course of action for the school administrator is to request an OSHA inspector to examine the various shops in the facility and evaluate the situation in terms of the regulations that concern schools. Each shop teacher should contact the Department of Labor and obtain information about the OSHA. This could become an important part of any shop and school safety education program.

PERSONNEL SYSTEM

Some form of a student organizational system within a shop or laboratory is usually required and is essential for good operation. These systems are commonly referred to as student personnel organizations, personnel systems, or clean-up systems. A system of this nature is usually not needed in a normal classroom situation but is essential to the organization and administration of a shop facility.

In the personnel system, students are assigned on a rotating basis to various shop assignments. These assignments vary from being a shop foreman to being a sweeper. A structure with a chain of command is the most workable system. Five or ten minutes before the end of the shop period, a signal is given that it is time to clean up and ready the shop for the next class. It is at this point that the assigned tasks of the personnel system are performed by the students. The shop foreman is responsible for reporting to the teacher on a daily basis. The teacher, of course, has the final responsibility for the condition of the shop and should make frequent checks on the operation of the personnel system.

The personnel system is of value to the teacher as well as the students. The teacher benefits in that it provides more time to work with individual students and to get organized for the next class. The students benefit from being part of an organizational system designed to accomplish a stated purpose. The students should gain some administrative or managerial experience during the period of time they serve as foreman.

The development of a personnel system is a good project and should involve pupil-teacher planning. The most effective system is one that the students had a part in designing. The teacher can describe the problem and then ask students for suggestions.

Various types of systems are designed to administer a personnel system. A well-designed personnel system should have a number of features including the following.

1. A chain of command
2. A detailed description of each position
3. A rotation schedule to assure that each student will have an opportunity to hold all positions during the course of the school year
4. An assignment every week for each student

The success of the personnel system will depend to a large extent on the planning that goes into its design. It will also depend on how well the teacher explains the purpose of the system and the cooperation he receives from the students.

DISPLAYS

The importance of shop appearance should be evident by this time. Many factors already mentioned contribute to the total appearance of the shop. You will want an attractive bulletin board, showcase, and wall charts since these add to the total environment of the shop.

A suitable bulletin board display is one that is neat in layout and contains materials of interest to the students. Do not fall into the trap that many teachers do, starting the school year with a neat bulletin board and ending with the same one. Make an honest effort to change the bulletin board display at least monthly or, better yet, every two weeks. The bulletin board is a good place to put industrial items of concern to your students.

If you have a display case in your shop or in the hall, fill it with items of interest to both students and visitors to the school. It is one way of showing others what type of activities and project work are going on in shop. Again, try to change the display at least every month.

Many companies supply free wall charts to schools. It would be worth your time and effort to request safety charts and instructional charts from industries appropriate to your specialization.

Attractive, well-designed bulletin boards and displays require time to design and put up. The effort or lack of effort you exert will be reflected in the type of program you end up with.

A few more suggestions for the shop teacher are listed below.

1. Keep a clean shop.
2. Have a suitable seating area for all the students.
3. Have an attractive bulletin board display.
4. Keep everything in proper order.
5. Have all machinery in good working condition.
6. Keep all hand tools in proper storage areas and in a ready-to-use condition.
7. Keep a suitable supply of materials available for use.
8. Have all necessary school forms available for your use.
9. Have proper locker space available for your students.
10. Have examples of class projects or experiments available for student inspection.

SHOP ORGANIZATION AND MANAGEMENT

SUMMARY

A well-organized and managed shop or laboratory will make your job somewhat less demanding. Time spent in shop organization and management will leave the teacher more time to get on with teaching. Adequate preplanning will make the first year of teaching a much more pleasant experience for the new teacher.

Shop organization and planning is a subject all its own and whole books have been written on this subject. Those involved in planning a new shop or school facility should consult these sources.

Some of the material presented in this chapter is rather general due to the nature of the topic. Special mention is made of shop safety, eyeglass protection, first aid, teacher liability and safety standards, but specific regulations and laws vary from state to state. This subject should not be taken lightly and the teacher should check into these areas before entering the shop or laboratory for the first time. Additional information on some of these topics can be found in the Source Materials listed at the end of this chapter.

A well-established and administered vocational school will have a professional resource library for the staff that should contain additional information on many of the subjects mentioned in this chapter.

SOURCE MATERIALS

Department of Labor. *Occupational Safety and Health Standards. Federal Register,* June 27, 1974.

Department of Labor. *Training Requirements of the Occupational Safety and Health Standards.* Washington, D.C.: U.S. Government Printing Office, 1973.

Kigin, Denis J. *Teacher Liability in School-Shop Accidents.* Ann Arbor, Mich.: Prakken Publications, 1973.

Meckley, Richard F. *Planning Facilities for Occupational Education Programs.* Columbus, Ohio: Merrill, 1972.

Strong, M. L., ed. *Accident Prevention Manual for Shop Teachers.* Chicago: American Technical Society, 1975.

3

TEACHING AND LEARNING

Most of the formal educational process takes place in school. Learning, of course, takes place both in and out of school. The major concern of this book is the formal learning situation that exists or should exist in our shops and laboratories. This is referred to as the teaching-learning situation. It is the responsibility of both the teacher and the student to create the best possible teaching-learning situation with the given physical conditions.

This chapter will describe some of the factors that might influence the teaching-learning situation and factors that may have a bearing on the success or failure of the teacher.

DEFINITION

Courses of study, instructional strategy, instructional materials and lesson plans all contribute to the development of a sound teaching-learning situation. These situations include both in-school and out-of-school programs.

The burden of responsibility rests with the teacher for establishing the climate for the teaching-learning situation. Figure 3-1 diagrams the suggested procedure the teacher is to follow, starting with a statement of instructional objectives and ending with a teacher evaluation of the process. Modifications of objectives are then made and the process starts over again.

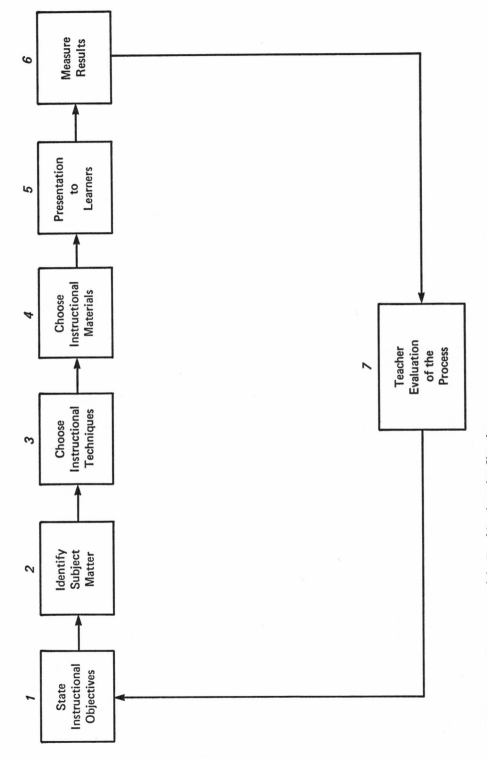

FIGURE 3-1. Components of the Teaching-Learning Situation

PRESSURES ON THE SCHOOL

To some extent the teaching-learning situation is influenced by the pressures that are brought to bear on the whole school system, such as school board policy and available funds. All school systems face the constant pressures and influences of a tax-supported system. Additional pressures are exerted by the various boards of education that must determine policy for the school system. Active parent groups can also influence the direction of the school program. In recent years, we have seen student activism demonstrated on both our college campuses and at the secondary level. All of these factors influence or exert pressure on the system and, in turn, on the teaching-learning situation.

Vocational education programs by their nature are responsible for supplying trained manpower to industry. The success or failure of the vocational program to meet this need is always under evaluation by employers in the community.

The world of work has a strong influence on any vocational education program. Those individuals responsible for the vocational education program must be well acquainted with industrial developments that are and will be occurring. They must be concerned with the technological advances of industry and the needs of industry as related to employment requirements (skills) and employee needs.

Well spelled-out objectives will help the industrial community know what your graduates are capable of doing and what level of expertise they can expect them to exhibit. The active participation of your curriculum advisory committee will assure some level of understanding between the school and the industrial community.

You will notice some of these pressures more than others. The important thing is to get on with the job and provide the best instruction you can under the given conditions.

MAKING THE PROGRAM RELEVANT

A common word among educators and students at the present time is *relevant*. The students' plea is that the school program be relevant to the society that exists outside the bricks and mortar of the school building. Educators use the word in speeches and articles for publication. Both teachers and students are concerned about how relevant the school curriculum is to the problems and conditions that exist outside the school. If vocational education programs are not relevant to industrial employment needs of the community, state, and country, a low rate of job placement will be noted in follow-up studies of vocational graduates.

As a vocational educator, it is to your advantage to keep as up to date in your specialization as possible. Attempt to incorporate the latest industrial advances into your course of study.

It would be to your students' advantage as well as yours for you to contact the various employers of your graduates. Their feedback can prove helpful in making changes in your course of study. This technique plus the active involvement of a curriculum advisory committee should help you keep your program relevant to the needs of students.

A relevant education program involves more than just the skills and knowledge essential for employment. The educational program should prepare students for life. With the rapid changes in technology, it may be necessary for an individual to change his specialization a number of times during his lifetime. Educators should build into the curriculum the essential elements of study needed for life.

As a vocational educator, you are in a unique position to provide a really meaningful and relevant program for your students. In order to do this, you must be willing to keep up with advances in your specialization and the skills necessary to master them. A vocational educator should be a unique individual who is able to "make it" as a teacher in the public school system or as a skilled craftsman in his specialization. Try not to find yourself outdated in your specialization after five years as a shop or laboratory teacher.

THE TEACHER'S ROLE

The teacher is the subject matter expert in the teaching-learning situation. The subject may be English, social studies, mathematics, machine design, or cosmetology. The teacher has the necessary expertise, including both theory and practical experience, to give instruction and assistance to learners. The teacher is responsible for keeping up with advances in his field as well as in educational theory. The teacher is responsible for setting the teaching-learning situation in operation and keeping it moving from the simplest to the most complex material to be covered in the course. The instructional content is the responsibility of the teacher. Well-stated course objectives are essential in order to keep the level of the course up to where it should be.

When the door to the shop or classroom closes, the teacher leads the way in establishing the climate for the teaching-learning situation. Traditional teachers will stick to traditional methods and techniques. Innovative teachers will experiment and seek new and exciting techniques to improve instruction. At this point, the stage is set and students either become actively involved in the process or passive. The question is, "Which will you be?"

TEACHING

The vocational teacher has to understand his or her role in the instructional process. Teaching is defined a number of ways: to show how to do some things; to give instruction; to train; to give lessons to a student or pupil; to give lessons in a certain subject; to provide the learner with knowledge or insight. Teaching occurs in many settings with different people, including church-related work, in the military, in industry, in on-the-job training as well as in the formal school structures.

The vocational teacher is called on continually to make decisions that will influence the teaching-learning situation. Many of these decisions will influence the learning situation and the curriculum process. What should be taught; when it should be taught; how it should be taught; what instructional devices and materials are needed; how teaching should be evaluated; how learning should be evaluated; how learning occurs; whether everyone learns at the same rate; what the best way is to individualize instruction within the group; what the instructional objectives are for the program or course, are all questions the teacher will have to consider.

A person cannot be prepared to teach effectively unless he or she knows how learners learn. A broad understanding of learning and learning theory should be stressed in all teacher education programs. Most programs, for example, require one or more courses in human learning or educational psychology. Even experienced teachers from time to time need some in-service work to bring their understanding of contemporary learning theory up to date. More will be said about learning and how it occurs later in this chapter.

THE STUDENT

Some have said that the teaching profession would be great if it were not for students. No doubt this statement was said in jest. We must always remember that students come to school as consumers of what the school has to offer. They leave for the world of work as products of the school. If students had their choice of schools and teachers, just like we have our choice of physicians, dentists, lawyers, skilled tradesmen, and many other specialists, many classrooms and schools might be empty.

All educational personnel are accountable for the program they provide the students. Accountability does not just rest with the superintendent or principal, but is the responsibility of every staff member in the school. In preparing your lessons, never lose sight of the fact that you are in the shop or laboratory to provide a service to the consumers, the students. Many self-centered individuals lose sight of this fact and feel they are providing a great service to education by their presence in the school. At this point, it is easy for a teacher to turn bitter and almost hate students.

Student Needs

It would be nice if all teachers could assume that students are in the shop or laboratory because they want to be. That assumption may be more reasonable with older students. The secondary-level vocational instructor may find students who are placed or referred to vocational education programs who are not 100 per cent certain that they want to be in such a program. As the age and maturity level increases, the instructor can be more certain that students are in certain programs because they want to be. This is more apt to hold true for students at the post-secondary, community college, private trade school and adult education levels. It must be pointed out that even at these levels exceptions can and do occur. Instructors who teach in programs in which students are paid to attend classes (MDTA, CETA, or remedial) may often find students who are going to school only for the salary they receive by taking the program. You will find that it is easier to work with highly motivated students who are in the program because they want to be than with others who are not as serious.

Students are human just like you and should be treated with the respect and dignity with which you expect others to treat you. No two students are exactly alike. Each student has problems, ambitions, and bad days just like everyone else, including teachers.

Students need to be accepted by fellow students and the teacher. Call them by name and show an interest in each one, both as learners and as individuals. Encourage small group work as opportunities present themselves. The instructional setting should duplicate as closely as possible the situation students will later face in industry as employees. This involves both the social and the technological climates that exist in the industrial setting.

Students need a sense of security. The teaching-learning situation should make students feel they have a place in the situation. They must feel part of the setting and be secure in the situation. When students have done a good job, tell them that you are pleased with their progress. Provide opportunities for your students to discuss items of concern to them in private with you. See to it that the physical and instructional climates are as good as you can make them.

Students need approval from others. Encourage the most advanced students to do even better work. Let them know their work is very good and they are making excellent progress. Encourage slower students, and when they make advances let them know you are pleased. The teaching-learning situation should be geared to success, not failure. Many educators talk about a "zero-reject" system in which even the slowest student is not destined to failure. You will set the tone for the shop or laboratory and determine whether it is geared to success or failure.

Many students like to help others. Advanced students may be asked to help some of the slower students in the shop. Encourage group projects and assignments as a means of encouraging group interaction and a sharing of learning experiences.

Students must be constantly reminded that they are preparing for employment when they leave the vocational program. Their success to a large extent will depend on the level of skill they develop in the vocational program. Employment security and economic independence are major considerations for your students. Your skills and planning will help the students achieve these goals after they graduate.

The Student's Role

The student is the learner in the teaching-learning situation. Teachers should view students as consumers or customers in the educational setting. The student is attending school to prepare for his future, which might involve still more formal education or immediate employment.

In the teaching-learning situation, the instructional strategy and course content depend mainly on the teacher. Students should enter and be a part of the teaching-learning situation to get as much out of the experience as possible. Many students, if conditioned properly by past experiences, will attempt to get the very most out of the teaching-learning situation. Other students will play a much less active role. The expert teacher will attempt to draw them out and get them involved in shop and laboratory activities that are under way.

If the teacher has laid the stage properly, students will take an active part in the teaching-learning situation. Much will depend on their past educational experiences and contacts with other teachers. Many students, due to the nature of the educational system, are apt to take a passive role in class. It will be difficult for students of this type to adjust to the new-found freedom of being in a teaching-learning situation where the learner is expected to be an active participant.

The student should feel comfortable in the teaching-learning situation. The student needs to have a sense of security and belonging in the educational setting. It is the teacher's responsibility to develop the setting and make the students' feel a part of the action. This does not mean a free-wheeling, do-nothing atmosphere should exist in the shop or laboratory. The educational process is still under way and active involvement is encouraged to facilitate the teaching-learning situation.

Students should realize the importance of getting as much practical experience as possible during their limited stay in school. They must be made to realize that schooling is preparation for life, and that imparting the skills and knowledge essential for entering the world of work is the important function of the teaching-learning situation.

Just as the teacher has the responsibility to decide on the instructional strategy and content, the student has the responsibility to learn the material and master the skill involved. Well-stated behavioral objectives will assist both teacher and student in defining what is expected of both.

Individual Differences

No two people are alike. There is only one you with your strengths and your weaknesses. No two students in your class will be identical in aptitude, ability, and behavior.

Each time you plan a new school term or an individual lesson, try and remember that all the students with whom you will use the lesson plan are different. In a class of fifteen, it would no doubt be best, time permitting, to prepare fifteen lesson plans, one for each student. Planning time, of course, does not permit this type of preparation, so we manage with one plan.

Just as the physical characteristics of individuals vary to a large extent, so do the non-physical characteristics. No one would ask the ninety-pound weakling in the class to carry a heavy object any great distance. Yet we may well be expecting great things from a student with limited mental ability. It is important to be aware of the individual characteristics of our students.

Gather as much information about your students as is available. Such information is usually obtained from the guidance counselor. Some items of concern would be:

1. Any special physical disability that might delimit a student's career
2. Past academic achievement in school
3. Reading grade level based on standardized tests
4. Mathematics grade level based on standardized tests
5. IQ score

Each of the indicated items are best explained by a properly prepared guidance counselor who can interpret IQ scores and scores on standardized tests.

When students enter your class for the first time, let them know you will form your opinion of them on the basis of their involvement and behavior in your class. Anything that might have happened in past years and with other teachers is not of concern to you. Each student should start with a clean record in your class. If you look for a problem from a particular student, you will probably create one.

A good teacher will attempt to observe and understand each student in his class. The teacher should believe in the dignity of the individual and treat each student as he himself likes to be treated.

Course work in educational psychology, learning theory, and vocational guidance will all help to improve one's understanding of individual differences. Always remember that you are teaching students. The subject matter, be it baking or sewing, is the content and is of secondary importance to your influence on students. Attempt to relate to your students and get to know them as individuals in the class setting.

LEARNING

Robert Mager, in his book, *Developing Attitude Toward Learning*, states the following:[1]

> Consider any of the instruction you yourself have given. Why did you lecture, or tutor, or otherwise assist the student to learn? Wasn't it because you hoped he would, as a result of your efforts,
>
> • Know more than he knew before.
>
> • Understand something he did not understand before.
>
> • Develop a skill that was not developed before.

1. Robert F. Mager, *Developing Attitude Toward Learning* (Palo Alto, Calif.: Fearon, 1968), p. 8.

- Feel differently about a subject than he felt before, or
- Develop an appreciation for something where there was none before?

One could go on and list many more definitions of learning but this example is sufficient for the present discussion.

Senses Through Which We Learn[2]

SIGHT. We acquire most of our knowledge through the sense of sight. Observation of action and the study of drawings, diagrams, models, and pictures are indispensable in trade training. (Reading printed words is considered more related to hearing than sight.)

HEARING. Through hearing we are able to learn from the experiences of others. It also enables us to receive instruction and to recognize the proper operation of tools, machines, and the like.

TOUCH. Through the sense of touch we become aware of the quality and texture of materials, degree of roughness and smoothness, heat and cold, and, to some degree, the shapes of objects.

INTELLIGENCE. Briefly stated, intelligence is the ability to respond quickly and successfully to new or unusual situations. It enables the learner to "tie up" new ideas with past experiences and knowledge. The so-called native intelligence of a person changes very little throughout a lifetime and is not increased by education.

PAST EXPERIENCES. A person's background of experiences forms the basis for receiving additional knowledge.

CONCENTRATION. It is difficult for a person to fix attention on one idea for very long. Yet one may refocus one's attention quickly when one's mind wanders. The ability to do this repeatedly over a period of time is known as "power of concentration."

MEMORY. A person's ability to remember is extremely important in learning. Factors which influence memory are vividness, uniqueness, frequency, and relative importance.

2. *The Preparation of Occupational Instructors* (Washington, D.C.: Superintendent of Documents, 1965), pp. 69–77. (Note, the contents up through "Four-step Plan of Instruction" have been slightly modified from the source indicated.)

WELL-BEING. Mental and physical comfort increase one's power of concentration. On the other hand, pain, discomfort, and such emotions as grief, irritation, anger, and worry greatly hinder mental processes. The good teacher tries to put the group in a cheerful frame of mind before presenting the lesson.

SELF-CONFIDENCE. People learn something better if they think they can. Fear of bodily injury, fear of failure or spoiling a job, and fear of criticism or humiliation make learning difficult, if not impossible. The good teacher never purposely assigns students tasks beyond their ability to perform, nor says or does anything that would tend to make learners lose confidence in themselves.

IMAGINATION. Imagination is the power to form mental pictures of things not actually present. It helps the craftsman to visualize the finished job before beginning it. A person without imagination can never learn to read a blueprint.

The Teaching Process Influences Learning

The teacher plans, presents, tests, and thereby helps the learner to understand or develop a skill.

The learner develops new knowledge, new qualities, and new abilities and is able to apply them to a situation.

Even though the learner will not learn without taking an active part, the instructor is primarily responsible for success. "If the learner hasn't learned, the instructor hasn't taught."

1. The good instructor makes the most effective possible use of the learner's senses.
   a. We learn faster by seeing and hearing than by hearing alone.
   b. We learn still faster when doing or saying is added to seeing and hearing. It is doing which makes learning permanent.
2. The good instructor designs the lesson and course to take advantage of the three principles of learning.
   a. *Readiness.* You learn a thing when you feel a need for it. You must be interested. Conditions must be right.
   b. *Effect.* You must get satisfaction out of learning. Satisfaction comes from the success you have in learning the

job. The more certain you are of success, the greater the desire to learn.

c. *Practice.* You like to repeat those things you have learned to do well, so practice becomes a pleasure rather than drudgery. The more you do a thing, the better you are able to do it.

3. People differ in many ways, and these differences affect:
   a. The reasons they have for wanting to learn something. An argument that convinces one person of the need for a lesson may not convince another.
   b. The speed and thoroughness at which each person learns. A teaching approach that works with one person may not work with another. That is why it is important to make frequent checks to see if individuals are learning, reteaching as needed, using various approaches to get the job done.

4. The instructor must remember that students:
   a. Usually can see relationships between what they know and what they are studying. If an instructor knows a learner's background, he may be able to discuss the lesson in terms the learner already understands.
   b. Are usually active learners and need a chance to apply what they are learning.
   c. Are serious, almost always seeking a specific goal.

Four-Step Plan of Instruction

STEP I. PREPARATION OF THE LEARNER

   a. Put learners at ease.
   b. Find out what they already know.
   c. Get them interested in learning.

STEP II. PRESENTATION

   a. Tell, show, demonstrate, illustrate, and question in order to put over knowledge or operation.
   b. Instruct slowly, clearly, completely, and patiently one point at a time.
   c. Check, question, and repeat.
   d. Make sure the learner really learns.

PREPARATION

STEP III. APPLICATION (PERFORMANCE TRYOUT)

    a.   Have learners perform the operation.
    b.   Ask questions beginning with "Why," "How," "Who," "When," "Where," or "What."
    c.   Observe performances, correct errors, repeat.
    d.   Make sure the learners really learn.

STEP IV. TEST (FOLLOW-UP)

    a.   Test to determine if they have learned.
    b.   Put them on their own.
    c.   Check frequently and be sure they follow instructions.

Both beginning and experienced vocational teachers are well advised to take one or more courses in the area of human learning or educational psychology to keep current in the field of learning theory.

TREATMENT OF STUDENTS

Students can have bad days just as teachers often have days when things do not go just according to schedule. Many students come to school each day with personal problems not known to the teacher. Illness, family problems and other factors often plague students just as they do teachers. The experienced, student-orientated teacher will develop a sense of understanding for the problems that at times influence student behavior.

No one likes a person who acts one way one time and another way at another time. It is difficult to work for a boss who runs hot and cold depending upon his mood. As you move through your first years of teaching, you will in a sense be establishing your own procedures. Consistent treatment of students should be an essential ingredient of your policies. A treatment that varies from day to day will gain the teacher little respect from students.

Many times teachers have to make decisions under trying classroom conditions. Be cautious of making snap judgments that influence other people. If you lose your temper, try to "cool off" before making a decision that you may regret later. Do not be afraid to admit an incorrect decision and attempt to correct the situation.

What technique works for one teacher may not work for another. It is difficult to play a role and act differently than you normally do.

Be *firm, fair,* and *consistent* in the treatment of students. The first few days with any new class are the most important of the year, as they set the stage for what is to follow. It is much better to be too strict early in the year, as you can always ease off. If you fail at the beginning to exercise good control, it is very difficult to regain it as the year goes on. It is essential that the teacher establish some ground rules on procedures necessary for the operation of the shop or laboratory. Such ground rules should be subject to change as conditions dictate.

Teaching is not a popularity contest. Do not be concerned about being the good guy and the buddy of your students. You can lose students' respect if you put yourself on their level. You are the teacher, a paid professional, and they are the students. The relationship between the teacher and students should be kept at a professional level in the classroom situation. Many good guy, buddy-type teachers do not survive the first year of their teaching careers. A friendly atmosphere should exist in the classroom, but one in which the student and teacher both know their respective roles.

As problems occur involving students, remember the three key words —*firm, fair, consistent*—and let them guide you in the situation at hand. You must be firm and let the student know you mean business. Be fair and treat all students alike. Do not deal out unreasonable punishments for minor violations. Be consistent in your treatment of students and in the rules and regulations that need to be enforced in the shop. Safety regulations are of special importance in the shop, and violations should be dealt with immediately.

Students will respect the teacher who plays by the rules and treats them with respect and fairness. They should realize that every minute of class time used by the teacher in playing policeman is multiplied by the number of students in the class. In a class of fifteen, if the teacher is forced to discipline a student and such action takes five minutes, it amounts to seventy-five minutes of wasted time for the whole class. The shop teacher should always relate the shop atmosphere to the on-the-job atmosphere in industry. Time is valuable and means money to the employer. The goof-off will soon be among the unemployed.

Discipline

Try to handle all your discipline cases yourself. The teachers who continually send students to the office soon lose the respect of the administration as well as the students. Certain school policy violations, by regulation, may have to be reported to the office, but try to handle any problems in your shop or laboratory by yourself.

There will be times when you need to send a student to the person who handles discipline cases. Usually it is a good idea to accompany the student to the office, so that a full discussion of the situation can take place. However, a shop instructor should *never* leave his students unsupervised for even a second. If it is impossible to accompany the student to the office, call the office, if you have a phone in the shop. If you cannot call, give the student a note to take to the office, and as soon as you can, go to the office to follow-up on the situation. Check your local policy or building manual for the suggested procedure in your school.

To be meaningful, discipline must occur at the time of the violation or problem. It does little good to delay disciplinary action for a day or week. If there is to be some form of punishment, it should be carried out as soon as possible. Again, make sure you review local school policy on discipline before you find yourself in violation of school policy.

Discipline should be handled in a firm, fair, and consistent manner. If some form of punishment is dealt out, it should be consistent with the violation.

You must find your own system and techniques as a disciplinarian. It is one of the unpleasant tasks involved in being a teacher, but it is essential for the smooth operation of your class and the school. All teachers and students must work together to provide the best conditions for the teaching-learning situation.

Handling Special Problems

Use all the resources of the school to handle student-centered problems that you might be involved in. If you notice that a student seems to have a special problem, it is usually best to speak to the student's guidance counselor. Such problems might be physical, emotional, achievement centered, or personal in nature. The guidance counselor might have information available about the student, or if it seems necessary to have additional information and reports, can obtain the necessary information. Consultative services of professional psychologists, physicians, and social case workers can be made available. There is usually a clear school policy on the procedure to be used in requesting such special services which usually starts with the student's counselor.

Case studies of various student problems could be related. However, their value to the classroom teacher may be limited since in an entire teaching career a teacher may never experience a similar case. The best advice to the beginning teacher is to consult with the counselor of a student you feel may have a special problem. The classroom teacher is just not prepared to be everything to every student. Make use of the various professionals that are usually available to serve the school system.

SUMMARY

This chapter has presented material dealing with the teaching-learning situation and the wide range of factors that may influence both teaching and learning. Teaching and learning have been defined for all teachers but especially vocationally orientated teachers.

Figure 3-1 presented a model for a basic teaching-learning strategy suitable for vocational instruction.

The roles of both teacher and student were discussed along with various pressures on the school. The teacher's obligation to make the learner a more satisfied customer was discussed along with ways in which the learning environment might be improved. The treatment of students and students with special needs was also discussed.

This chapter should be considered a general overview of learning and teaching. Some of the references suggested in the section "Source Materials" should be given serious consideration. This chapter has only scratched the surface of basic learning theory.

SOURCE MATERIALS

Bruner, Jerome S. *Toward a Theory of Instruction.* New York: W. W. Norton, 1966.

Gagné, Robert M. *The Conditions of Learning.* New York: Holt, Rinehart and Winston, 1970.

Kemp, Jerrold E. *Instructional Design.* Belmont, Calif.: Fearon, 1971.

Mager, Robert F. *Developing Attitude Toward Learning.* Palo Alto, Calif.: Fearon, 1968.

Skinner, B. F. *The Technology of Teaching.* New York: Appleton-Century-Crofts, 1968.

LESSON PLANNING

Part II

4

DETERMINING WHAT TO TEACH

The material in this chapter will point out some of the basics of determining what to teach. More detailed information can be obtained by using the references that are suggested at the end of the chapter.

The traditional vocational curriculum is usually divided into smaller units which are offered on a semester or yearly basis. If a three-year program in plumbing is offered, it will typically be divided into three one-year courses such as Plumbing I, Plumbing II, and Plumbing III. It also could be divided into six smaller units and divided into six one-semester courses. As stated earlier, this is traditionally how vocational programs and courses are established and is not intended as an argument for or against the traditional system. Since most courses and programs are structured this way, the established format will be followed.

Program is defined as the pursuit of a certain specialization such as cosmetology, electronics, etc. *Course* is defined as one segment of the total program. A *unit* is a still smaller sub-division of a course.

A typical modern-day vocational curriculum for a large vocational school program can be seen in Figure 4-1. This is a recent listing of programs offered at the secondary and post-secondary levels in the Camden County Vocational and Technical Schools (New Jersey) and illustrates a very compre-

POST-SECONDARY PROGRAMS
(Technical Institute and Trade Preparatory)

	Years*
Air-Conditioning & Refrigeration Tech. (2 to 7 p. m.)	1
Architectural Drafting Technology	2
Auto Body Repair & Painting Technology	2
Automatic Heating Technology	2
Automotive Technology (2 to 7 p. m.)	2
Beauty Culture	1
Building Trades Technology (2 to 7 p. m.)	2
Cabinet-Making & Millwork	2
Chemical & Nuclear Technology	2
Commercial Baking	2
Culinary Arts	2
Distributive Education	2
Electrical Technology	2
Electronics Technology	2
Food Processing Technology	1
Library Technician	1
Machine Drafting Technology	2
Machine Trades Technology	2
Masonry	2
Plumbing & Heating Technology (2 to 7 p. m.)	2
Printing	2
Radio & TV Service Technology	2
Sheet Metal	2
Stationary Engineering Technology	2
Water & Waste Water Technology	2
Welding	2

HEALTH OCCUPATIONS (9 to 20 months, includes affiliation)

Dental Assistant	9 mo.
Dental Laboratory Technician	11 mo.
Medical Assistant	9 mo.
Medical Laboratory Technician	20 mo.
Practical Nursing (both campuses)	12 mo.

*Approximate. All courses based on completion of units of instruction.

DAY HIGH SCHOOL PROGRAMS

OFFERED AT BOTH CAMPUSES

	Years*
Air-Conditioning & Refrigeration	2**
Auto Body Repair & Painting	2
Automatic Heating	2
Auto Mechanics	4
Beauty Culture	2**
Cabinet-Making & Millwork	4
Carpentry	4
Culinary Arts	4
Electric Shop	4
Electronics	4
Machine Drafting	4
Machine Shop	2
Maintenance Mechanics	4
Plumbing & Heating	4
Printing	4
Radio & TV Repair	2**
Sheet Metal	4
Welding—Electric & Gas	2 or 4

AT PENNSAUKEN ONLY

Design Tailoring & Home Furnishing Careers	2 or 4
Ornamental Horticulture	
(a) Landscaping	2
(b) Floriculture	2

AT GLOUCESTER TOWNSHIP ONLY

Architectural Drafting	2**
Chemical & Nuclear Technology	4
Commercial Baking	4
Distributive Education	4
Masonry	2
Stationary Engineering	2**

*Approximate. All courses based on completion of units of instruction.
**11th and 12th grade only.

FIGURE 4-1. Vocational Curriculum

hensive curriculum based on local needs. The program offerings are listed by years needed to complete a given program and would typically be sub-divided into courses and units of instruction.

It is first necessary to consider the product (student) who is about to enter the vocational program. Second, it is necessary to establish some level of behavioral performance to be expected of the student upon completion of a program in his chosen specialization. Third, the sequence of development from the input (when the student enters the program) to the output (graduation) must be carefully broken into small segments which can be called units. The product (student) upon completion of the program should be evaluated in terms of the stated objectives of the program. Likewise, the program should develop from the simplest to the most complex units in order to achieve the level of behavioral performance stated in the objectives of the program.

OBJECTIVES OF VOCATIONAL EDUCATION

Chapter 1 discussed the objectives of education and those especially concerned with vocational education. Now the subject of the program and course objectives must be considered. Course and program objectives conform to the philosophy of the school.

Perhaps it would be helpful to read such statements of philosophy by various schools. The schools and locations have not been identified, but the statements themselves were taken from materials published in formal form by the various schools.

1. VOCATIONAL EDUCATION. The main purpose of vocational education is to prepare qualified individuals for useful employment.

This is interpreted to mean preparation not only in the hand skills necessary to be successful in any given occupation, but also to develop those traits necessary in becoming a satisfied and productive citizen. Therefore, the goal of vocational education is the development of the student socially, academically and civically.

To accomplish this goal, prospective students should have the following interest and abilities.

1. Interest in pursuing education in a trade in terms of pre-employment training.
2. Ability to profit from the instruction.
3. Meet the entrance tests and requirements that indicate ability to profit from the training.

Vocational high school programs usually provide for one-half of the time to be spent in the shop and the remainder in related and academic work. Therefore, it is evident that the shop course is the core of the vocational high school program.

The related subjects of mathematics, science and drawing are scheduled in proportion to their use in the trade being studied. All related subjects have a practical relationship to the fundamentals, and, therefore, emphasis is placed on applying those principles.

2. INSTITUTE PURPOSE AND OBJECTIVES. The County Technical Institute offers college level technical programs designed to equip graduates for immediate employment in specialized fields. The programs are so arranged that each student acquires some degree of competence in manual skills, plus supporting knowledge in mathematics, science, English and the humanities. Basic supporting courses are presented in sufficient depth to provide insurance against obsolescence in technology. Graduates will be qualified, either immediately or after appropriate work experience, for such positions as are listed under each program description.

3. GENERAL STATEMENT OF PHILOSOPHY. The Board of Trustees of the _____ has, as its central purpose and objective, the goal of providing high quality education and specialized skill or technical training for the youth of _____ County who aspire, and are qualified by interest and ability, to prepare for a career in a craft or specialized occupation.

We recognize that implementation of this objective involves interrelation of many functioning parts: the staff, the facilities, the student and the curriculum. We therefore shall endeavor, in every way possible, to develop an effective blend of all aspects and the several functioning parts recognizing that the key to the success of the total program is the instructional staff, and, hence, the individual teacher.

4. AREA VOCATIONAL CENTER. The vocational education program provides education and training in a specific occupational area, closely following industrial and technical practices of private industry. The primary purpose is to make an individual employable in one group of occupations. Completion of a program should prepare individuals for gainful employment as semi-skilled or skilled workers, technicians or sub-professionals, or to prepare individuals for enrollment in advanced technical programs.

As one reads the four statements, the philosophies and objectives of the various schools become apparent. Program evaluation should be based on the statements made. The board of education, administrators, and faculty should stand accountable for the various programs which attempt to meet these broad statements.

Many schools will operate with just a general statement of philosophy such as those listed earlier but others may have more specific school-wide objectives such as those that follow:

1. Upon completion of an occupational education program (65%) of the students will rate the experience satisfying.
2. Upon completion of an occupational education program (65%) of the students will indicate that they would tend to take the same program again if they had to make the choice over.
3. Upon completion of an occupational education program (60%) of the students, available for employment or advanced education, will indicate that they plan to enter the area of specialization they prepared for or go on to advanced training/education in their area of specialization.
4. Seventy-five (75%) per cent of the graduates of any licensed occupation program will pass the appropriate examination. (i.e., cosmetology, L.P.N., etc.).
5. Within six (6) months after graduation (60%) of the graduates, available for and having sought employment, will be employed full-time.
6. Within six (6) months after graduation (35%) of the graduates, available for and having sought employment in their specialization, will be employed full-time.
7. Within six (6) months after graduation another (15%) of the graduates, available for and having sought employment in their specialization, will be employed full-time in a position they considered related to their area of specialization.

The important point to remember in planning for the program or course that you are responsible for is to consider the statement of philosophy, goals, and objectives which have been approved by the board of education and set the direction for the vocational program. The teacher is responsible for conforming through his courses to the central thrust of the school. Only a few examples can be shown in this book; you must search out the objectives that establish the direction for the program you are a part of.

OBJECTIVES OF YOUR COURSE

The instructor, in most cases, determines the objectives of a particular course. It is a good idea to accept the advice of the members of an advisory committee in listing the objectives of a particular course.

DETERMINING WHAT TO TEACH

Remember, a course is but one part or segment of the learning activities making up the program. If a three-year program in electronics is offered, it will probably be broken into three one-year courses or six one-semester courses. A three-year electronics program might be divided into Electronics I, Electronics II, and Electronics III. The relationship among the three must be carefully determined in advance of the curriculum development effort. The student should be able to proceed from the simplest elements of Electronics I to the most complex items in Electronics III. It is therefore essential that the staff member assigned to teach Electronics I be well acquainted with the relationship between Electronics I and II and III. In simple words, it must fit into the total program.

The program objectives should be closely related to the stated objectives of the school. If the main purpose of vocational education is to prepare qualified individuals for useful employment in a certain specialization, then the major program objective would probably be the same. In a practical nursing program, the primary objective would, no doubt, be to prepare qualified individuals for useful employment as practical nurses. And, likewise, this would be the primary objective of all the other specializations offered in the school. The primary objective of a college entrance program is the preparation of individuals for some form of higher education. The practical nursing program would, or should, be evaluated in terms of the number of graduates who enter the field for which they trained. The college entrance program should be evaluated in terms of the number of students who are successfully admitted to colleges.

The classroom teacher will be mainly responsible for determining and stating the objectives of a particular course. His objectives are, or should be, greatly influenced by the objectives of the school and the program his course is a part of. A student completing the requirements for the first course should meet the entrance requirement for the second course, and so forth. At the end of this course of study, the student should be prepared for entry-level employment in his specialization.

Figure 4-2 shows the course-to-program relationship that is typical for most vocational education programs. Early exiting before program completion should not be encouraged since what typically can happen is a beginning class may start with twenty-five students and end three years later with ten to fifteen.

Each course can be subdivided into still smaller segments called units. The unit method allows the student to move from the simplest to the most complex unit within the individual course. In fact, a total program could be developed on the unit method principle which would eliminate the need for a course structure. This is a somewhat untraditional approach but still worthy of note and experimentation. The unit approach is simply a means of dividing course content into smaller packages than the traditional semester or year

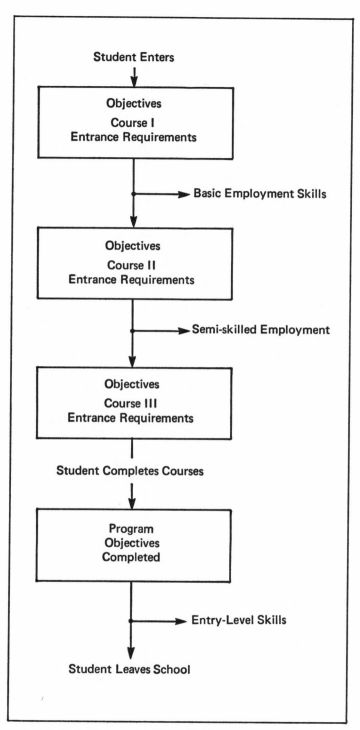

FIGURE 4-2. *Relationship of Course to Program*

courses. The unit method of course construction will be used in this book, but it will be limited to the course level rather than the program level.

It is suggested that course objectives be stated in behavioral terms in order to let the student and teacher both know when a stated objective has been met. Much has recently been written about behavioral objectives. References are cited at the end of this chapter that will be helpful to the teacher in writing behavioral objectives. A few examples of objectives that require demonstrated behavior on the part of the student follow.

1. The student will be able to *identify* the advantages of gas-shielded arc processes.
2. The student will be able to *operate* a T.I.G. unit and compare the results with other welding techniques.
3. The student will be able correctly to *select* and *prepare* instruments, equipment, and materials for each dental procedure.
4. The student will correctly *mix* dental materials.
5. The student will *describe* the normal functioning of the kidney and its elimination of toxic substances from the body. To accomplish this, the student will
   a. *describe* the overall function of the urinary system and *list* its parts.
   b. *list* the factors affecting the amount of urine produced.
   c. *list* the differences between the male and female urethra.
6. The student will be able to *test* toggle switches, wires, lamps, fuses, tubes, resistors, capacitors, transformers, and potentiometers, and *determine* their serviceability as component parts.
7. The student will be able to *identify*, 75 per cent of the time, in a five-minute physical inspection, damaged wires, cables, transformers, capacitors, resistors, tubes, and hardware in a typical power supply.
8. Given the audible output from a normal or defective amplifier, the student will be able to *describe* the tonal quality in terms such as normal, A.C. hum, motorboating, etc.

The following is an example of a course objective that is related to the total program.

At the completion of the two-year Nursing Assistant program, the student should be able to successfully complete the required examination and acquire certification from the Nursing Assistant Association allowing him/her to practice as a Nursing Assistant in any health field.

LESSON PLANNING

It takes time to write suitable objectives, but the effort will be well appreciated in the long run. Final evaluation should be based on the stated objectives and necessary records, so that both the student and teacher know what progress is being made.

A well-written objective will state the *conditions* and the *criteria* for acceptable performance. A student should know when he has met the criteria and then be able to move on to the next objective.

SCOPE AND SEQUENCE

Scope and sequence refer to the depth and order of subject matter. A program could be divided into fifty or more smaller units and placed in a logical sequence. A student might move from unit to unit at his own pace. This is called "self-pacing."

Scope refers to depth and variety within the individual unit. The content of the individual unit determines the scope of the unit.

Figure 4-2 is a practical example of scope and sequence. The various courses indicated I, II, and III taken in logical order would be the sequence. The content of each course would be the scope and, likewise, the content of all the courses making up the program would form the scope of the total program. Basically then, scope refers to the content of the individual courses and may also refer to the scope of the total program.

Traditional programs have usually been divided into convenient semester or year packages. The semester program is designed for about eighteen weeks, and the year program for about thirty-six weeks. No doubt, the only reason for this was to fit the school calendar. This is a rather weak reason, no doubt, and perhaps is due for a change. It seems to make more sense to divide the subject matter into smaller units and base the content as much as possible on behavior-oriented objectives for each unit.

The teacher concerned with individual differences and using individualized instruction could make it possible for students to progress at their own rate. As a student completed the stated objectives and the evaluation of one unit, he would be allowed to move on to the next unit in the sequence. The successful completion of any unit would be based on some demonstrated competency on the student's part.

For example, a traditional electronics program would have a unit on power supplies. A teacher interested in the unit method and self-pacing technique might divide his unit on power supplies into eight or more parts.

1. Half-wave rectifier
2. Full-wave rectifier

3. Full-wave bridge rectifier
4. Half-wave voltage doubler
5. Full-wave voltage doubler
6. Voltage tripler
7. AC to DC converter
8. Silicon controlled rectifier

CURRICULUM ADVISORY COMMITTEE

The shop or laboratory teacher will want to develop a working relationship with the local industrial and trade leaders in his teaching specialization. In addition to the informal relationship that is desirable, some formal relationship should exist. A curriculum advisory committee made up of members of the industrial community can provide such a relationship.

Some well-established vocational schools will have working curriculum advisory committees for each program, and the new teacher will more or less work with the existing group. However, individual committee members usually serve a one- or two-year term, and new members are appointed to replace the retiring members. If you start your teaching career in a new vocational center, you will probably have the responsibility of selecting members for an advisory committee.

The principal may work with a total program curriculum advisory committee. One of the members from each of the specialized subject committees should be represented on the principal's committee. The laboratory or shop teachers would work with a small committee of perhaps six or eight members who have expertise in a certain specialization such as carpentry. If a school is big enough to have more than one laboratory or shop instructor in a certain specialization, then all the teachers in the specialization would work with a common committee. In other words, a curriculum advisory committee should exist for every program that is offered in the school district.

The committee should be an active, functioning group. Its main responsibility is to keep the various courses and programs up to date with modern industrial practices. Their advice should be sought when purchasing new machinery and equipment.

If you are faced with the task of developing a course of study, try to involve your curriculum advisory committee early in the developmental phase. They can be a valuable sounding board for your ideas and plans.

LESSON PLANNING

INDUSTRIAL NEEDS

The curriculum advisory committee is one of the major methods of keeping the school staff informed about local industrial needs. This does not imply that the major function of the vocational-technical school is to meet local industrial needs. A well-planned vocational curriculum should prepare students both for entry-level employment and for higher education. However, this is a local school matter which should be discussed in the philosophy and objectives of the school.

Since vocational education is charged with preparing students for entry-level employment, the school, its board, and the staff must constantly be aware of the industrial needs of the community. The staff should be in touch with the local industrial scene, and the various teachers fully informed of industrial needs in their specialization. Three items are worthy of note.

1. Seek the *advice* of local industrial and trade organizations. Key personnel should be asked to serve on curriculum advisory committees. Curriculum evaluation should be an on-going activity of the various committees.
2. Staff members should be fully informed about the industrial *needs* of the community, including the number of personnel required and the preparation needed for entry-level employment.
3. Discover what *skills* are needed by students seeking employment in local industry. This information should be of the utmost concern to the shop and laboratory teacher. If possible, encourage local industrial leaders to list employment skills in terms of performance objectives.

Cooperation between the school and industry is essential if a meaningful program is to exist. School personnel should take the initiative in establishing such a relationship and continue to make it an active involvement.

PRESSURES OF SOCIETY

Pressures from society are on all of us. Public schools and their staffs are constantly in the public eye. It is essential that students be prepared to meet the three basic needs of food, clothing, and shelter. Surely then, one of the most basic pressures on the school is to prepare students for productive

DETERMINING WHAT TO TEACH

employment in the modern world. Employers are mainly concerned with the individual's basic skills.

Higher education is the goal of many students. Thus, schools, while preparing students for gainful employment, should take care not to close the door to higher education. Our programs should be tailored to meet the needs of students as much as possible.

Occupational program planners must give considerable attention to present and future trends in society. National, as well as local, trends must be considered in program planning. Some important factors are urbanization, mobility of the population, racial integration, automation, rapid change, specialization, and mechanization. These items should be investigated in detail to determine their relevance at the local planning level.

THE STUDENT

Each teacher should gain as much information as possible about the students in class. Many vocational teachers will be involved in the selection process of incoming students; in other cases, the selection will be made by the home district or someone in pupil personnel work. Figure 4-3 is a typical application form used by an area vocational center in New York State. You will note that it asks for a number of items, including a statement of the student's career plans, parental approval, health information, counselor recommendation, and personal data. If such information is available to you in your school it is worth your time to review the application form before you meet the student in class. Pay special attention to the health data since you must be aware of any physical disabilities that may affect your students' ability to function in your shop or laboratory.

OCCUPATIONAL ANALYSIS

A number of different terms are used in writing about occupational analysis techniques. Some writers say job analysis, others task analysis, and still others, structural analysis. But basically, occupational analysis is the study of activities in which an individual in a particular occupation is engaged.

If you are not fully acquainted with a trade or occupation, the best way to make an analysis is to observe someone actively engaged in that trade or occupation and note all activities over a period of time. An observation of this nature reveals the skills and knowledge necessary to become a successful practitioner.

Many industries spell out the requirements for positions in the orga-

BOARD OF COOPERATIVE EDUCATIONAL SERVICES
First Supervisory District, Erie County, New York 14225

APPLICATION FOR OCCUPATIONAL EDUCATION

HARKNESS CENTER	POTTER ROAD CENTER	KENTON CENTER
99 Aero Drive	705 Potter Road	151 Two Mile Creek Road
Cheektowaga, New York 14225	West Seneca, New York 14224	Tonawanda, New York 14150
634-6800 Ext. 268	634-6800 Ext. 265	634-6800 Ext. 264

PLEASE READ BACK PAGE BEFORE COMPLETING THIS APPLICATION

PERSONAL DATA - TO BE COMPLETED BY STUDENT

NAME	Last	First	Middle	DATE OF BIRTH	Month Day Year	PRESENT DATE	Month Day Year

HOME ADDRESS — No. & Street — Post Office — State — Zip Code

HOME PHONE	HOME SCHOOL	PRESENT GRADE

SOCIAL SECURITY NUMBER — OCCUPATIONAL CENTER FOR WHICH YOU ARE APPLYING

PROGRAM FOR WHICH YOU ARE APPLYING — DATE YOU EXPECT TO ENTER THIS PROGRAM — Month Year

FATHER'S NAME	FATHER'S OCCUPATION	FATHER'S BUSINESS PHONE

MOTHER'S NAME	MOTHER'S OCCUPATION	MOTHER'S BUSINESS PHONE

IF PARENTS UNAVAILABLE WHOM TO CONTACT IN CASE OF EMERGENCY — TELEPHONE

FAMILY DOCTOR — DOCTOR'S PHONE

ACTION TAKEN ON APPLICANT - FOR HOME SCHOOL USE

ACCEPTED ☐   WAITING LIST ☐   NUMBER ON WAITING LIST _____

FIGURE 4-3. *Application for Vocational Education*

CAREER PLANS - TO BE COMPLETED BY STUDENT

OCCUPATION WHICH YOU PLAN TO ENTER UPON GRADUATION FROM HIGH SCHOOL

HOW WILL THE VOCATIONAL PROGRAM FOR WHICH YOU ARE APPLYING ASSIST YOU IN REACHING YOUR OCCUPATIONAL GOAL?

HAVE YOU EVER VISITED THE OCCUPATIONAL CENTER TO WHICH YOU ARE APPLYING?	SIGNATURE OF APPLICANT

OPEN HOUSE

If you have not had the opportunity to visit one of the Occupational Centers, you are encouraged to do so. Open House programs will be held during the evening hours at each of the Centers in the Spring, usually during March or April. Announcements of these Open House programs will be made in local newspapers and at each of the home schools.

PARENTAL APPROVAL - TO BE SIGNED BY PARENT OR GUARDIAN

I approve of my (son/daughter's) application to the _____
Program at the Occupational Center designated. If he/she is selected for participation in the program I agree to provide the necessary uniforms or equipment needed for the course in which he/she is enrolled and insure to the best of my ability that he/she abides by the rules established by the Center.

SIGNATURE OF PARENT OR GUARDIAN

FIGURE 4-3 continued

HEALTH DATA - TO BE COMPLETED BY HOME SCHOOL NURSE

STUDENT'S HEIGHT	STUDENT'S WEIGHT	DAYS ABSENT:	Last Year		Current Year To Date	

PLEASE CHECK IF STUDENT HAS A HISTORY OF PROBLEMS IN ANY OF THE FOLLOWING:

Tuberculosis	Epilepsy	Hearing Disability
Heart Disease	Fainting Spells	Visual Disability
Diabetes	Skin Allergies	Psychological Evaluation Available
Hernia	Physical Disability or Handicap	Other

PLEASE GIVE ANY PERTINENT DETAILS REGARDING THE ABOVE CHECKED ITEMS, OR ANY OTHER INFORMATION YOU FEEL MAY HAVE AN INFLUENCE UPON THIS STUDENT'S FUNCTIONING IN A VOCATIONAL PROGRAM.

SCHOOL NURSE'S SIGNATURE

COUNSELOR RECOMMENDATIONS - TO BE COMPLETED BY HOME SCHOOL COUNSELOR

DEGREE OF INTEREST APPLICANT HAS EXPRESSED IN THE PROGRAM FOR WHICH HE HAS APPLIED: HIGH ☐ MEDIUM ☐ QUESTIOÑABLE ☐

DO YOU FEEL THE APPLICANT NEEDS REMEDIAL HELP IN THE FOLLOWING AREAS:

READING   Yes ☐   No ☐   MATH   Yes ☐   No ☐

SPECIFIC RECOMMENDATIONS OR COMMENTS WHICH WILL ENABLE OCCUPATIONAL CENTER PERSONNEL TO WORK EFFECTIVELY WITH THE APPLICANT:

COUNSELOR'S SIGNATURE	COUNSELOR FOR NEXT SCHOOL YEAR

FIGURE 4-3 continued

TO STUDENTS AND PARENTS

This application is to be completed by all students whose interest is in one of the occupational programs operated by the Board of Cooperative Educational Services, First Supervisory District, Erie County, New York. Programs are offered at the Harkness Center in Cheektowaga, the Kenton Center in Tonawanda and the Potter Road Occupational Center in West Seneca. Completion of the application by the student and approval of the application by the parents in no way guarantees admission to an occupational program. The following information may be helpful as you consider your application to an occupational program.

Information Concerning Programs. Costs for sending students to an occupational program are paid by the home school district and involve a considerable amount of tax money in the school budget. Therefore, it behooves any student who is considering an application to find out as much as he possibly can about the program for which he is applying. Information about the occupational programs is available in the home school guidance offices. More detailed information and answers to specific questions can be obtained by contacting the student program coordinator's office at each of the vocational centers. Visits to the centers are encouraged and can be arranged by contacting the Harkness Center (634-6800, Ext. 268), the Kenton Center (634-6800, Ext. 264), or the Potter Road Center (634-6800, Ext. 265).

Student Selection. Selection of students to attend the occupational centers is made by your home school administrators and guidance counselors and is usually based on a number of factors including such things as completion of course prerequisites, attendance, teacher and counselor recommendations, and the degree of student interest displayed in the course. Students who are currently enrolled in a Multi-Occupations program at one of the centers and are applying for other one or two year programs are also selected on the basis of the recommendations of their Multi-Occupations teachers. Preference in selection is given to those students who intend to work in the occupation for which they are training. Questions concerning the status of your application should be referred to your home school guidance office.

Deadline for Applications. Applications for the next school year should be turned in to your home school guidance department on or before _____ . You will be notified before the summer vacation whether you have been chosen for a program or not.

Costs. Although the home school district pays the enrollment costs for students in occupational programs, there are certain items of personal equipment which must be purchased by the students or their parents. Costs will vary according to the program chosen. More details concerning costs may be obtained by contacting the home school guidance office or the occupational center student program coordinator's office.

Special Note for Cosmetology Applicants. Each year there appears to be some misunderstanding concerning the requirement for cosmetology students to have their hair cut. One of the first basic procedures to be learned by the future beautician is hair cutting. Since state law prohibits the use of outside models by beginning students, it is necessary that the students practice hair cutting on each other. The number of hair cuts and the length of the hair must be determined by the professional judgment of the instructor. The applicant for cosmetology must agree to this course requirement and failure to comply could result in the student's dismissal from the program.

FIGURE 4-3 continued

nization in behavioral terms, and naturally they require individuals to have certain skills to hold positions at various levels.

Basically the concern of the shop or laboratory teacher is to prepare the student with the skills and related technical knowledge necessary for entry-level employment in a trade. One basic technique for determining what to teach is an analysis of the trade or occupation you are teaching.

You should analyze occupations in behavioral terms and then gear your course of study, lesson plans, and daily procedures to the listed behaviors. A possible procedure might include the following.

1. Read the philosophy and objectives of the school.
2. Do an occupational analysis.
3. Get active assistance from the advisory committee.
4. Develop a course of study based on items 1, 2, and 3.
5. Develop daily lesson plans based on the course of study.
6. Do continual evaluations of the course.

The six statements list basic procedures from occupational analysis to continual course evaluation. The occupational analysis should start with the simplest activity and proceed to the most complex. This will give a much more systematic approach to the procedure and make for less work in constructing the course of study. For example, in preparing to solo (fly alone) an aircraft for the first time, one must first acquire some basic skills. It would be foolish to practice landings if you had not learned and mastered the proper take-off procedures. One should first learn to take off and fly level, and then master the landing procedure. Proceed from the simplest to the most complex. State the tasks to be mastered in behavioral terms:

1. The student pilot will be able to demonstrate the proper take-off procedure.
2. The student pilot will be able to demonstrate the basic turns and level flight required in the landing pattern.
3. The student pilot will be able to demonstrate the proper landing procedure.

The previous example was given for a very special reason. When the flight instructor signs off a student for his first flight, the student is on his own. The flight must end in a safe landing, a faulty landing, or a crash. Although most of us are not flight instructors, the future of many students rests in our control. Occupational analysis is one technique which, when properly used, will help us provide the best occupational programs possible.

An occupational analysis is a technique used to determine the skills needed by someone to be adequately prepared for a certain type of occupation. The level of skill attainment might vary from entry-level employment to more advanced positions within the specialization. Members of your advisory committee should be helpful in determining what skills and experiences are essential for someone interested in employment in the particular specialization.

If you were developing a course of study for a service station attendant program, the best way to determine course content would be to first observe a number of "successful" attendants. This observation period might last from one to many days.

A priority would be assigned to those behaviors which are most often required. One of the most basic procedures for a service station attendant is making change for a customer after a sale is made. It would be difficult to place a graduate in a service station position if he lacked this basic skill. It is not a technical skill associated with automobiles, but rather a basic skill necessary for every sale the man makes. It is, however, the type of skill that might be overlooked by someone constructing a course of study, yet if a service station attendant was observed, it would probably be the most often used skill observed.

The occupational analysis should be completed, reviewed, and approved by your curriculum advisory committee before work is started on the course of study. The course of study will be good or bad depending on the quality and quantity of your efforts.

The same technique of observation could be applied to any occupation. This procedure is seldom used, but it is the practical way to determine what is expected of a person in a particular occupation. Of course, some skills that are necessary in a particular occupation are seldom used and would not be noticed unless a great deal of time was spent observing. For this reason, expert advice from those closely associated with the particular specialization is usually of value in an occupational analysis.

Determine the content for your unit, course, or program on the basis of established school objectives, the basic needs and abilities of the learners, and the occupational analysis of the area you teach. Entire books have been written on the subject of occupational analysis and most vocational teacher education programs have as part of their curriculums at least one course dealing with occupational analysis. Space will not permit a complete review of analysis techniques that are used. Those who desire more information should check the references at the end of this chapter.

SUMMARY

This chapter discussed determining what to teach. In some cases, much research and effort, including an occupational analysis, will have gone into the development of the course of study. In other cases, a limited amount of planning and time may have gone into its preparation.

The intent of this chapter was to present a brief overview of many of the items that must be considered in determining what to teach. Foremost consideration must be given to the philosophy and objectives of the school that you are teaching in. What are the objectives of the vocational education program? That should be a key question because that will indicate how the staff and school will be evaluated by the members of the community.

This chapter also discussed the importance of the relationship between course objectives, program objectives, and the overall school philosophy and objectives. In addition, the needs of the student are an important consideration. What do students expect from a vocational program? Why do they choose to attend a vocational school in the first place? Do vocational schools exist to prepare students for industry or do they function to meet the needs of the learners?

In the following chapters, we will get more at the "nuts and bolts" issues of planning, but such planning should be based on the questions and issues raised in this chapter.

ACTIVITIES

1.   Obtain a copy of the philosophy statement of the school that you are teaching in.

2.   Obtain a copy of the objectives of the school that you are teaching in.

3.   Review your present course of study. List its strong points and weak points. When was the course of study last updated? Can your present course of study be improved?

4.   List the objectives, in behavioral terms, for the specialization you are prepared to teach. These objectives may be for the program or for just the course you teach.

SOURCE MATERIALS

Fryklund, Verne C. *Occupational Analysis: Techniques and Procedures.* New York: Bruce, 1970.

Krishan, Paul K. and Braden, Paul. *Occupational Analysis of Educational Planning.* Columbus, Ohio: Merrill, 1975.

Larson, Milton E. *Teaching Related Subjects in Trade and Industrial and Technical Education*. Columbus, Ohio: Merrill, 1972.

Mager, Robert F. *Preparing Instructional Objectives*. Palo Alto, Calif.: Fearon, 1962.

Mager, Robert F. and Beach, Kenneth M. *Developing Vocational Instruction*. Palo Alto, Calif.: Fearon, 1967.

McMahon, Gordon G. *Curriculum Development in Trade and Industrial and Technical Education*. Columbus, Ohio: Merrill, 1974.

5

THE COURSE
OF STUDY

In planning a cross country flight, the pilot will use a number of aids in arriving at his final flight plan. The driver planning a long automobile trip on strange roads should review the road map and plan his route. The conscientious teacher will also plan well in advance and follow some form of instructional outline in his day-to-day preparation. The teacher's road map should be a well-planned and up-to-date instructional outline called a course of study.

It is true that many teachers have courses of study, but some seldom use them in planning their instructional strategy. Many are dust covered and out of date. Some teachers will not update their courses of study until administrative pressure is placed on them to do so.

The conscientious teacher will always attempt to keep his course of study current with modern industry and look for means to improve it. Updating of course content should be a continual process and not something that happens every five or ten years. The well-constructed course of study should be close at hand and used in weekly planning and lesson plan construction.

The unit method of course construction will be discussed in this chapter. The course of study should be divided into small instructional segments called units. It is suggested that the units be placed in a loose-leaf notebook or binder so that units may be added or deleted as needed. You may want to consider making the individual units available to your students as they progress from one instructional unit to the next. This informs the student about the instructional content of each unit and the method of evaluation that will be used to evaluate his performance. If you attempt to construct your units using behavioral objectives and levels of acceptable performance, the students should receive copies of the various instructional units. The course of study can be as valuable to the student as it is to the teacher.

COURSE OF STUDY

A course of study is a comprehensive resource which, when properly constructed, updated, and followed, will aid teacher and students in meeting the specific objectives of the course and program. The word *curriculum* generally refers to all the learning experiences, both formal and informal, which come under the school's control. When you take all the formal courses and programs, together with the informal experiences that students are exposed to in and out of school, you have the school curriculum. A course of study may in some cases be referred to as a course outline, but generally an outline is not as fully developed as one would expect for a course of study.

A course of study may be constructed for a one-day, one-week, one-month, one-year, two-year or longer course. For example, a three-year program in machine shop may be included in one course of study that in turn is subdivided into smaller parts called units. Or this same three-year program may be subdivided into three courses of study and called Machine Shop I, Machine Shop II, and Machine Shop III. In turn, each of the three levels of machine shop could be subdivided into still smaller parts we will call units.

Most school administrations seem to favor the level approach to curriculum design of a course of study. This means that a three-year program in secretarial science would be broken into three levels and three courses of study when put together as a package. However, it is possible to construct the course of study as one package made up of units of instruction. Whatever method or system best suits the administrative structure and organization of your school could be used. The teacher in planning or developing a course of study is doing curriculum planning and development work. The teacher in this situation is truly functioning as a curriculum worker.

LESSON PLANNING

PURPOSE

The course of study is like a road map for the instructor's use in preparing lesson content for his class. Usually, the course of study is school approved and adopted whereas lesson plans are the teacher's individual property. The teacher's main problem is planning what to teach using a course of study and adding lesson plans as the school year progresses.

The course of study is useful in the event the teacher becomes ill; the substitute teacher can then have an outline to follow. If a teacher decides to leave his position during the school year, the replacement teacher can carry on along the specified lines laid out in the course of study.

The course of study can also be placed in a loose-leaf binder and kept on the teacher's desk. Students should have a copy made available to them and be encouraged to use it as needed.

REASONS FOR USING A COURSE OF STUDY

If the shop and laboratory teachers are not convinced of the value of a well-planned course of study, little would be achieved in forcing them to construct one. Teachers must first be convinced of the value of a course of study.

A number of items must be considered and undertaken before a course of study is constructed. The philosophy and objectives of the school must be considered since they relate to the philosophy and objectives of the various courses of study. An occupational analysis of the occupation (electrician, practical nurse, etc.) would also have to be undertaken. The advisory committee would have been involved from the beginning stage on through to their approval of the completed program.

DEVELOPING A COURSE OF STUDY

A systematic procedure should be used in constructing the course of study. The following is a suggested procedure.

1. Consider and review the philosophy and stated objectives of the school. With the assistance of your curriculum advisory committee, write a statement of philosophy and state the

course objectives, preferably in behavioral terms. Take into consideration the age and grade level of your students and their educational backgrounds and abilities. Also, consider the practical elements of the amount of instructional time that will be available and the equipment and facility in which the instruction will take place.

2. An occupational analysis should be conducted at this point with the assistance of your advisory committee. Since the members of your committee might very well be the future employers of your students, let them take part and help in the occupational analysis. What level of performance and what skills are needed by a student to enter the specialization that you are teaching? This is the basic question, and the instructional content of the course of study should result from the occupational analysis.

3. Keep your advisory committee actively engaged from the very start. Do not do all the work yourself, and then ask them for their approval. Make them feel a part of the total effort. Even after they approve the course of study, keep them involved in continual evaluation and updating of the course. As they will be employing some of your students, they will be in an ideal position to evaluate the finished product—the student.

4. Start to write a course of study based on the previously mentioned three items. The technique suggested in this chapter will make use of the unit method of construction. The detailed procedure for the actual course of study will be discussed later in this chapter.

5. Weekly and daily plans should then be constructed based on the course of study. The course of study is a comprehensive outline and should not be too restrictive on the content of the daily plans. It should be flexible enough that the teacher has some variation in the actual lesson content.

6. Continual evaluation should be undertaken in terms of the stated objectives of the course of study. This evaluation should be an on-going process and should involve employers, students, and the school staff.

In the development of the course of study the teacher must keep in mind the purpose for which it will be used. The basic components of a teaching-learning situation (Figure 3-1) are reproduced below in Figure 5-1. This is the basic principle on which the design of the course of study and the lesson plans in this book are based. Keep this design in mind as you continue with the material in this text. The overall course of study, the various units that make up the course of study, and the lesson plans that result based on the units will all be based on this design.

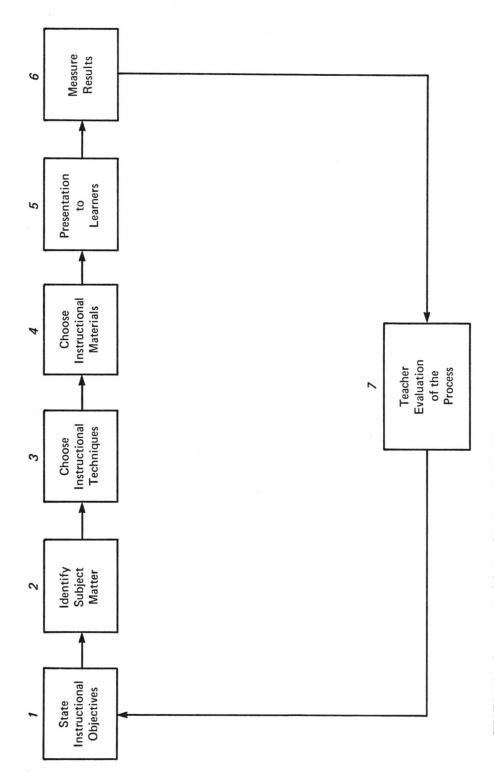

FIGURE 5-1. Components of the Teaching-Learning Situation

OUTLINE FOR THE COURSE OF STUDY

To be a really usable item the course of study should be contained in some form of loose-leaf binder, so that units can be modified, deleted, or added to as needed. Also, as lesson plans are constructed by the teacher during the course of the year, they can be added to the proper unit in the course of study. It is generally much easier to update and modify a course of study assembled in this manner than it would be to change a bound copy.

The following items are essential to every course of study.

1. Title page
2. Introductory statement
3. Philosophy of the school
4. Objectives of the course—desired outcomes
5. Student requirements—prerequisites
6. Length of the course
7. Relationship of course to all-school program
8. Topical unit outline
9. Instructional units
10. Advisory committee statement

Each item of the outline will now be considered in detail.

TITLE PAGE. The title page should contain the following information: (a) course title (Machine Design, Machine Design I, Plumbing, etc.); (b) duration of the course (one-year course of study, three-year course of study, etc.); (c) name of the school; (d) department, and (e) date.

INTRODUCTORY STATEMENT. This should be a basic statement in which are explained the reasons such a course is to be offered. You might mention the employment demand for students who complete such a program of study. The statement should be in plain, noneducational terminology so that students, parents, and employers can understand it. Note the assistance rendered by the curriculum advisory committee and indicate that the committee has approved the course of study.

PHILOSOPHY OF THE SCHOOL. Obtain the board of education's approved statement of philosophy and include it at this point in the course of study. As you are aware, this statement should have guided the total course of study development to this point. If school-wide objectives have been approved by the board of education, also include them at this time.

OBJECTIVES OF THE COURSE—DESIRED OUTCOMES. This is perhaps the most important item in the course of study. It is necessary at this point that you list in simple language the stated objectives of the course. It is on the basis of these stated objectives that the total course of study, the program, the student, the board of education, the administrative staff, and the teacher are evaluated.

Use care in writing objectives for the course of study. Do not make statements that are either too vague, too specific, or too difficult to achieve in the time available. It would be best to write statements that refer to desired student behaviors at the completion of the course.

In the licensed occupations we have excellent examples. An objective of a cosmetology course might state, "Upon completion of this course of study, the student should be able to pass the state board examination in cosmetology." The cosmetology program may consist of only one or two courses of study, perhaps more. The objectives of each course of study should be consistent with the program objectives and lead to success on the state board examination.

In nonlicensed occupations, much more is involved in writing objectives. It might be best to list the desired behavioral outcomes in detail. These would be statements such as the following.

> The student will be able to do a complete engine tune-up in _____ minutes, and do it successfully 75 per cent of the time.

> The student will be able to troubleshoot a transistor radio in _____ minutes, localize the trouble, and do it successfully 75 per cent of the time.

The above two statements are only examples, and the percentages would vary depending upon your own measure of successful performance.

STUDENT REQUIREMENTS—PREREQUISITES. You should now list the prerequisites necessary for the course. This is comparable to certain college classes for which certain courses are prerequisites. Rather than list courses, it is possible to require a certain level of reading or mathematical ability based on standardized tests.

You should also list any special physical conditions that are desirable and, likewise, physical conditions that would prevent a student from working in the specialization.

For example, students with skin conditions should be advised to seek professional assistance before electing a barbering or cosmetology course. This writer knows of students who completed cosmetology courses and were never advised that certain skin conditions could prevent them from obtaining a state board license.

THE COURSE OF STUDY

Electronics students should be advised that color blindness is a handicap in the electronics industry. This is due to the fact that many electronic components are color coded for identification.

Levels of previous learning are important, but it is also necessary to investigate and spell out physical conditions that are desirable for the specialization for which you are preparing the course of study.

LENGTH OF THE COURSE. Indicate the number of days, weeks, months, or years that are usually necessary to complete the course. If you follow some of the previous recommendations and develop one course of study for the total program, this should be specified. In other words, if your school has a three-year electronics program and develops one course of study divided into units, you should make it clear that the course of study is for a three-year period based on three consecutive school years. You might indicate the approximate number of units that would be completed each year.

It is difficult to determine instructional time until you have taught the course a number of times. It is best to be overprepared, so have more material in the course of study than is required to meet the stated objectives of the course.

RELATIONSHIP OF THE COURSE TO THE ALL-SCHOOL PROGRAM. Indicate how the course relates to the school program as a whole. You should tell in what ways the course relates to the total learning experience of the student and how it fits into the curriculum offerings of the school.

TOPICAL UNIT OUTLINE. This is a topical listing of the various units in the total course of study. It should be listed in sequence from the simplest to the most complex learning activities. The unit topic should be listed as well as the major subtopics of the unit. A typical unit might appear this way in the topical unit outline.

UNIT V: VACUUM TUBES

1. Schematic symbols
2. Construction
3. Classification
4. Electron emission
5. Types of emission
6. The emitter (cathode materials)
7. Directly and indirectly heated tubes

LESSON PLANNING

8. Theory of diode operation
9. Plate (anode materials)
10. Fleming Valve
11. DeForrest Theory
12. Testing vacuum tubes
13. Life testing (aging)

In the example, "Vacuum Tubes" is the topic of Unit V. Unit V consists of thirteen subtopics which cover the objectives of the vacuum tubes unit. The complete course of study might be as follows.

UNIT III: Magnetism

UNIT II: Electron Theory

UNIT 1:   Direct Current Circuits

UNIT IV: Alternating Current Circuits

UNIT V: Vacuum Tubes

UNIT VI: Solid State Devices

Each unit would be broken down into a number of subtopics, and these together would make up the topical unit outline.

INSTRUCTIONAL UNITS. Later in this chapter, the unit approach method will be discussed in detail. The units are the most important elements in the course of study since it is from the unit content that the teacher develops the daily lesson plan.

The unit should not be confused with the daily lesson plan. A number of lesson plans would be necessary to cover the content included in the unit. As lesson plans are developed, they could be placed with the proper unit and then modified as needed for future use.

Figure 5-2 indicates the subtopics that should be included in an instructional unit as well as a brief statement about each topic. Each student should be encouraged or required to develop at least one instructional unit and have it reviewed by the instructor.

ADVISORY COMMITTEE STATEMENT. A brief statement by the members of the curriculum advisory committee should be included. The statement should indicate their assistance and approval of the course of study as well as a notation that evaluation of the course will be a continuous process.

THE COURSE OF STUDY

UNIT #1

Instructional Unit Format

INTRODUCTORY STATEMENT. The actual introductory statement that will be used to introduce the new unit to the students.

INSTRUCTIONAL OBJECTIVES. The desired behavior of the students after the completion of the unit. Demonstrated skills that the students will have at the end of the unit.

INSTRUCTIONAL CONTENT. Outline, in detail, of the instructional content to be included in the unit. It will be from this outline that the teacher will develop his lesson plans.

METHODS OF PRESENTATION. The instructional strategy used to present the material to the students. Individual instruction, large group instruction, small group instruction, lecture, programmed instruction, computer assisted instruction, etc.

INSTRUCTIONAL AIDS. A listing of the instructional aids that should be used. Films, slides, tape, T.V. computer assisted instruction, in-basket training, problems, etc.

REFERENCE MATERIALS. A listing of reference books, articles, charts, resource people that could be used for supportive information.

EVALUATION CRITERIA. How the students will be evaluated on their success or failure to complete the unit. Should be based entirely on the earlier stated behavioral objectives.

FIGURE 5-2. Outline of an Instructional Unit Format

THE INSTRUCTIONAL UNIT APPROACH

The unit approach to course construction is simply a technique that divides the subject content into a number of instructional units. These units or instructional packages, when assembled from the simplest to the most complex, would make up the course content. Successful completion of the objectives of the beginning unit would also meet the entrance conditions of the following unit.

The ultimate goal is to construct a number of instructional units with clearly defined behavioral objectives and the necessary evaluation criteria for each unit. Early in the school year the beginning students could be given a test to determine with what unit they should start. As an example, let us say the automotive mechanics program is divided into fifty instructional units. By means of a test, some students might be able to satisfactorily demonstrate their proficiency on a number of the beginning units. Perhaps one student has demonstrated a mastery of the first five units. Are you, as the teacher, still going to require him to redo the first five units, or will you allow him to start on unit six? The student should be allowed to start work on unit six. This is self-pacing and requires individualized instruction on your part.

The unit method is best suited to this type of instruction and, when combined with behavioral objectives and performance evaluation, can be a very rewarding experience for both the teacher and students.

After the occupational analysis is completed, those involved in the construction of the course of study would outline in systematic order the tasks one in that trade must be able to perform. The sequence (order) should be such that one unit forms the foundation for the following unit, and so on, until the stated objectives of the course have been met. However, the well-prepared course of study will have more complex material surpassing the stated instructional objectives. The purpose of these added units is to make sure the teacher is prepared for the students who fulfill the course objectives before the end of the school term. An alternative would be to allow those students to concentrate on the other subjects they are taking. Unfortunately, it will probably be a long time before such a secondary program is in existence.

The construction of each unit would be based on a number of subtopics. The basic structure of a unit is indicated in Figure 5-2.

The same format used to outline the style of the individual units of the course of study can be used for lesson plans as well, though greater elaboration is needed under the section labeled "Instructional Content."

Two exhibits follow which are based on the format suggested in this chapter. Exhibit 5-1 presents a sample topical unit outline for a course in welding technology. Exhibit 5-2 presents one completed unit from the course in welding technology. These are student-constructed examples making use of the format and procedure suggested in this chapter.

THE COURSE OF STUDY

EXHIBIT 5-1
EXAMPLE OF A TOPICAL UNIT OUTLINE
FOR A COURSE IN WELDING TECHNOLOGY

UNIT: I. Welding — An Essential Skill

1. Where welding is used
2. Types of welding processes
3. Selection of proper welding processes
4. Occupational opportunities in welding

UNIT: II. Metallurgy — As It Applies to Welding

1. Mechanical properties of metals
2. Classification of carbon steels
3. Alloy steels
4. Steel code classifying systems
5. Structure of metal
6. Effects of heat during the welding process
7. Welding defects
8. Residual Stresses
9. Controlling residual stresses
10. Jigs and Fixtures

UNIT: III. Oxy-acetylene Welding Machines and Accessories

1. Separating oxygen for use in welding
2. Separating acetylene for use in welding
3. The oxygen cylinder
4. The acetylene cylinder
5. Handling cylinders
6. The welding outfit
7. Regulators
8. Oxygen and acetylene hose
9. The welding torch
10. Protective clothing

UNIT: IV. Setting Up and Operating Oxy-acetylene Welding Outfit

1. Assembling the welding outfit
2. Selecting the proper welding tip
3. Lighting the torch
4. Adjusting the flame
5. Testing the flame
6. Flame control
7. Backfire and flashback
8. Shutting off the torch

UNIT: V. Shielded Metal-Arc Welding — Machines and Accessories

1. Welding current
2. Electrical terms
3. Electrical circuit
4. Welding machines
5. Transformers
6. Motor generators
7. Rectifiers
8. Personal equipment
9. Shop equipment
10. Cleaning tools

EXHIBIT 5–1, *continued*

UNIT: VI. Electrodes

1. What is an electrode
2. Identifying electrodes
3. Selecting the correct electrode
4. Conserving and storing electrodes
5. Special electrodes

UNIT: VII. Gas-Shielded Arc Welding — Gas Tungsten Arc — T.I.G.

1. Specific advantages of gas-shielded arc processes
2. Types of gas-shielded arc processes
3. Welding machines
4. Electrodes
5. Shielding gas
6. The filler rod
7. T.I.G. welding

UNIT: VIII. Gas-Shielded Arc Welding — Gas Tungsten Arc — M.I.G.

1. Specific advantages of M.I.G. welding
2. Types of metal transfer
3. M.I.G. welding equipment
4. Shielding gas
5. Welding wire
6. Power source

UNIT: IX. Testing Welds

1. Visual examination
2. Destructive testing
3. Tensile testing
4. Free-bent test
5. Etching test
6. Hardness testing
7. Ultransonic testing
8. Radiographic inspection
9. Eddy current testing
10. Magnetic particle inspection
11. Weld uniformity test

EXHIBIT 5-2

EXAMPLE OF ONE COMPLETED UNIT
FOR A COURSE IN WELDING TECHNOLOGY

UNIT VII
Gas-Shielded Arc Welding — Gas Tungsten — T.I.G.

INTRODUCTORY STATEMENT

The primary consideration in any welding operation is to produce a
weld that has the same properties as the base metal. Such a weld can
only be made if the molten puddle is completely protected from the
atmosphere during the welding process. Otherwise atmospheric oxygen
and nitrogen will be absorbed in the molten puddle, and the weld will
be porous and weak. In gas-shielded arc welding, a gas is used as a
covering shield around the arc to prevent the atmosphere from
contaminating the weld.

Originally gas-shielded arc welding was developed to weld corrosion
resistant and other difficult-to-weld metals. The T.I.G. process, as it is
commonly known throughout the welding industry, was first experimented
with in the 1940s, but practical development of the process took place in
the 1950s. Gas-shielded arc welding will eventually displace much of the
shielded metal arc and oxy-acetylene production welding due to the
superiority of the weld, greater ease of operation, and increased welding
speed. In addition to manual welding, the process can be automated, and
in either case can be used for both light and heavy gage ferrous and
nonferrous metals.

EXHIBIT 5-2, *continued*

INSTRUCTIONAL OBJECTIVES

GENERAL

On completion of this unit the student will *enumerate* the particular uses of the T.I.G. welding machine, *identify* the different components, *recall* their functions, and *demonstrate* the steps in setting up and operating the T.I.G. welding unit, following the recommended safety precautions.

SPECIFIC

The student will be able to:

    a. *identify* the advantages of gas-shielded arc processes,

    b. *describe* the types of gas-shielded arc processes,

    c. *recall* the various parts and their functions in a T.I.G. welding machine,

    d. *identify* the types and applications of electrodes,

    e. *select* a correct shielding gas for a specific function,

    f. *utilize* the proper filler rod for a specific assignment,

    g. *operate* a T.I.G. unit and compare the result with other welding techniques.

EXHIBIT 5-2, *continued*

INSTRUCTIONAL CONTENT

Detailed Outline

THEORY: 15 periods

1. T.I.G. processes
2. Type of machine
3. Slope control
4. AC/DC and A.C.H.F. applications
5. Types of torches

6. Types and application of electrodes
7. Selecting the shielding gas
8. Proper selection and purpose of filler rods
9. Techniques of operating the T.I.G. unit

PRACTICE: 20 periods

1. Setting up the T.I.G. unit

2. Safety precautions
3. Fusion beads on 1/8" aluminum

METHODS OF PRESENTATION

The theory part of the T.I.G. unit will be presented to the students as a group in the form of lectures. Because of the complexity of the topic, sketches, drawings, textbooks, and the T.I.G. machine itself will be used.

The practical aspects will be carried out as follows:

Setting up a T.I.G. unit, emphasizing all safety precautions and demonstrating a fusion bead on a 1/8" aluminum, will be presented to the students as a group. After the demonstration, the students will be divided into four groups. Each group will operate a T.I.G. unit. Further assistance will be given as the groups progress. If the need arises, individual instruction will be given.

EXHIBIT 5–2, *continued*

REFERENCES

Althouse, Andrew D., Carl H. Turnquist, and William A. Bowditch. *Modern Welding.* Homewood, Ill.: Goodheart-Willcox, 1967.

Giachino, J. W., William Weeks, and Elmer Brune. *Welding Skills and Practices.* Chicago, Ill.: American Technical Society, 1971.

Griffin, Ivan H. and Edward M. Roden. *Basic T.I.G. Welding.* Albany, N. Y.: Delmar Publishers, 1962.

Jefferson, Ted B., ed. *The Welding Encyclopedia, Sixteenth Edition.* Morton Grove, Ill.: Monticello Books, 1968.

Pamphlets on T.I.G. welding are available from the Canadian Welding Bureau, Montreal, Quebec, and the Institute of Welding Technology, Edmonton, Alberta.

EVALUATION CRITERIA

On completion of this unit, students will be evaluated as follows:

THEORY – Written Examination (Sample included)

PRACTICE – 1/8" Aluminum — Flat Butt

Time Allowed: two class periods

Machine Involved: T.I.G. Welding Unit Station

Materials Required:

Aluminum 4043 Size 1/8" x 2" x 5"

Aluminum 4043 Filler Rods 3/32"

Tungsten Zirconium Electrode 3/32"

Marking Scheme for Finished Weld:

Distortion Control – 20

Forward Bend – 15

Reverse Bend – 25

Rupture Test – 20

General Appearance – 20

100%

EXHIBIT 5-2, *continued*

INSTRUCTIONAL AIDS

A T.I.G. machine
A disassembled T.I.G. machine
Charts
Filmstrips
Transparencies for the overhead projector
Diagrammatic sketches
1/8" aluminum plates
3/32" zirconium electrodes
T.I.G. welding unit with A.C.H.F.
Mimeographed instructions to be handed out

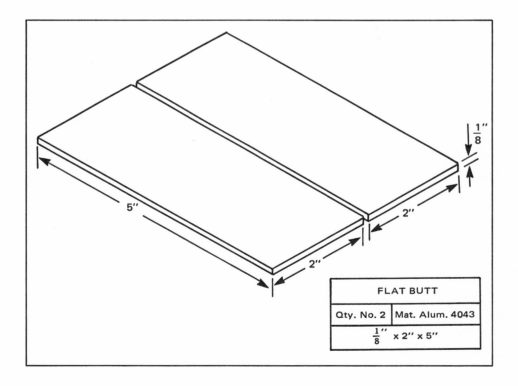

FLAT BUTT

Qty. No. 2	Mat. Alum. 4043
$\frac{1}{8}''$ x 2" x 5"	

SUMMARY

This chapter could stand by itself as a model for developing a total course of study or a unit within a course of study. Curriculum and the development of a course of study would be much more effective if the teacher who was going to use it had a part in its development.

As you introduce a new unit to your class, you might give each student a copy of the new unit so everyone in the class knows what is expected and how they will be evaluated at the end of the unit. This system works and if you develop a good course of study it will make your job easier.

Examples of a topical unit outline (Exhibit 5-1) and of one completed unit (Exhibit 5-2) are included in the chapter to give you a basic idea of what both look like on completion. You should feel free to modify either or both to fit your needs. Space does not permit the inclusion of a completed course of study.

It is suggested that you develop the materials in the manner presented in this chapter. Also, it is a good idea to use a loose-leaf notebook to keep the outline in, making it much easier to delete, modify or add to the existing course of study. Your efforts in preplanning will pay off when the actual teaching begins in your shop or laboratory.

ACTIVITIES

1. Prepare a topical outline for the program or course that you teach or plan to teach.

2. Prepare one instruction unit in the manner outlined in this chapter.

3. Evaluate the course of study that you are presently using or obtain a current course of study in your field of specialization and evaluate it.

SOURCE MATERIALS

McMahon, Gordon G. *Curriculum Development in Trade and Industrial and Technical Education.* Columbus, Ohio: Merrill, 1974.

Pucel, David J. and Knaak, William C. *Individualizing Vocational and Technical Instruction.* Columbus, Ohio: Merrill, 1974.

THE COURSE OF STUDY

Stadt, Ronald, et al. *Planning and Organizing Career Curriculum: Articulated Education.* New York: Sams, 1973.

Tyler, Ralph W. *Basic Principles of Curriculum and Instruction.* Chicago: University of Chicago Press, 1949.

6

PREPLANNING

It is assumed at this point that you are following a course of study that you either have constructed yourself or were given by the administration of your school. In any event, you should be following an outline or course of study appropriate to the subject and grade level that you are teaching. With the course of study as your "road map" it is now your responsibility to get on with the planning and then the instructional process. It is for you to decide on the instructional strategy to be used in the classroom. Only you will be able to find out what techniques and methods work best for you in the teaching-learning situation.

THE VALUE OF GOOD PREPLANNING

Preplanning is essential for any teacher, even experienced teachers. It insures maximum usage of instructional time during the teaching-learning situation. The ill-prepared teacher is guilty of wasting his own time and, more importantly, the time of his students. One minute of wasted time has to be multiplied by the number of students in the class.

Preplanning begins the moment one signs a teaching contract and ends the day of retirement. It should be an on-going process, and local administrators should provide suitable planning time in the daily schedule of each teacher.

Occupational analysis and outlining a course of study are examples of preplanning. Now, assuming that a course of study is to be followed, consideration must be given to the plan book, term plan, monthly plan, weekly plan and the daily plan.

Good preplanning should, and can, prevent embarrassing classroom experiences such as presenting a lesson in ten minutes that you had planned to make in thirty minutes. Preplanning can prevent your being in the middle of a demonstration and finding that you are missing a tool or instructional device essential to your lesson. Preplanning can prevent trouble occurring with audiovisual devices that you are using with your lesson. As indicated earlier, it is always better to be overprepared than underprepared.

The teaching-learning situation is illustrated in Figure 5-1. It represents what this book is all about. The content of each of the blocks in the diagram will be discussed in detail.

There are five characteristics of good planning:

1. Good planning will take into account the abilities, needs, and interests of the students.
2. Good planning will be flexible enough to allow for last-minute changes and emergencies.
3. Good planning will be such that a substitute teacher of equal ability could understand and continue using the existing plan.
4. Good planning will outline the instructional strategy (methods and techniques) to be used in the teaching-learning situation.
5. Good planning will constantly show an awareness of the stated objectives of the program and have some built-in method of evaluation.

THE PLAN BOOK

Most school systems will require faculty members to maintain a plan book of one type or another. A plan book is usually a commercially prepared item which is made available to the teachers. Space is provided in the plan book for the teacher to write out the term plan and weekly plans. The term plan is, as the name implies, the plan for a term (usually twenty weeks). The weekly plan is the plan for one week at a time, and sufficient space is usually provided for a forty-week school year.

The requirements for keeping a plan book vary from school system to school system. One known system requires the plan book to be kept in, or on, the teacher's desk. Plans for at least one week in advance are to be ready at any given time. Plan books are to be placed in the teacher's mailbox on Friday afternoon and kept there until Monday morning.

Any number of reasons can be given for maintaining a plan book. (It results in better teaching, and can be of assistance to a substitute teacher.) But the *teacher* must realize the need to keep his plan book up to date.

Segments are taken from the course of study and included in the plan book. The notation is usually in outline form, but with sufficient references and page numbers to be useful to the teacher or a substitute. The plan book is not to be confused with the daily lesson plan or the course of study. The course of study is the detailed content of the course. The daily lesson plan is the reference source to be followed by the teacher in presenting a lesson. The plan book holds a position between the course of study and the daily lesson plan. In its original condition, it simply has blank spaces for the user to write in his plans, references, and any other notation of value.

In most school systems, the plan books are collected at the end of the school year. They are usually kept on file for a number of years before being destroyed. Plan books may be called in weekly or from time to time by department chairmen or by the administration. Usually the contents are checked for content and preplanning.

Some plan books also have a section for class attendance and grades. A separate class book for attendance and grades is better than the combined type for two reasons. First, in some schools, plan books are not to be removed from the school. This makes it impossible to take the book home and record grades in it. Second, if plan books are called in, so is the class attendance and grades section of the combination book. Keeping separate books, one for plans and one for attendance and grades, seems to be a flexible arrangement.

The main value of the plan book is to the teacher. Careful planning should make for better teaching and utilization of instructional time. On Monday of each week, review the plans with your students so that they are aware of the week's events. Give them their assignments, if any, on Monday and indicate what day the assignment is due. Remember, the plan book is a tool to help the instructional process, and it will be as helpful as the instructor makes it.

The Term Plan

A section is usually included in plan books for writing in the term plan. The necessity for the term plan varies with the course of study. If a well-planned, comprehensive course of study is used for the course, an outline type of term plan is suitable. If the teacher is teaching without a course of study, then a detailed term plan is essential.

The term plan is a plan for one term of a school year. A term, sometimes referred to as a semester, is usually about twenty weeks in length.

The term plan, like a course of study, is an example of long-range planning. In a term plan, you should indicate what units will be covered and what level of skill you expect the students to have mastered at the end of the term.

Assuming that you are using a course of study, the term plan should be no problem. You can simply indicate on a weekly or monthly basis what units from the course of study will be covered in a given period of time. Then, you reference the term plan to your course of study and indicate where the course of study is kept. *It is suggested that you keep your course of study on your desk and in plain view of students and visitors.* You may want to have a special copy for students and a special copy for visitors.

The teacher operating without a course of study will have to be much more detailed in developing a term plan. But the term plan can later be used to develop a course of study.

The Monthly Plan

The monthly plan is simply the plan for one month. It would be considered a long-range plan. The monthly plan is based on the earlier discussed term plan. The monthly plan can be helpful in allowing the teacher to modify his long-range plans.

The Weekly Plan

The weekly plan is simply the schedule of shop activities for a one-week period. It is broken down into five days, and space is provided for the teacher to indicate shop activities on a daily basis.

The weekly plan is based on the content of the course of study. Individual lesson plans are prepared by the teacher, based on the weekly plan. For example, if some sort of demonstration lesson is planned for Thursday, the teacher will develop a lesson plan to aid him in presenting the lesson.

Teachers should attempt to make their plans at least one week in advance. In the event of illness, the substitute teacher will then have plans for at least one week. Planning much beyond five class sessions is not a good idea. If the stated material is not covered, a modification in the weekly plan will have to be made, and this will affect the preplanning.

The weekly plan is short range and is usually presented in the form of an outline of the topics or lessons to be covered on a day-by-day basis for a one-week period of time. The instructional strategy (method of presentation) and the types of audiovisual materials to be used should be indicated.

The weekly plan provides for a balance of activities, content, skills, and attitudes in all program areas. It allots time for stressing special interests, allows for unexpected events or developments, and includes working with individuals, groups, and the entire class.

One is not bound inflexibly by exact minutes. Approximate the time needed for each lesson. Include the following in your weekly plans.

Lesson topics

Instruction strategy

Reminders for the week

Duty assignments

Audiovisual aids

Assemblies

Joint lessons (team teaching, related science, etc.)

Preparation periods

Observations (planned visits by your supervisor)

Figure 6-1 presents a typical format for a plan book. This represents a plan for one week of instructional time designed for a vocational teacher responsible for two two-and-one-half-hour sections of Electronics I. The plan is generally made out for the week in advance and should be completed by the Friday before. The teacher, Mr. Thomas, is responsible for two sections of the same course. Time is not indicated on the one-week plan, but this is no problem because, as a lesson or experiment ends, the balance of the assigned time is available for individual project or experiment work. Mr. Thomas assigns one new experiment each week and, in addition, each student is working on an individual project. Such a plan relates directly to the course of study used for Electronics I.

PREPLANNING

WEEK OF MARCH 15

TEACHER: THOMAS
SUBJECT: ELECTRONICS I

Section	Monday	Tuesday	Wednesday	Thursday	Friday	Comments
A.M.	(1) Film on transistors	Individual Project and Experiment Period	(1) Do Exp. 15 from text	(1) Short quiz on transistors	Teacher Conference	30-week marking period ends next week
	(2) Assign Chapter 15 for Thursday		(2) Students to complete Exp. 15 during this period	(2) Review Chapter 15 from text	No class	Prepare suitable evaluation
	(3) Do Nos. 1–10, p. 195, for Thursday			(3) Review assignment from p. 195, Nos. 1–10, text		
P.M.	Individual Project and Experiment Period	Same as Monday A.M. Section	Same as A.M. Section	Same as A.M. Section	Same as A.M. Section	Same as A.M. Section

FIGURE 6-1. One-Week Plan

The Daily Plan

The daily plan is the organizational plan of events for one day. It is based on the normal schedule of activities assigned to a given teacher. It can start with homeroom period and continue through dismissal at the end of the school day. If the school day is based on eight periods, the daily plan will indicate what the teacher is doing each of the periods. The daily plan is one day of the weekly plan and involves no more planning than that involved in weekly planning.

When the weekly plan is complete, you automatically will have the daily plan for each of the next five school days. The daily plan is in outline form and is not to be confused with the lesson plan. Lesson plans and lesson plan construction will be discussed fully in chapter 7.

The weekly plan for Mr. Thomas, as shown in Figure 6-1, consists of five different daily plans. On Monday, for example, in the A.M. session, Mr. Thomas will show a film dealing with transistors. After the film, he will allow some time for discussion and questions. He then plans to assign Chapter 15 for Thursday and questions 1 through 10, from page 195 of the text, also for the same date. The remaining class time will be spent on individual project work. For the afternoon section, the daily plan for Monday indicates that the class will have the whole period for individual work on their projects and experiment. During this period of time, Mr. Thomas will be moving from student to student and offering instruction on an individual or small group basis as needed.

As suggested earlier, it is a good habit to review the whole plan for the week with students on Monday of each week, so that they can plan their time for assignments from the electronics course as well as their other courses. This procedure is also helpful if a student is missing during the week. In other words, the assignment due Thursday is given on Monday, not Wednesday. The student who misses class on Wednesday cannot then say, "Gee, Mr. Thomas, I didn't know about the assignment!"

The daily plan is one small part of the weekly plan. If it is well organized the day will generally go more smoothly than if it is planned as it goes along.

USE OF THE PLAN BOOK

The plan book will be as useful to the teacher as he makes it. It is much like the course of study in that respect. The best course of study is of little value in the back of a file cabinet. Likewise, the teacher who makes satisfactory plans in his plan book but never uses them will find little value in pre-planning.

The plan book should be used daily by the teacher and modifications made as required. Students should be told Monday what the plan for the week is.

Continual use of the plan book should help guard against repeating the same lesson a number of times or skipping over essential material.

The plans included in the plan book should be based on the contents of the course of study. Going it alone, without a course of study, is not suggested practice but, if it has to be done, it is better to use a plan book and plan as well as possible, until a course of study is developed.

The plan book is an aid to the teacher in the teaching-learning situation. Good preplanning will usually make the job easier. The teacher who plans from minute to minute and plays it by ear will usually have a more difficult time than the teacher who believes in and does adequate pre-planning.

TEACHER–TEACHER PLANNING

Teacher-teacher planning involves two or more teachers meeting together to plan for class. In vocational-technical education, such planning should be encouraged between teachers teaching the same subject. Teacher-teacher planning is also suggested to coordinate the instructional program between shop teachers and related-subjects teachers. Teachers of mathematics, science, and English should attempt to coordinate their teaching with what is scheduled by the shop instructor.

Joint planning should result in a much more coordinated instructional program, which will be of utmost advantage to the students.

Assignments required of students can be organized to meet the requirements of two or more teachers. If a research assignment is required by the shop teacher, the assignment can be reviewed by the English instructor for usage, grammar, and style and then passed on to the shop instructor for technical accuracy. The same procedure can be used in mathematics and science courses. Such a program might lend itself to a "team approach" to planning. Teacher-teacher planning makes a lot of sense and should be encouraged by administrators.

It is essential that teachers have a schedule that will make teacher-teacher planning possible. The administrator who wants to encourage such planning should provide teachers with suitable planning time, office space, and expert advice.

PUPIL–TEACHER PLANNING

Pupil-teacher planning provides for, and encourages, student contributions to the development of the instructional process. The teacher and his pupils plan together for topics, units, routines, trips, special events, programs, and projects. Lessons can be planned with the entire class, with small groups, or with individual students.

The teacher who has not had experience with pupil-teacher planning should ease into it rather than rush into it blind. Start with involving students in planning small projects and then move onto larger ones. Pupil-teacher planning is not something that every teacher can use.

Planning between the teacher and pupils encourages critical thinking and self-expression. It also encourages the students to be a part of the teaching-learning situation and thereby helps them feel a closer relationship to the process.

PLANNING FOR THE SUBSTITUTE TEACHER

Suitable preplanning will also be of assistance to the person called upon to substitute for you when, due to circumstances of illness, family, or business, you are unable to teach. The form displayed in Figure 6-2, Instruction Sheet for Shop Substitute, should be completed and kept in the front of your plan book. This form should be completed as early in the school year as possible and placed in the plan book as suggested. Figure 6-3 displays a somewhat different form entitled "Classroom Instructions for Substitute" and can be used in the event you know you will not be in school for the next day or so. The form in Figure 6-2 is always available for that unexpected day when, due to last-minute illness or family problems, you are not able to go to school. Both of these forms will help the person called into substitute for you.

The Burr D. Coe Vocational and Technical High School in New Jersey asks substitute teachers to complete the form displayed in Figure 6-4. The information obtained is passed along to the regular teacher. A review of the content of this form will give you a basic idea of how to prepare for days when you are not able to meet your classes.

BURR D. COE VOCATIONAL AND TECHNICAL HIGH SCHOOL SHOP TEACHER SUBSTITUTE

Instruction Sheet for Shop Substitute

Shop Teacher: Keep the following information clearly visible in the front of your daily plan book:

A. Shop Routine:

B. General Outline of a Typical Day's Activity in the Shop/Class A.M. and P.M.

C. A List of 2 or 3 Students from Each Class Group Who Will Provide the Best Assistants to the Substitute:

D. Times for Clean-up and Dismissal:

E. Other Special Instructions:

FIGURE 6-2. *Instruction Sheet for Shop Substitute*

LESSON PLANNING

CLASSROOM INSTRUCTIONS FOR SUBSTITUTE

I. Welcome to my room. Thank you for substituting for me. I wish you a good day!

II. My name is: _____

III. You are in room _____

IV. I teach the following subjects in this room:

SUBJECTS   CLASS TITLES

V. The books for the above subjects may be found:

VI. My daily schedule
     Plan book
     Seating charts
     Grade record book
     Attendance record book   May be found: _____

                                 _____

                                 _____

                                 _____

VII. My lunch period is: _____

VIII. Special instructions are:

FIGURE 6-3.   Classroom Instructions for Substitute

BURR D. COE VOCATIONAL AND TECHNICAL HIGH SCHOOL

Shop Teacher Substitute Report

Sub's Name _____

Subbing for: _____ Date: _____

Morning Class:

A. Home Room (if applicable)
Was the roll call book readily available?   _____

Were absentee slips readily available?   _____

Was information on the regular teacher's routine
provided?   _____

B. Shop Classes   A.M. and P.M.
Was the roll call book readily available?   _____

Were the shop keys complete and identifiable?   _____

Was equipment convenient and in working order?   _____

C. Your suggestions and criticisms will be appreciated.

Did the regular instructor provide enough information on the operation
of the shop?

_____

_____

Is there anything we can do or provide which will make future substitutes
in this shop more effective?

_____

_____

FIGURE 6-4. Shop Teacher Substitute Report

Do you personally feel that learning was taking place today? If not, why not?

_____

_____

(PLEASE TURN IN THIS REPORT TO THE PRINCIPAL'S SECRETARY AT THE END OF THE DAY)

FIGURE 6-4 continued

SUMMARY

This chapter discussed the importance of a course of study in day-to-day activity of the shop or classroom.

Discussion was based in part on the diagram shown in Figure 5-1, Components of a Teaching-Learning Situation, and all planning has the good of the learner as its basis. The value of good planning and the use of the plan book was discussed in some detail, for example, to assist the substitute teacher on days you are not able to be in school.

Just as a well-designed and prepared course of study will make your job a little easier, so will adequate planning. With your course of study as a base, the plan book will help organize your course work for a term, week, or day, as the case may be. From these planning tools will emerge your lesson plans. A procedure for lesson plan development is presented in the next chapter.

SOURCE MATERIALS

Kemp, Jerrold E. _Instructional Design_. Belmont, Calif.: Fearon, 1971.

Petrequin, Gaynor. _Individualizing Learning Through Modular-Flexible Programming_. New York: McGraw-Hill, 1968.

Pucel, David J. and Knaak, William C. _Individualizing Vocational and Technical Instruction_. Columbus: Merrill, 1975.

7

THE LESSON PLAN

A lesson plan is an instructional aid for the teacher. The most helpful lesson plans are those prepared by the teacher and then put to immediate use in the shop or related classroom situation. Lesson plans prepared by others and then adopted for use will be of limited value to the user. Part of the value of lesson plan construction is the preparation phase of the process. In the preparation phase, the logical sequencing of instructional content can take place, and instructional aids and media devices can be selected.

All teachers are able to profit from the use of some form of lesson plan. The most experienced teacher who has taught the same lesson a hundred times only kids himself when he dispenses with lesson plans. The first-year teacher presenting a lesson for the first time should have a very elaborate plan. In fact, most public speakers have some kind of plan to aid them in logically organizing and presenting their material. A well-constructed lesson plan will not save the day for a "poor" teacher, but it can help him. If lesson plans could make anyone a teacher, no doubt there would be many companies preparing and selling tried and proven lesson plans to the public school systems. There is no substitute for practical ability and know-how. The lesson plan is an aid, not a crutch for the poorly prepared teacher.

Policies vary from school to school regarding the preparation of lesson plans. You may be employed in a school that requires that daily lesson plans be submitted each day or each week. On the other hand, you might be employed in a school that has no formal policy on lesson plans. Policies mean little, since the important thing is that teachers believe in the lesson plan. Forcing teachers to submit lesson plans probably does very little to improve the instructional process, if the various teachers do not believe in their value.

DEFINITION

The teacher should consider lesson plans management aids for providing the best teaching-learning situation possible. The plan itself cannot guarantee good instructional presentations, but it should help.

A well-prepared lesson plan can also be used as an instruction sheet. Instruction sheets are usually given to the students to assist them in course work. Lesson plans need not be secret weapons to be used against students; rather they can be used jointly by teacher and student.

Organizational formats vary widely. It is not the style of a lesson plan that is important. What is important is whether the format works in the situation for which it is designed. In most military schools, an agreed-upon format is established, and all instructors are required to follow the format. There is at least one community college that has an established lesson plan format and requires all evening school instructors to place a copy of their plan in the office each night before class meets.

The lesson plan format suggested in this chapter is compatible with the course of study technique outlined in Chapter 5. The style of plan does not matter; the important thing is to use some form of lesson plan.

The suggested lesson plan format for the Middlesex County Vocational and Technical High Schools is shown in Figure 7-1. The plan format is printed on five-by-eight-inch cards, and the printed cards are available for the teachers to use.

You will find that most lesson plan formats are divided into at least four major areas. These four areas are

    I.   Preparation phase
    II. Presentation phase
    III. Application phase
    IV. Evaluation phase

A very simple lesson plan format could be established using the four items just listed, and probably prove suitable to most teachers. However, as indicated earlier, this book will relate the lesson plan construction to the course of study development procedure discussed in Chapter 5.

This four-step approach is a proven technique for shop and laboratory

THE LESSON PLAN

LESSON PLAN
OBJECTIVE INFORMATIONAL

MIDDLESEX COUNTY
VOCATIONAL and TECHNICAL HIGH SCHOOL

LESSON_____CLASSIFICATION_____

OBJECTIVES:

1. _____
2. _____
3. _____

STEP I. PREPARATION

A. Teacher

1. Tools, Supplies, Equipment _____
_____

2. Books, References, Instruction Sheets, Visual Aids_____
_____

B Student

1. Introducing the lesson --- Motivation _____
_____

2. Association or connection with previous lesson_____
_____
_____

STEP II. PRESENTATION Underline methods to be used :

Demonstration, Lecture, Illustration, Discussion, Experimentation

Teaching Points:

1.	6.
2.	7.
3.	8.
4.	9.
5.	10.

STEP III. APPLICATION Underline methods:

Job, Exercise Work, Production Work, Written Assignment, Oral Quiz, Study Guide

Assignment :
_____
_____
_____

STEP IV. TESTING Underline methods:

Inspection of Work, Performance Test, Written Questions --- Problems, Oral Questions, List Inspection
Points, Questions, Problems.
_____
_____
_____
_____

FIGURE 7-1. Sample Lesson Plan Format

instructors, but for these purposes, it is suggested that the more detailed lesson plan format appearing in Figure 7-1 be used by both beginning and experienced teachers.

THE LESSON PLAN AND ITS RELATIONSHIP TO THE COURSE OF STUDY

The course of study represents the total sum of the learning experiences that students will be exposed to in a certain program. Assuming that the course of study was broken down into units, lesson plans should be developed using the outline presented in a unit as a guide to lesson planning.

A unit in a course of study will probably represent a wide range of instructional content, along with audiovisual aids and various reference sources. The course of study unit is very broad in range compared to the contents of a lesson plan. The unit structure used in the course of study will determine the number of lesson plans per unit. Also, to a large extent, the ability of the students will influence the length of any one given lesson. Some units from the course of study might need twenty lesson plans and others, only two. This will depend on how broad an area each unit covers. On the other hand, if great depth and planning were involved in the development of the units, the individual units might very well be used as lesson plans. This is usually not the case and is not advised as a technique.

The lesson plan represents the smallest segment of the material in the course of study. Much greater depth and instructional strategy will be required in the lesson plan as compared to the course of study.

THE LESSON PLAN AND ITS RELATIONSHIP TO THE WEEKLY PLAN

The weekly plan represents the total plan of activities for a five-day period. The plan is the schedule of activities under the direction of one teacher. If a teacher instructs two three-hour classes per day, the weekly plan would be designed for only two classes. This might mean one or two different preparations per day. On the other hand, a related-subjects teacher might teach five different groups of students per day and his weekly plan would be designed for five different classes.

One lesson plan might be needed each day for each class for which a teacher is responsible. This might mean two lesson plans for the shop teacher and five lesson plans for the related-subjects teacher. It is less time consuming to construct two lesson plans than five. Some lessons will probably take longer than the time available, so one lesson plan may be suitable for two or more days. However, this is a decision that you, the teacher, will have to make. A lesson plan does not have to be under twenty or thirty minutes of instructional time. One lesson might take ten hours to complete. This time would, of course, include application of lesson content by the students. As an example, it might take thirty minutes to present a lesson on Ohm's Law, and then one hour to apply the law to various practical problems.

In other words, some weeks you might need five or six lesson plans, and others, not a single one. This depends on your strategy and technique in lesson planning for the teaching-learning situation.

THE LESSON PLAN AND ITS RELATIONSHIP TO THE DAILY PLAN

The daily plan is the schedule of activities under the direction of the teacher. The auto mechanics teacher on one day might need two different lesson plans and on another day, none. This all will depend on the type of activities planned for the day. Much shop instruction is on an individual basis, and lesson plans are not generally required in such situations.

IMPLEMENTING THE LESSON PLAN

A lesson plan has a number of advantages.

1. Preplanning for the lesson
2. Logical sequence of presentation
3. As an aid to the actual presentation
4. Information sheet for the students
5. Student evaluation

No doubt, the above list could be expanded to include a few more items, but we will concentrate on these five here.

PREPLANNING FOR THE LESSON. The teacher who walks into the shop or laboratory without a scheduled lesson is apt to be ill-prepared to present a meaningful lesson to the students. Students can tell the level of preparation a teacher puts into preplanning. How many times have you been in a class in which a tool or some item was missing, and the instructor had to stop and search for the missing item? Preplanning and a good lesson plan can help prevent such embarrassing situations.

LOGICAL SEQUENCE OF PRESENTATION. This does not just happen; it results from thinking out a situation and then putting it into some organizational pattern. In developing an occupational analysis and then the course of study, a great amount of time is involved in determining the logical sequence of learning experiences. This same systematic reasoning should be used in preparing a lesson plan for your class. If you use performance and behavioral objectives in your class, it is essential that all instruction be sequenced from the simple to the complex. This procedure should be followed in the construction of your lesson plans.

AS AN AID TO THE ACTUAL PRESENTATION. After you go to the effort to prepare a lesson plan, use it during your presentation. It is easy to put it aside and operate without it, but the value of it is lost. This does not imply that you should read directly from the plan, but rather follow it much like you follow a road map on a cross country trip. It is an aid, your aid to presenting as good a lesson as possible.

AN INFORMATION SHEET FOR THE STUDENTS. Some lesson plans will also be usable as information or instruction sheets for the students. Let's say you have prepared a demonstration lesson for hair coloring in a cosmetology class. Why not use it as a handout for students? It is not a secret weapon reserved for teachers. Get as much use out of your lesson plans as possible.

STUDENT EVALUATION. This is a topic by itself but is closely related to the lesson plan. If you write performance objectives for your lesson, then evaluation of students should be based on those objectives. Therefore, any test you construct or require students to take should be based on the stated objectives in your course of study and lesson plans. Do not list an objective unless you intend to measure the end performance.

WHY USE LESSON PLANS?

The major argument for the use of lesson plans is to provide the best learning situation for students.

The teacher who puts time and effort into planning his lesson considers many different aspects of his presentation phase. Some questions he might ask himself are:

1. Is the material or demonstration of *sufficient importance* to present to the class as a group lesson? Perhaps it is better suited to small group or individual instruction techniques.
2. Is the material or demonstration such that the best *method of presentation* is the lecture/demonstration technique? Perhaps the material could be covered by a reading assignment, instruction sheet, video tape, film, single-concept film, or some other form of educational technology.
3. Does the plan focus on the *main thing* to be learned by the students? Are the objectives of the lesson stated in a clear and concise form so that the focus is clear?
4. Is the lesson content of such *length* that it can be presented within the normal interest span of the students? The normal interest span of individuals varies. After a few lessons, most instructors can determine how long they will have their students' attention.
5. Is the lesson content appropriate to the learners and their *past experiences?* Does the lesson in question relate to their previous experiences?
6. Does the lesson proceed from the *known to the unknown?*
7. Does it proceed from the *simplest to the most complex?*
8. Does the lesson plan have a *measurable outcome?* If you have attempted to base your instruction on performance objectives, then the outcome should be measurable.

VARIOUS TYPES OF LESSONS

Instructional strategy is a necessary part of the teacher's "bag of tricks." We all get tired of hearing and seeing the same technique used day in and day out. Put yourself in the students' place. Better yet, have someone video tape your lesson and play back the tape so you can evaluate yourself. Chapter 10 presents a number of techniques to individualize instruction in the shop or laboratory setting and presents a variety of instructional strategies.

In shop classes of fifteen to twenty-five students, it is usually necessary to use many formal lesson presentations. The entire subject of lesson plan construction to this point has been concerned with formal lesson presentations. Most formal lessons presented by shop teachers fall into two basic types, the demonstration lesson and the theory lesson.

The *demonstration lesson* is a lesson planned for the learning of some skill involving active demonstrable performance on the part of the teacher as well as the students. Such lessons as the following would be demonstrations.

Proper Use of the Cross-Cut Saw

Adjusting the Breaker Points in an Automobile

Hair Coloring

Giving Injections

The *theory type* lesson is one planned for the learning of information or principles needed in the practice of a trade. Such lessons as the following deal with theory.

Nail Sizes

Theory of Internal Combustion

Diseases of the Heart

Parts of the Human Body

The important thing is not whether a lesson is a demonstration or related lesson, but the instructional strategy used to present the lesson. The lesson plan format suggested in this chapter is suitable to either type of lesson.

LESSON PLAN CONSTRUCTION

The lesson plan form outlined in Figure 7-2 is a suggested format for your own plans. The format is related to the structure presented in Figure 5-2. The suggested lesson plan format is suitable for demonstration and theory lessons.

Further elaboration of each of the items suggested for inclusion in lesson plans follows.

INTRODUCTORY STATEMENT. This statement introduces the lesson to the students. Think of yourself as a salesman selling a product. If the lesson content is important enough to be a lesson, then tell the students so, and why. You might review what preceded and what will follow the lesson.

BEHAVIORAL OBJECTIVES. It takes time to write behavioral objectives, but the results should be worth the effort. Well-written behavioral objectives

LESSON PLAN

TOPIC: *How to Use This Plan*

INTRODUCTORY STATEMENT

The actual introductory statement that will be used to introduce the lesson to the students.

BEHAVIORAL OBJECTIVES

The desired behavior of the students after completion of the lesson or after application of the principles or skills. Skills that the students should be able to satisfactorily demonstrate in order to meet the stated objectives.

REFERENCES

A brief listing of the reference source or sources that students can consult for additional material on the subject.

INSTRUCTIONAL AIDS

A listing of the aids that are essential for the lesson. Hand tools, machine parts, measurement devices, films, slides, charts and anything else you may need during the lesson.

THE PRESENTATION (INSTRUCTIONAL CONTENT)

Outline in sufficient detail of the instructional content to be included in the lesson. You will present the lesson from this outline. The material should be arranged starting with the simplest and proceeding to the most complex.

DISCUSSION

At the completion of the lesson, ask if the students have any questions. If not, have a series of your own questions to test their understanding of the material just presented.

APPLICATION

Assignment or practical work which will allow students sufficient practice to master what is expected of them.

EVALUATION CRITERIA

How the students will be evaluated. Should be based entirely on the stated behavioral objectives. This evaluation may take a number of forms including pencil-and-paper and performance tests.

FIGURE 7-2. Sample Outline of a Lesson Plan

will tell students what is expected of them some time in the future. The future might be immediately after the lesson, in one week, one month, or at the end of the school year, but whatever the time, the knowledge or skill gained is the result of the lesson being taught. The objective will also indicate the conditions under which the student will be expected to perform and to what level of accuracy. A few examples of behavioral objectives associated with lesson presentations follow.

1. The student, given a Weston Model 611 tube tester, should be able to test and indicate the condition of a conventional vacuum tube in _____ minutes and do it successfully _____ per cent of the time.
2. The student, given a rough draft of a one-page business letter (one hundred words in body), should be able to type it with perfect accuracy in _____ minutes.
3. The student, shown fifteen different woodworking tools, should be able to identify _____ per cent of them in _____ minutes.

The examples all have a number of things in common. Each describes some *action* on the part of the student, and each has some *time* allotment involved in the statement (although you may not be concerned with time in some of your objectives). Each has some *criterion* of performance, such as the percentage of the time the student should be correct.

In the examples, the time and per cent are determined by the teacher's knowledge of the students' levels. It is plausible to establish one criterion of performance for students one week after the lesson and another performance level for their final evaluation. As students gain more experience through doing, you could establish higher standards. Make sure the students are fully aware of the process and your reasons.

REFERENCES. It is a good idea to tell students about the various sources (books, etc.) that you used in developing the lesson plan, so that they, too, can go to them for additional or review information. These sources will also be available to a substitute teacher.

INSTRUCTIONAL AIDS. In this section of the lesson plan, you should list *everything* you plan to use during the lesson. If you are giving a lesson on driving nails into lumber, make sure you list the hammer, nail, and lumber.

You should also list audiovisual devices that you plan to use, including the title and source of films and filmstrips. If you plan to give students an instruction sheet, indicate it and attach a copy to the lesson plan.

THE PRESENTATION. This is the major section of the lesson plan that you will be working from on the day of your lesson presentation. It should be an outline, in sufficient detail, of the instructional content to be included in the lesson. The outline could be a list of teaching points arranged from number one on. Remember, it is mainly for your use and, perhaps, the use of a substitute teacher.

Think through or make a "dry run" of your lesson to check on the instructional procedure. Pick out the key points, always remembering that safety is the most important item.

DISCUSSION. At the completion of your formal presentation, allow time for, and encourage, class discussion or questions from students regarding the lesson. Always include a few pertinent questions so that, if the class does not interact, you can encourage discussion through your questions.

APPLICATION. Now that the lesson has been presented, do not leave it without first telling the students how you expect them to apply it in the shop or laboratory. Most demonstration-type lessons will involve immediate practical application.

EVALUATION CRITERIA. Tell the students how they will be evaluated on the material just presented. The evaluation should be based entirely on the stated objectives of your lesson. This evaluation might be demonstrated performance on a "live job," a project, or a pencil-and-paper-type test.

SUMMARY

The intent of this chapter was to state the importance of good planning and the relationship of the lesson plan to the course of study, term plan, weekly plan and daily plan. The lesson plan format suggested makes use of an eight-step approach which should prove suitable to both the inexperienced teacher as well as the experienced teacher in need of upgrading. Sample lesson plans are included as exhibits to show how the process can work in an actual teaching-learning situation. The lesson plan format is similar in design to the course of study. The suggested format is used by many shop and laboratory teachers who have found it a valuable method to improve their teaching skills.

One exhibit (7-3) presented a list of words the reader may find helpful in preparing behavioral objectives for the lesson plans. Much has been written about behavioral objectives and a number of good references are listed under the section on Source Materials. The teacher who spends time preparing objectives will do the students a favor by letting them know exactly what is required of them in the course.

EXHIBIT 7-1

SAMPLE LESSON PLAN

TOPIC: *How to Prepare a Lesson Plan*

INTRODUCTORY STATEMENT

The purpose of today's lesson is to give you introductory material on how to prepare a lesson plan. Shop and laboratory teachers will find lesson plans a great help in presenting both new and review materials to their students. Upon completion of the lesson you will be expected to prepare a lesson plan of the demonstration type designed to last for at least fifteen minutes.

BEHAVIORAL OBJECTIVES

1. Upon completion of this lesson, each student will be expected to *list* the eight parts of the lesson plan format.
2. By next class each student will be expected to *plan* and *write* a fifteen-minute demonstration lesson plan using the eight-step format.
3. By the completion date of this course each student will be expected to *plan* and *write* a thirty-minute demonstration lesson plan using the eight-step format. The lesson will then be *presented* to this class and videotaped for students to evaluate their own performances.

REFERENCES

1. Pautler, Albert J. *Shop and Laboratory Instructor's Handbook.* Boston: Allyn and Bacon, 1978 (Chapter 7).

INSTRUCTIONAL AIDS

1. Sufficient copies of this lesson plan for each student to serve as an instruction sheet.
2. Text as indicated above in reference section — special reference to be made to Figure 7–2, Lesson Plan. Topic: How to use this plan.
3. Examples of lesson plans from previous students who have used this eight-step format.
4. Overhead projector.
5. Chalkboard, chalk, eraser.

THE PRESENTATION (INSTRUCTIONAL CONTENT)

1. Read introductory statement.
2. State the three behavioral objectives as listed.
3. Distribute copies of the lesson plan.

EXHIBIT 7-1, *continued*

4. Refer to Figure 7–2 in the text. This is the format for a lesson plan outline students are encouraged to use in this course.
5. Discuss each of the eight parts of the plan from Introductory Statement to Evaluation Criteria.
6. Encourage questions during the discussion.
7. Make available at this time sample lesson plans that previous students have developed in the course. Allow the class ten to fifteen minutes to review some of the plans.
8. Start into the discussion phase.
9. Assign the work listed in the application phase of this plan.
10. State the evaluation criteria that appear last on this lesson plan.
11. Ask for final questions, comments, etc., from the class.

DISCUSSION

1. What seems to be the most important item in preparing behavioral objectives that make sense to learners?
2. How much detail should be included in the presentation part of the lesson plan format?
3. What relationship exists between the lesson plan and the course of study? The plan book?

APPLICATION

1. By next class you are expected to *plan* and *write* a fifteen–minute demonstration lesson plan using the eight-step approach.
2. By_____ you are expected to do the same but this time for a thirty-minute demonstration plan. You will be expected to present this lesson to the class and you will be video taped for self-evaluation and a class critique.
3. On a piece of paper, *list* the eight-step format with which this plan has been constructed.

EVALUATION CRITERIA

Each student will be expected to complete the three items specified under application. Since this is the students' first attempt at lesson plan development, a minimum standard of evaluation will be applied to the product.

EXHIBIT 7-2

SAMPLE LESSON PLAN

The Oscilloscope: Frequency Measurement
Using Lissajous Patterns

INTRODUCTORY STATEMENT

The oscilloscope is an indispensable tool for an electronic technician. Just as a physician uses X-rays to observe the internal functioning of the human body, the electronic technician uses an oscilloscope to observe the internal functioning of electrical circuits. This is the first of two lessons concerning the use of the oscilloscope for frequency measurements.

BEHAVIORAL OBJECTIVES

Each student, given a Tektronix Model 561 oscilloscope with a type 3A6 dual-trace amplifier and type 2B67 time base, will be able to:

- Determine an unknown frequency, when given a lissajous pattern and a known frequency, accurately three out of four times with one minute per display.
- Determine an unknown frequency by setting up the oscilloscope properly for a lissajous pattern using a signal generator and an unknown frequency from an unmarked signal generator. Four trials of five minutes each will be allowed and successful completion will require three out of four correct responses at an accuracy of 2 per cent or less.

REFERENCES

Allied Radio Corporation. *Understanding and Using Your Oscilloscope.* Chicago: Allied Radio Corporation, 1968.

Schultz, John J. *Electronic Test and Measurement Handbook.* Summit, Pa.: TAB Books, 1969.

Herrick, Clyde N. *Instruments and Measurements for Electronics.* New York: McGraw-Hill, 1972.

Zwick, George. *The Oscilloscope.* Summit, Pa.: TAB Books, 1969.

Prensky, Sol D. *Electronic Instrumentation.* Englewood Cliffs, N. J.: Prentice-Hall, 1971.

Thomas, Harry E. *Handbook of Electronic Instruments and Measurement Techniques.* Englewood Cliffs, N. J.: Prentice-Hall, 1967.

INSTRUCTIONAL AIDS

- Overhead projector
- Oscilloscope transparency set
- Oscilloscope frequency measurement transparencies

EXHIBIT 7–2, *continued*

- Overhead projector felt pens (blue, green, and red)
- Color chalk and chalkboard
- Chalkboard drawing instruments
- Model 561 oscilloscope with 3A6 and 2B67 plug-in units
- Two sets of Tektronix scope probes
- Two HP signal generators
- Two 6.3 VAC transformers
- Oscilloscope cart
- Four sets of clip leads

PRESENTATION

a. Lissajous pattern development
b. Scope input connections
c. Establishing the scope pattern
d. Pattern ratios and shapes
e. Applications
f. Instructor's demonstration

DISCUSSION

a. Ask Jay Albert to set up the scope for a lissajous pattern.
b. Have Mary Foster determine the unknown frequency set up by Jay.
c. Direct discussion to any problems encountered during the student participation.

APPLICATION

Students will be directed to perfect their expertise in setting up and interpreting lissajous for measuring unknown frequencies. A laboratory experience will be provided following this demonstration lesson.

EVALUATION

Students will be evaluated individually when they believe they are ready to take the performance test. The criteria for successful completion are stated in the objectives.

EXHIBIT 7–3

VERBS YOU MAY FIND HELPFUL IN PREPARING BEHAVIORAL OBJECTIVES

analyze	inspect	recite
apply	flush	speak
compute	test	spell
create	repair	state
demonstrate	rotate	summarize
evaluate	design	write
interpret	rewrite	chart
listen	synthesize	find
locate	compare	name
perform	defend	note
recognize	explain	organize
speak	plan	record
translate	substitute	add
use	choose	calculate
write	collect	compute
recite	describe	divide
identify	detect	calibrate
differentiate	subtract	demonstrate
solve	pick	operate
construct	point	replace
list	select	set
compare	separate	fix
contrast	edit	grind
replace	outline	sew
adjust	read	type

The lesson plan in itself is not always the most important product. More important is the time spent thinking about how to present a certain topic or lesson and then organizing for the presentation. After you gain experience teaching, the lesson plan format may be modified to suit your needs and abilities. For that reason, please feel free to modify the format to suit your own needs.

ACTIVITIES

1. Using the format suggested in Figure 7-2, prepare a fifteen-minute lesson plan of either the related or demonstration type for your area of specialization.

2. Write ten behavioral objectives for your instructional specialization. These should be short-range objectives, not course objectives.

3. Find one of your old lesson plans and compare it to the one you prepared for item 1 above.

4. Prepare a lesson plan using the suggested eight-step format. Present a lesson to your class this week.

SOURCE MATERIALS

Gronlund, Norman E. *Stating Behavioral Objectives for Classroom Instruction.* Toronto: Collier-Macmillan Canada, 1970.

Mager, Robert F. *Preparing Instructional Objectives.* Palo Alto, Calif.: Fearon, 1962.

Mager, Robert F. and Beach, Kenneth M. *Developing Vocational Instruction.* Palo Alto, Calif.: Fearon, 1967.

PRESENTATION

Part III

8

THE FIRST DAY
OF CLASS

The first day of a new school year can be very trying for the ill-prepared teacher. If advanced planning was well done, the day will be more bearable. Any number of first-day problems can occur through no fault of the teacher. Students can be somewhat confused if they are in a new school and there are usually some scheduling problems. If the advanced planning suggested in the first three chapters was followed, the first day should be easier.

SCHOOL PROCEDURE

The first day of school in some districts may last only a few hours. Other districts may start with a half-day or full-day session. The important thing is to be well prepared for the time you must spend with your classes the first day. If your school starts with a full-day session, you may have your shop or laboratory students for as long as two or three hours. This can be a long time for the teacher who is prepared to work with his class for only fifteen or twenty minutes. It is best to be overprepared. It is generally the unprepared teacher who runs into discipline problems with his students. If students are kept busy in meaningful shop work, few problems will occur.

First day procedures vary from district to district. The following are some items of concern to the shop teacher.

1. Check your attendance list and make sure all are in your classroom. Report those whose names appear but are not present.
2. Complete any forms that are required by the local administration. You may want to have students complete some form of data sheet for your own shop use. (If students are making out forms, make sure they understand the directions.)
3. Locks and lockers may be issued and assigned on the first day of class. Follow directions from the administration as to correct procedure and location of lockers.
4. Textbooks may be issued (loaned) to students on the first day. Note procedure and records to be used in issuing textbooks.

The four items listed above are in no way complete, but are given as an illustration of some of the things that might be necessary on the first day of school. You will have to look over your local school district's procedure for the opening of school for full particulars.

BE OVERPREPARED

It is much better to be overprepared than underprepared when you meet your classes. To say the least, it is rather embarrassing to complete the lesson or demonstration and find that you still have a half-hour or more remaining before the end of the period. This is an especially bad situation early in the school year when students are not ready to work on their shop projects or assigned jobs.

The wise instructor will always be ready to go on with new material or review old material so that no time is wasted. In planning your lessons, include questions, assignments, and practical applications of the lesson material. These items, in addition to being of instructional value, will occupy time in the shop or laboratory.

If the students are interested and the instructor is well prepared, there should be little wasted time. Remember too that busy students engaged in a meaningful learning experience are not going to cause discipline problems.

PRESENTATION

DISCIPLINE

A smoothly operating school is the responsibility of the administration, teachers, and students. All must work together to make the instructional setting as interesting and free from problems as possible. One weak link in the chain can cause all sorts of problems. The one weak link, be it an administrator, teacher, or student, must be dealt with in a firm, fair, and consistent manner.

One never knows when a problem will arise, and it is almost impossible to be prepared in advance to deal with all situations. When classroom problems do arise, stay cool and act in a firm, fair, and consistent manner. This is easier to say than do, but remember that your students are human beings and expect to be treated fairly. It could be that you, the teacher, may be the cause of some of the problems that exist. Did you get up on the wrong side of the bed this morning? Did you have an argument with your wife or husband at breakfast? Did you stay out too late last night? Are you in a bad mood? Are you poorly prepared for the day's lesson? Students, too, may have personal problems that affect their school behavior, so there are a multitude of things than can go wrong.

When a problem does occur, stay cool, and think before you act. Do not run hot and cold from one day to the next.

Many teachers are asked to leave a teaching position because of their inability to maintain discipline. It is a good idea to start off as a strong disciplinarian and then ease off as the year goes on. It is the teacher who starts off the year as a weak disciplinarian and then attempts to tighten up control who runs into difficulties.

Try to handle your own discipline cases. Do not rely on the assistant principal or principal to handle your problems. Only in the most serious cases, should you make use of administrative help. Of course, you should seek the advice of your administrators and experienced fellow teachers, but handle your own discipline cases as they arise. Both students and administrators will respect you for handling your own classroom problems. The teacher who is continually sending students to the office for discipline develops a reputation with both the office staff and the students.

The main purpose of discipline in a classroom or shop is to permit the most effective use of instructional time. This does not mean that military control is necessary. Control that is conducive to good learning is what is desired.

A few suggestions worthy of your consideration follow:

THE FIRST DAY OF CLASS

1. Act in a firm, fair, and consistent manner when handling discipline cases.
2. Do not make snap judgements or decisions in handling discipline cases. Think before you act.
3. Never act when you are angry. Cool off; consider the situation and act only when you are fully composed.
4. Never make fun of, or humiliate, a student. Students are human beings and should be treated that way.
5. Never use corporal punishment in handling a discipline case. So serious a case should be handled by the administration.
6. Do not punish an entire class in order to discipline one or two students.
7. Being well prepared is one way to avoid problems. Most problems occur during periods of wasted instructional time.
8. Establish a definite procedure for pupils to enter and leave the classroom.
9. Be consistent. Use disciplinary action suitable to the offense.
10. Handle discipline cases in private, not in front of the class. But make sure that the other students are aware that the situation will be dealt with.

If all else fails and you need help from the central office regarding a discipline case, usually some type of form is used to report the situation. The form shown in Figure 8-1 is one example of a student disciplinary report. The problem or situation should be described as fully as possible on the form. In some cases, the completed form should be taken by the student and teacher directly to the person assigned to handle such matters. More detailed information can then be heard from all parties concerned.

The teacher who uses such a form only with the most serious problems will get quick and firm action. Teachers who have to use the forms on almost a daily basis will soon develop an unfavorable reputation with the person handling such cases and the action will be generally less prompt and less severe. The best advice is to try to handle your own problems and resort to the administration only in the most serious cases or for those incidents in which school policy requires office action. Even in these cases, the teacher may want to play a role as decision maker. The teacher generally knows the students better than anyone in the central office and is in many cases better qualified to handle certain cases.

STUDENT RECORDS

It is a good idea to review the school records of your students before the first day of class. The records will provide you with some background in-

BOARD OF COOPERATIVE EDUCATIONAL SERVICES
First Supervisory District, Erie County

Harkness Center
Kenton Center
Potter Road Center

STUDENT DISCIPLINARY REPORT

Student's Name _____ Home School _____

Teacher's Name _____ Course _____

Date _____ Time _____

Incident Description: _____
_____
_____

Previous Incidents not referred to Principal: _____
_____
_____

Action taken by Principal: _____
_____
_____

Copy to: Original   —   Principal's copy
            Pink   —   Student's file
            Canary   —   Teacher

FIGURE 8-1. Student Disciplinary Report

APPLICATION FOR ADMISSION

BURLINGTON COUNTY VOCATIONAL and TECHNICAL HIGH SCHOOL

Woodlane Road, Mount Holly, New Jersey   (609) 267-4226

INSTRUCTIONS FOR COMPLETING PART I - Please Print All Information in Ink. This Application Must Be Approved by Your Parent or Guardian. Indicate Your 1st, 2nd and 3rd Choice of Programs as Listed in the School Information Brochure. Return this Application to your School Principal or Guidance Counselor for Completion of Part II.

PART I

			Male ☐ Female ☐	Today's Date
Applicant's Last Name	First	Middle Initial	Sex	Month Day Year

1st Choice Program	2nd Choice Program	3rd Choice Program

Applicant's Signature	Parent or Guardian Signature	Telephone No.

PART II

Schools may substitute own form for Part II providing it contains information requested. Please return completed Application to Burlington County Vocational and Technical High School.

			Date of Birth	Month Day Year
Applicant's Last Name	First	Middle Initial	Today's Date	Month Day Year

Street Address	City	State

Present Grade School Attending	Address	Telephone No.

Test Score	Name of Test	Date Given

Test Score	Name of Test	Date Given

Test Score	Name of Test	Date Given

English	Math	Science	Social Studies	Shop

AVERAGE MARKS LAST YEAR

English	Math	Science	Social Studies	Shop

AVERAGE MARKS THIS YEAR

Good Fair Poor	Good Fair Poor	Good Fair Poor
Attendance	Relationship with Teachers	Relationship with Students

Good Fair Poor	Good Fair Poor	If Poor, Explain
General Behavior	Physical Health	

Additional Comments: _____

_____

_____

School District	School Officials Signature, Position

FIGURE 8-2.   *Application for Admission (Burlington County Vocational and Technical High School)*

Date _____   Interviewer _____

1. Mathematics desired for 9th Grade. _____ General Math - _____ Algebra I - _____

2. Student's reason(s) for attending Burlington County Vocational and Technical School. _____
   _____

3. Student's understanding of Program.   Good - _____ Fair - _____ Poor - _____

4. School visited.   Yes _____ No _____

5. Apparent Speech Difficulty   Yes _____ No _____   _____

6. Apparent hearing difficulty   Yes _____ No. _____   _____

7. Parents at interview   Yes _____ No _____

8. Additional Comments: _____
   _____
   _____

PART IV

Action taken by Burlington County Vocational and Technical High School Admission Committee.

Accepted _____ Program _____ Math _____

Placed on waiting list _____ Program _____ Math _____

Hold _____ Additional Information _____ Additional Testing _____

Rejected _____ Reason _____
_____

Student Folder Received _____ Date _____ Initial _____

Comments: _____
_____
_____
_____
_____
_____
_____
_____
_____

School Official's Signature   Position   Date Notification Letter Sent

FIGURE 8-2 continued

APPLICATION BLANK

Middlesex County Vocational and Technical High Schools
ADMINISTRATION OFFICES
256 Easton Avenue, New Brunswick, N. J.
CHarter 7 - 3832

Date_____

I, _____ , hereby make application for admittance to the Middlesex County Vocational and Technical High School. School [Check One] New Brunswick _____ Perth Amboy _____ Woodbridge _____ This application must be approved by a parent and returned to the school principal.

_____
PARENT OR GUARDIAN'S SIGNATURE

_____
ADDRESS   TELEPHONE NO.

This part is to be detached before sending the top part home for approval. This part should then be filled out by an authorized school official and returned with the top part to the Middlesex County Vocational and Technical High School concerned.

Applicant's Name _____
           Last   First   Initial

Address _____

Date of Birth _____ Grade Completed _____ Date _____

Name of school last attended _____

IQ _____ Name of Test _____ Date Given _____

Reading Grade Equivalent _____ Test _____ Date Given _____

Arithmetic Grade Equivalent _____ Test _____ Date Given _____

Attendance _____ Satisfactory _____ Unsatisfactory _____

Scholarship _____ Excellent _____ Good _____ Fair _____ Poor _____

Work Habits and Attitudes: _____ Excellent _____ Good _____ Fair _____ Poor _____

Tuition [If out of county] Paid by District _____ Paid by Parent _____

District _____

_____
SCHOOL OFFICIAL'S SIGNATURE

FIGURE 8-3.   Application Blank (Middlesex County Vocational and Technical High Schools)

formation about your students and their past level of achievement. In order to avoid an improper interpretation of the information, ask the counselor to look over the records with you.

School policies vary, so do not be shocked if the records are not made available to you. In recent years the right of access of students and parents to files has created some changes in school policy regarding what records are kept and who may see them. Find out what records are available to you. The materials displayed in Figures 8-2 and 8-3 illustrate two different application forms used by two vocational schools. Much of the information on these forms would be valuable to the teacher. Some of the information on test scores may better be explained by the school counselor. You should be aware of any students in your class with health problems that may need emergency treatment. You should have a clear understanding of what you as the teacher can do and should do in emergency situations. Would you know what to do if an epileptic student had a convulsion in your class? It seems to this writer that the administration has an obligation to inform teachers about such problems and tell them what they may do to render aid in an emergency.

INTRODUCTION OF SELF AND STUDENTS

If you are meeting the students in your class for the first time, introduce yourself and relate industrial experiences you have had in the past. Ask each student to introduce him or herself and say something about past education and work experiences.

This procedure will set the stage for the year and should be of value to both the students and the teacher.

FIRST IMPRESSIONS

The students will be gaining their first impression of you and, likewise, you of them. No matter what you may have heard about a student (or students) in your class, make it clear to them that they are starting the year with a "clean record." You will form your impression of each student as the school year moves on. Make this clear to students the first day of class. First impressions are important, but impressions based on a term or two are much more valid.

THE FIRST DAY OF CLASS

INTRODUCTION OF COURSE AND OBJECTIVES

It is important that you introduce the course and its stated objectives to your students on the first day of class. In a sense, you are selling the course to the students, but in another sense, you are telling them what they can expect. On the basis of your presentation, some students may decide they have made a wrong decision and do not want to take the course after all. Make provisions for them to see their counselor and arrange a transfer to some other program or specialization.

It is important that the class be as fully informed as possible about the course and its relationship to the total program. If you are teaching the first-year course in electronics, relate it to the whole three-year program. In other words, relate the course you are teaching to the long-range program leading to graduation.

It is desirable to teach from a course of study, and the stated objectives should be included in this. Chapter 5 dealt with the course of study in much more detail, as well as with the writing of behavioral objectives.

Relate the objectives of the course to students so they are aware of what will be expected of them at the end of the course. It will help the student to state the objectives in behavioral terms. A few examples follow.

ELECTRONICS

The student, given a properly functioning radio receiver of the eight-transistor type, must be able to *take* and *record* the proper voltage readings in fifteen minutes.

The student, given the necessary parts to make a power supply, must be able to *assemble, wire,* and *solder* them in a one-hour time period.

The student must be able to correctly *solve* at least five simple Ohm's law problems in twenty-five minutes.

DRAFTING

Given an object (model, tool, etc.), the student must be able to correctly *draw* an assembly drawing of it in a two-hour time period.

HAIRSTYLING

Given an illustration (photo), the student must be able to *style* the model's hair in a similar manner in forty-five minutes.

PRESENTATION

It is possible to state your instructional objectives in behavioral terms. The key is action verbs, with stated conditions and times. Students should be made aware that they will be evaluated in terms of the stated instructional objectives. This evaluation will occur during, and at the end of, the course.

If you make use of student progress charts, this is a good time to make them available to the students as an example of the kind of activities, projects, and jobs that they will be required to perform in the course. Figures 8-4 and 8-5 present two examples of progress charts, one in the area of architectural drafting and the other in plumbing and heating. This is another way of introducing the course and the long-range program of study to new students.

METHOD OF STUDENT EVALUATION

The method of student evaluation outlined above should be based on the stated instructional objectives. Just as the instructor informs the class of the instructional objectives of the course, he should tell the students how their final grade will be determined. Well-written instructional objectives stated in behavioral terms will make it possible for students to assess their own progress.

All schools have some sort of structured marking system for reporting student progress to parents. The shop teacher just as any other teacher in the school system will have to operate within the structure of the marking system. For example, Smithville Vocational High School reports student grades to parents every ten weeks. There are four ten-week marking periods plus a final examination. The final grade is arrived at by averaging the four quarter grades and the final examination grade. Each grade counts 20 per cent toward the final grade. As seen in Figure 8-6, the final grade of 81 resulted from the average of the four quarters and the final examination grade.

Though the teacher must operate within the marking system used in the school, he is responsible for arriving at the grades to be reported each quarter. This information should be conveyed to students during the first day of class. Will you base the quarter grades on shop work, pencil-and-paper tests, or assignments? How will you record grades in your classbook?

Students should be informed of the school's marking system and how it operates. Students should also be informed how the teacher will arrive at their quarter grades. Pupil-teacher planning can be used by the teacher to arrive at a fair system of student evaluation. Evaluation, if it is to be effective, should not be kept secret from the students. After all, it is the students who are being rated.

THE FIRST DAY OF CLASS

STUDENT PROGRESS CHART   CAMDEN COUNTY VOCATIONAL   ARCHITECTURAL DRAFTING
                               and TECHNICAL SCHOOLS
Gloucester Township Campus _____
Student's Name _____

		Date Completed	Instructor's Signature
I.	Junior Architectural Draftsman _____		
	(Trade Manipulative Units)		
A.	Introduction to Architectural Drafting	_____	_____
B.	Drafting Equipment and It's Use	_____	_____
C.	Architectural Lettering	_____	_____
D.	Basic Technical Drawing	_____	_____
E.	Architectural Drafting Expression and Techniques	_____	_____
F.	Freehand Sketching and Approximate Perspective	_____	_____
G.	Presentation Drawings	_____	_____
H.	Architectural Model Building	_____	_____
I.	Floor Plan Preparation	_____	_____
J.	Exterior Elevation Preparation	_____	_____
K.	Plot Plan and Survey Plan Preparation	_____	_____
L.	Landscape Plan Preparation	_____	_____
M.	Building Section Preparation	_____	_____
N.	Architectural Detail Preparation	_____	_____
O.	Basement, Footing and Foundation Plan Preparation	_____	_____
P.	Framing Plan Preparation	_____	_____
Q.	Electrical Plan Preparation	_____	_____
R.	Plumbing Plan Preparation	_____	_____
S.	Heating and Cooling Plan Preparation	_____	_____
T.	Modular Component Plan Preparation	_____	_____
	(Trade Information Units)		
A.	Architectural Blueprint Reading	_____	_____
B.	Survey of Building Construction	_____	_____
C.	Operations Preliminary to Building	_____	_____
D.	Concrete Construction	_____	_____
E.	Footings, Foundations, Slabs & Basement Construction	_____	_____
F.	Sill and Wood Floor Construction	_____	_____
G.	Frame Wall Constructions and Coverings	_____	_____
H.	Masonry Wall Construction	_____	_____
I.	Ceiling Joists, Roof Construction and Roofing	_____	_____
J.	Post, Plank and Beam Construction	_____	_____
K.	Doors	_____	_____
L.	Windows	_____	_____
M.	Stairs and Stair Framing	_____	_____
N.	Fireplaces and Chimneys	_____	_____
O.	Modular Construction	_____	_____

FIGURE 8-4. *Student Progress Chart (Architectural Drafting)*

	Date Completed	Instructor's Signature
II. Junior Architectural Design Draftsman (Residential)	_____	
A. Introduction to Residential Planning		
B. Client, Community and Site Considerations	_____	_____
C. Overall Floor Plan Considerations and Planning		
D. Planning Individual Areas and Rooms	_____	_____
E. Exterior Design	_____	_____
F. Site Planning	_____	_____
G. Planning Residential Lighting and Wiring	_____	_____
H. Planning Residential Plumbing	_____	_____
I. Planning Residential Heating, Cooling and Insulation		
J. Estimating and Financing Building Costs	_____	_____
K. Creative Residential Design	_____	_____
III. Junior Architectural Design Draftsman (Commercial)	_____	
A. Introduction to Planning Specific Building Types		
B. Planning Merchandising Facilities	_____	_____
C. Planning Offices, Banks and Medical Offices and Clinics		
D. Planning Food Stores, Restaurants and Cafeterias		
E. Planning Motels and Parking Facilities	_____	_____
F. Planning Shopping Centers and Bowling Centers		
G. Planning Churches	_____	_____
H. Planning Industrial Buildings	_____	_____
I. Planning Educational Buildings	_____	_____
J. Commercial Building Construction Principles		
K. Creative Commercial Building Design	_____	_____

FIGURE 8-4 continued

STUDENT PROGRESS CHART   PLUMBING AND HEATING

CAMDEN COUNTY VOCATIONAL AND TECHNICAL SCHOOLS

Gloucester Township Campus _____   _____Pennsauken Campus

Student's Name_____

		Date Completed	Instructor's Signature
I.	Plumber Helper_____		
A.	Hand Tools	_____	_____
B.	Pipe Cutting	_____	_____
C.	Pipe Threading	_____	_____
D.	Cut Copper	_____	_____
E.	Sweat Copper	_____	_____
F.	Flair Copper	_____	_____
G.	Pipe Threading Machine	_____	_____
H.	Plastic Piping	_____	_____
II.	Steel Pipe Fitter_____		
A.	Steel Pipe	_____	_____
III.	Installation Man_____		
A.	Steel Pipe	_____	_____
B.	Cast Iron Pipe	_____	_____
C.	Copper Installations to Sketch	_____	_____
D.	Soldering with Live Flame & Soldering Iron	_____	_____
E.	Fixtures	_____	_____
F.	Hot Water Heating Systems	_____	_____
G.	Steam Heating Systems	_____	_____
H.	Bathrooms	_____	_____
I.	Gas Fittings	_____	_____
J.	Gasoline and Fuel Oil Tank	_____	_____
K.	Grease Trap	_____	_____
L.	Home Humidifier	_____	_____
IV.	Plumber Maintenance_____		
A.	Plumbing Maintenance	_____	_____
B.	Lead Wiping	_____	_____
V.	Plumber_____		
A.	Multiple Zone Heating Systems	_____	_____
B.	Dual Plumbing Systems	_____	_____
C.	Three Sink Mock Up with Drawing	_____	_____
D.	Multiple Zone Heating System	_____	_____
E.	Radiant Hot Water Heating	_____	_____
VI.	Blueprint Layout and Estimator_____		
A.	Blueprint Reading	_____	_____
B.	Material Layout	_____	_____
C.	Estimation	_____	_____

FIGURE 8-5. *Student Progress Chart (Plumbing and Heating)*

10th week	20th week	30th week	40th week	Final Exam	Final Grade
80	85	75	90	75	81

FIGURE 8-6. Numerical Grading System

Two methods of reporting student progress are displayed in Figures 8-7 and 8-8. A more complete discussion of student evaluation, test construction, and grading will be presented in Part IV.

STUDENT REQUIREMENTS— QUALITY AND QUANTITY

Closely associated with student evaluation is the topic of student requirements and the quality of workmanship expected of the students. The students should be told what the course requirements are and what level of craftsmanship is expected of them for successful completion of the course. The experienced teacher will do it in such a way as to arouse student interest in the project or activities the class will be involved in.

The requirements should not be presented in such a way as to make them seem a barrier to successful course completion. This will only scare off some students and shock others, which is not the purpose of reviewing course requirements. The experienced teacher will do little more than relate the experiences, activities, jobs, projects, and assignments that the students must master before the end of the course, the level of achievement and craftsmanship expected of them by the end of the course. It should be a positive, rather than negative, approach.

Examples of the work, projects, and achievements of former students should be shown or related to the class. A former graduate or student might be asked to come in and relate his experiences to the new students.

SHOP TOUR

If it is the first time the students have been in the shop, it would be a good idea to conduct a tour. During the tour, the instructor can point out the

MARKING SYSTEM

ACHIEVEMENT			EFFORT	
Letter Grade	Numerical Equivalent		Numerical Grade	
A = Excellent	90 - 100		1 = Outstanding	
B = Very Good	80 - 89		2 = Satisfactory	
C = Satisfactory	70 - 79		3 = Poor	
D = Poor	60 - 69			
E = Failure	Below 60			

EXPLANATIONS

1. "D" is a passing grade but indicates unsatisfactory work; close to failure and not worthy of recommendation.

2. "E" for a final grade requires that the subject be repeated if credit toward graduation is desired.

3. "ab" indicates the pupil was absent for more than half of the checking level.

4. A checking level covers approximately 45 school days.

PARENT'S SIGNATURE

1. _____

2. _____

3. _____

4. _____

No. ....

Name ....

Year Ending .... 19 ....

Shop ....

Report Card
Middlesex County Vocational and Technical High Schools

.... New Brunswick   .... Perth Amboy   .... Woodbridge   .... East Brunswick

SUBJECT	COURSE	CHECKING LEVEL 1 Achievement	1 Effort	2 Achievement	2 Effort	3 Achievement	3 Effort	4 Achievement	4 Effort	FINAL Achievement
Shop										
Mathematics										
Science										
Drawing										
English										
History										
Health										
Physical Education										
Days Absent										
Times Tardy										

FIGURE 8-7. Report Card (Middlesex County Vocational and Technical High School)

EMPLOYABILITY PROFILE

OSWEGO COUNTY BOARD OF COOPERATIVE EDUCATIONAL SERVICES
MEXICO, NEW YORK 13114
PHONE: 315-963-7251
1974 - 1975

Name _____ Home School _____ Grade _____

Course _____HEAVY EQUIPMENT OPERATION_____ Date _____ Quarter 1st__ 2nd__ 3rd__ Final

The following is a list of operations and skills that the above student has been exposed to, and instructor's appraisal of his/her entry level employ-ability in these areas. These operations have been accompanied by a significant amount of classroom work in related theory.

GENERAL SKILLS
- ☐ Proper Attire for work
- ☐ Participation in VICA
- ☐ Safety & O.S.H.A. training
- ☐ Preventive maintenance supervision
- ☐ Job-site supervision
- ☐ General supervision of student personnel
- ☐ Service manual interpretation
- ☐ Parts book interpretation
- ☐ Shop math
- ☐ Metric measurements & interpretation
- ☐ Precision measuring tool utilization
- ☐ Steam cleaning operation
- ☐ Chemical cleaning operation
- ☐ Jacking & blocking operations

EQUIPMENT MAINTENANCE
- ☐ Daily Maintenance
- ☐ Schedule Maintenance
- ☐ Hand Lubricating
- ☐ Power Lubricating
- ☐ Oil & Filter Change
- ☐ Air Cleaner Service
- ☐ Fuel System Service
- ☐ Hydraulic System Service
- ☐ Cable Lubrication
- ☐ Cable Cutting

RECONDITIONING
- ☐ Cleaning
- ☐ Inspection
- ☐ Estimating repair costs
- ☐ Remove dents
- ☐ Straightening
- ☐ Fill dents & holes
- ☐ Fabricate pants
- ☐ Stripping
- ☐ Sanding
- ☐ Masking
- ☐ Priming
- ☐ Painting

HYDRAULICS,
- ☐ Basic Principles
- ☐ Hydraulic Terms
- ☐ Symbols & Circuit Interpretations
- ☐ Check hydraulic pressures
- ☐ Utilize flow & pressure tester
- ☐ Change hydraulic filters
- ☐ Cutting & flaring tubings
- ☐ Install hydraulic hoses & tubing
- ☐ Check, locate, & repair leaks
- ☐ Replace 'O-Rings'
- ☐ Inspect & Service value assemblies
- ☐ Replace Packings & Seals
- ☐ Test & adjust relief values
- ☐ Inspect pumps
- ☐ Test pumps
- ☐ Test cylinders
- ☐ Troubleshoot hydraulic system problems

BASIC SURVEYING
- ☐ Telescopic level set-up
- ☐ Interpretation of measurements
- ☐ Planning & layout with instruments
- ☐ Grade stake locations & interpretations
- ☐ Leveling to a specified grade
- ☐ Ditching to a specified grade

TRACKS & UNDERCARRIAGE
- ☐ Cleaning & Inspection
- ☐ Lubrication
- ☐ Adjust tracks
- ☐ Remove tracks
- ☐ Install tracks
- ☐ Remove rollers
- ☐ Install rollers
- ☐ Remove sprockets
- ☐ Install sprockets

WELDING
- ☐ Safety
- ☐ Gas Welding
- ☐ Cutting
- ☐ Brazing
- ☐ Soldering
- ☐ Arc Welding, horizontal
- ☐ Arc Welding, vertical
- ☐ Hand surfacing

**EQUIPMENT SAFETY OSHA.
OPERATIONS, & MAINTENANCE
LIGHT VEHICLES**
- ☐ Trucks, 2x4
- ☐ Trucks, 4x4
- ☐ Trucks, 4x6
- ☐ Trucks, 6x6
- ☐ Tractor-Trailer Combinations
- ☐ Tractor-Trailer Combinations
- ☐ Learner's permit
- ☐ Class 3 license
- ☐ Class 1 license
- ☐ Forklifts
- ☐ Backhoes
- ☐   Digging holes
- ☐   Digging square holes
- ☐   Digging flat-bottom trench
- ☐   Digging trenchs to grade
- ☐ Tractor loaders
- ☐ Skid-steer loaders, friction drive
- ☐ Skid-steer loaders, hydrostatic
- ☐ 4 Wheel drive loaders, straight frame
- ☐ 4 wheel drive loaders, articulated
- ☐ Crawler-type loaders
- ☐ Bulldozers, hydraulic blade
- ☐ Bulldozers, hydraulic 6 way blade
- ☐ Bulldozers, cable controlled blade
- ☐ Hydraulic Excavators
- ☐ Gradalls
- ☐ Drag line
- ☐ Clam buckets
- ☐ Lifting crane
- ☐ Graders, straight frame
- ☐ Graders, articulated
- ☐ Scrapers
- ☐ Rollers
- ☐ Industrial tractors & attachments
- ☐
- ☐
- ☐
- ☐
- ☐
- ☐
- ☐

WORK HABITS	IGNORES DIRECTIONS	FOLLOWS SOME DIRECTIONS, WORKS INEFFICIENTLY	FOLLOWS DIRECTIONS AND WORKS SATISFACTORILY	STEADY CONSCIENTIOUS WORKER	VERY ACCURATE RESOURCEFUL AND EFFICIENT	MOTIVATION	APATHETIC	SPORATICALLY MOTIVATED	GENERALLY MOTIVATED	INTERESTED IN EXCELLING	HIGHLY INVOLVED AND MOTIVATED
SAFETY HABITS	SLOPPY AND HAZARDOUS	FAIR, NEEDS IMPROVEMENT	GENERALLY WORKS SAFELY	MEETS REQUIRED SAFETY STANDARDS	NEAT, CONSCIENTIOUS AND CAREFUL	INITIATIVE	REQUIRES CONSTANT PRESSURE	NEEDS OCCASIONAL PRODDING	DOES ASSIGNED WORK	OCCASIONALLY SEEKS EXTRA WORK	SEEKS AND RECOGNIZES WORK TO BE DONE
WORK AREA NEATNESS	VERY SLOPPY AND INCONSIDERATE	FORGETFUL AND UNCONSCIENTIOUS	ADEQUATE	THOROUGH	PRIDE IN OVERALL APPEARANCE OF FACILITIES	EFFORT	"QUITTER"	APPLIES MINIMAL EFFORT	SHOWS SATISFACTORY EFFORT	SHOWS GROWING DETERMINATION	DETERMINED, PERSEVERING AND DILIGENT
WORK AREA ATTENDANCE	OFTEN NOT IN WORK AREA	MAKES EXCUSES TO LEAVE WORK AREA	GENERALLY IN WORK AREA	SELDOM LEAVES WORK AREA	ALWAYS WHERE ASSIGNED	PEER RELATIONS	UNCOOPERATIVE	SOMETIMES HARD TO WORK WITH	GENERALLY COOPERATIVE	WORKS VERY WELL WITH OTHERS	OUTGOING WARM AND COOPERATIVE
SELF-ESTEEM	NO SELF-CONFIDENCE	INSECURE, SELF-CONSCIOUS DEFENSIVE	BALANCED ATTITUDE	POSITIVE SELF EVALUATION	SELF-CONFIDENT AND SECURE	LEADERSHIP	UNABLE TO LEAD	RESIGNS TO FOLLOW	SHOWS LEADERSHIP WHEN REQUESTED	VOLUNTARILY DISPLAYS LEADERSHIP	MAKES THINGS GO
INTEGRITY	NOT TRUSTWORTHY	ERRATIC	SINCERE	RELIABLE AND DEPENDABLE	EXCEPTIONALLY TRUSTWORTHY	REACTION TO AUTHORITY	HOSTILE	INDIFFERENT	ACCEPTING	GENERALLY COOPERATIVE	EXCEPTIONALLY COOPERATIVE
RESPONSIBILITY	UNRELIABLE	SOMETIMES RELIABLE	USUALLY RELIABLE	CONSCIENTIOUS	ASSUMES RESPONSIBILITY VERY WELL	Total Days Absent			Excused		Unexcused

TEACHER'S COMMENTS _____

_____

_____

_____
              _____

FIGURE 8-8. *Employability Profile*

various features, machines, and areas of the shop to the students. Special consideration should be given to safety zones and other safety features. The tour should be more than a quick walk through the shop. Questions should be encouraged. It should be obvious that advance preparation of the shop was carried out by the instructor. It would be foolish to take students on a tour of a messy shop facility.

SAFETY INSTRUCTION

Safety regulations and procedures were discussed in detail in Chapter 2. They are included in this chapter only to remind the teacher that safety instruction should begin the first day of class and continue each and every day of the school year.

The instructor will have to decide how much time to spend on safety instruction the first day. At least some mention of safety should be made. A review of the shop safety regulations should be conducted as early as possible in the school year.

DAILY PROCEDURE

The students should be informed about what the daily procedure will be in the shop. This procedure can, and no doubt will, vary from shop to shop and teacher to teacher. When the students enter, should they be seated, change to work clothes, or go to work? Explain what procedure you want the students to follow. One example follows.

1. When you enter the shop, sit in your assigned seat.
2. Attendance will be taken. Announcements will be made. A lesson, if scheduled, will be presented.
3. Change to suitable shop dress. (Optional depending on specialization.)
4. Carry on with shop assignment, project, or work as required.
5. When the clean-up signal is given, stop work, replace tools, and do your assigned job.
6. When your clean-up assignment is completed, change from work clothes and return to your assigned seat.
7. Wait until dismissed by the instructor. (The bell is not for students, it is for the instructor.)

The above is just an example. You should decide on a procedure and make sure that it is followed. A set procedure will save you many problems and result in a smoother operation.

SUMMARY

Part III of this book was concerned with instructional presentation with major consideration given to the first day of class. Chapter 8 presented materials on school procedure, discipline, student records, and evaluation, to mention only a few of the headings. It concluded with a suggested daily procedure. Be well prepared for that first day of class. Many problems can occur since you and the students may be in a new situation for the first time. Since first impressions are so important, try to get things off to a good start and gain the students' respect. Adequate preplanning should help the first day go by without any major problems.

SOURCE MATERIALS

Doros, Sidney. *Teaching as a Profession.* Columbus, Ohio: Merrill, 1968.

Foster, Herbert L. *Ribbin', Jivin', and Playing the Dozens: The Unrecognized Dilemma of Innercity Schools.* Cambridge, Mass.: Ballinger, 1974.

Proctor, James O. and Griefzu, G. Edward. *TNT—Techniques, Notes, Tips for Teachers.* Albany, N.Y.: Delmar, 1949.

Skinner, B. F. *The Technology of Teaching.* New York: Appleton-Century-Crofts, 1968.

9

THE LESSON
PRESENTATION

This chapter focuses on the presentation of a formal lesson to a group of students. The formal lesson presentation is only one technique and may or may not be used depending on the teaching style of the instructor. Most instructors will find it necessary to present formal lessons and demonstrations to the entire class at various times, even though most of the other instruction is individualized. It is but one technique and should be used when suited to the needs of the students and teacher.

By this time you should have had the opportunity to develop a few sample lesson plans based on the format for lesson plan construction suggested in Chapter 7. Now you should have the opportunity for a practice run. If a video tape recorder is available, it is a good idea to have someone video tape the presentation and then rerun it for your own evaluation. If this is not possible, at least tape record the presentation and then listen to the tape. Video tape recording has proven a valuable experience for many teachers.

THE IMPORTANCE OF THE PRESENTATION

Even with the best of lesson plans to work from, you have no guarantee of your ability to present the lesson to a group of students. However, you will be much better off with a good lesson plan than without. The preplanning spent in developing the lesson plan should pay off in the presentation.

The presentation is important for a number of reasons.

1. The content of the lesson is important enough to teach.
2. The formal lesson presentation method is the best means of presenting the lesson content to the students.
3. The application of the lesson content to students' practical situations must be made clear.
4. Timing the presentation is important. Timing does not refer to the minutes or hours necessary for the actual presentation, but to its proper place in the instructional process. The presentation should be applicable within a short period of time.
5. The teacher is on display during a formal lesson presentation. His ability to present a lesson to the class but yet relate to each individual is being evaluated by each student. His preparation, teaching style, and mastery of subject matter are all on display.
6. The presentation is time consuming. It is essential that instructional time not be wasted by either the teacher or the learner. A well-prepared teacher and well-prepared student will guard against lost instructional time.

PREPLANNING

The importance of preplanning was discussed earlier in the chapter concerned with the construction of lesson plans. The time spent in preparing the course of study and the lesson plans should now begin to pay off in the quality of the actual lesson presentation. Many rather embarrassing situations can be avoided by good preplanning. The following could all have been avoided if sufficient preplanning had taken place.

1. You prepared a lesson plan and estimated that it would take thirty minutes to make the presentation. The actual presentation time was fifteen minutes and left you unprepared for the remaining fifteen minutes. That extra time can be very long to the underprepared teacher.
2. You are in the middle of a demonstration lesson and find that you are missing an essential part or tool. It is especially embarrassing if you cannot locate the part or tool in the shop.
3. You have started your presentation to the class and are now ready to use a filmstrip projector. You turn it on, and the bulb

does not light. The well-prepared instructor would have a spare bulb handy to replace the defective one.

4. You have started a demonstration-type presentation and find it essential to use a mathematical formula before you can continue with the demonstration. In preparing for the presentation, you neglected to review the formula and find yourself unable to continue with the demonstration.

Be Overprepared

It is much better to be overprepared for a presentation than underprepared. This does not imply that you would continue with the presentation beyond the time you usually spend in your lesson presentations. It means that you have built-in safeguards in the form of follow-up or review questions which follow the presentation. Another safeguard is to require individual laboratory work so that students can apply the material just presented. To be of the most value, the presentation should be of immediate need and use to the students. A delay in application will probably require review of the presentation and wasted instructional time.

The student teacher or in-service teacher is most apt to overestimate the time necessary to present a certain topic. For this reason, it is essential that he be overprepared and have back-up questions or an immediate application procedure for the students to follow.

Setting the Stage

The teacher, lesson plans in hand, must set the physical stage for the actual presentation. The physical setting is an important ingredient to consider in the preplanning. A number of suggestions are worthy of note at this time.

PHYSICAL FACILITY. The location for the presentation should be the setting in the shop or laboratory most conducive to the teaching-learning situation. You should be concerned about the comfort of your students. At times, especially for demonstration-type lessons, it is necessary for the students to stand in order to see a demonstration on certain machines or equipment. The students will be seated for most of the presentations. Provide proper chairs for the students. It is very difficult for students to sit on benches during a lesson presentation and be expected to pay attention and take notes. Do not require students to sit in an area in which you would not want to sit.

Use care in the selection of your position to present the lesson. Do not position yourself in front of a large window area or bright lights that would require students to look into glaring sunlight or bright lights. Guard against outside distractions in selecting the instructional area. Outside distractions are of two types, those that exist outside the shop and can be seen through the windows, and those that may or may not be visible depending on whether there are windows in the door or wall facing the corridor.

Be aware of crowding, especially during demonstrations on machines or live work. If a lesson is presented on the lathe, it is essential that students stand back far enough so that everyone can see. The instructors must constantly think about crowding and lack of visibility. Closed circuit television (CCTV) and video tape recording (VTR) equipment can help the instructor who is willing to use such equipment in the shop and laboratory. CCTV and VTR equipment should be especially helpful to shop and laboratory instructors with demonstration lessons which are difficult to present to large groups of students. The thoughtful instructor will always be aware of and attempt to improve the instructional setting.

LIGHTING, HEATING, AND VENTILATION. Before the start of a lesson or any activity in the shop, make sure that you have proper lighting, temperature control, and ventilation. Even on the coldest day, fresh air is essential where a large group of people are assembled. Temperature control is essential and should be maintained between seventy and seventy-two degrees Fahrenheit. Lighting should be suitable since it is controlled by building specifications of the various state departments of education. Shades or blinds of one or more types should be available to shut off outside light if visual aids such as movies, slides, single-concept films, etc., are to be used.

STUDENT COMFORT. Many of the items previously mentioned were concerned with student comfort. Student comfort does not imply that the shop or laboratory be a plush recreation area. The shop or laboratory should approximate the conditions students will face when they enter employment in industry. Any other type of situation does not do justice to the student or the occupation. But it is essential that the setting be conducive to learning.

From time to time, the wise instructor might ask for student comments on what can be done to improve the shop. Remember, the shop is designed for learners and any input is worthy of consideration.

THE LESSON PLAN

Lesson plan construction and format were discussed in detail in Chapter 7. Figure 7-2 presented a sample outline of a lesson plan. The lesson plan format is consistent with the individual instructional units recommended for the course of study and discussed in Chapter 5.

The concern now is to present the lesson, making use of the lesson plan that you have prepared. If CCTV or VTR equipment is available, it would be a good idea to tape your presentation and then play it back for self-evaluation. If video equipment is not available, at least audio tape your lesson presentation. For purposes of this book, the lesson presentation will be based on the lesson plan format suggested in Chapter 6.

THE PRESENTATION

The outline of the presentation will be based on the following lesson plan format.

Title page

Introductory statement

Behavioral objectives

References

Instructional aids

The presentation (instructional content)

Discussion—questions

Application

Evaluation criteria

The material to follow will be presented in procedural order, which is not based on time sequence.

INTRODUCTORY STATEMENT. Opening remarks will set the stage for what is to follow. The introductory statement should be carefully worded when first written in the lesson plan; it should then be used as written during the presentation. The statement should state the necessity or importance of the lesson to be presented. Think of yourself as a salesman selling a product. You might briefly review what preceded and what will follow the lesson.

BEHAVIORAL OBJECTIVES. You, no doubt, spent considerable time in writing the behavioral objectives that appear now in your lesson plan. Let the students know what behavior (this refers to performance, not discipline) will be expected of them after the lesson presentation. In basic terms, you are indicating what technique will be used to evaluate their performance when you state the one or more behavioral objectives for the lesson. If the lesson topic is the use of the Weston Model 611 tube tester, one objective might be: "The student, given a Weston Model 611 tube tester, should be able to test and indicate the condition of a conventional vacuum tube within 2 minutes and do it successfully 90 per cent of the time." (Underlined numbers may vary accordingly.) This should indicate to the students that, if given a Weston Model 611 tube tester and one conventional vacuum tube, within a two-minute period, they should be able to check and indicate the condition of the tube and be correct 90 per cent of the time (nine out of ten in twenty minutes). The students then will know what level of performance on such an objective is expected of them. The teacher must provide sufficient equipment, tubes, and class time to allow the students to practice. A student will clearly know when he reaches the level of performance expected and, at that time, ask the teacher to evaluate his performance.

REFERENCES. It is a good idea to let students know what references on the lesson are available in the shop and elsewhere. Such references might include textbooks, instructional manuals, charts, single-concept films, trade publications, etc. It is to your advantage to have a few sample references available to show and share with the students. If you like the idea of using the lesson plan as an information sheet, the students will then receive a copy of the plan for their notebooks.

INSTRUCTIONAL AIDS. The instructional aids are indicated in the lesson plan and may or may not be an actual part of the lesson presentation. Much will depend on the type or types of instructional aids or materials you have decided to use. If a 16 mm film is to be used along with your lesson, indicate the title of the film, supplier, and running time. It will be obvious to the students in the class that the film was used as an instructional aid. It is included on the lesson plan to remind the teacher that the film, projector, and screen are all essential to the lesson.

If the instructional aid used is an information sheet, a copy should be attached to the lesson plan. The information sheet could very well be the most important ingredient in the lesson. The teacher will want to make certain that sufficient copies are readily available for the students.

The instructional aids you have selected should be of help to you in making the presentation. They should be of value to the students in making the lesson content easier to understand and easier to apply to their actual performance activities.

The wise teacher will use a variety of aids. Too much of any one type might lose its effectiveness after a while. The selection of instructional aids is but one item in your instructional strategy.

THE LESSON PRESENTATION

THE PRESENTATION (INSTRUCTIONAL CONTENT). Many different types of strategies have been suggested for this section of the lesson plan. They boil down to the presentation of the instructional content in a logical sequential order. The procedure you select can, and should, vary with your teaching style. Nothing is wrong with a simple numerical listing of topics or items which are essential to the demonstration. Systematic procedure proceeding from the simplest to the most complex ingredients should be presented in procedural order.

You might highlight or underline the most essential elements of your lesson plan by underlining various key words. You should be encouraged to experiment with a number of ways to construct this section of the lesson plan and then present the lesson. After all, lesson plans are for the use of teachers and to be most effective must suit the teaching style of the individual teacher.

A good lesson requires the teacher to have a thorough knowledge of the material he is about to present to the class. It includes a definite plan of procedure.

A good presentation will include interwoven questions to check the understanding of the students as the presentation moves along. Safety instruction, if appropriate, should be included with the material being presented to the students. The short-range and long-range objectives of the lesson should be tied in with the presentation.

DISCUSSION—QUESTIONS. It is a good idea to summarize the presentation by one technique or another. One way is to prepare five or more questions which can be asked of the students at the conclusion of the lesson. Questions can be selected that will summarize the lesson as well, and give the teacher some feedback concerning how well the students understood the lesson. The questions can raise additional questions and a discussion may logically develop.

APPLICATION. *Immediate reinforcement of the demonstration or lesson should be built into the lesson plan and the presentation.* This can be referred to as the application phase. If the presentation was important enough to be made in the first place, then immediate application of the presentation should be required of the students.

If a lesson dealing with Ohm's law is the topic of the presentation, then the application might be to require students to work out a number of Ohm's law problems. If the presentation was a demonstration lesson on the use of the cross-cut saw, then the application might be actual supervised practice requiring students to use the cross-cut saw. Whatever application is involved, it should be consistent with the stated behavioral or performance objectives.

PRESENTATION

Due to the nature of most shop and laboratory subjects, the "hands-on" type of application is an important phase of instruction. Usually, each succeeding lesson or demonstration builds on what preceded it. Shop and laboratory teachers have long made use of progress charts which indicate to both the student and the teacher what progress has been made. In many cases, such progress charts reflect behavioral or performance objectives.

Application should occur as soon as possible after the presentation if the most advantage is to be gained from the presentation.

EVALUATION CRITERIA. When you list the various behavioral or performance objectives on your lesson plan, you are more or less indicating to students what level you expect them to reach. The evaluation criteria should be consistent with the stated behavioral or performance objectives. Any other form of evaluation is unfair, and students will soon lose faith in you.

Objective criteria should rule your decision regarding evaluation criteria. Subjective judgement has little room in shop and laboratory teaching. Action verbs should be your key in writing objectives and in selecting evaluation criteria. Words such as the following will prove helpful: list, calculate, identify, locate, design, draw, calibrate, install, replace, repair, inspect, service.

Following a presentation of a lesson on Ohm's law, one method of evaluation might be:

The student should be able to mathematically calculate correctly, to the nearest tenth, nine out of ten *simple* Ohm's law problems. (Simple might refer to no value larger than 10 or less than .001.)

Be conscious of speaking habits, posture, and mannerisms at all times in the shop and laboratory. Be constantly on the alert for ways to evaluate your teaching ability and improve your style. Self-improvement should be given high priority by all teachers. How would you like to be a student in your own class?

THE FOUR-STEP LESSON

The teacher is advised to consider the material presented in Figure 9-1, taken from a publication entitled The Preparation of Occupational Instructors, when preparing lessons. The four-step lesson is compatible with the lesson plan format suggested in this book. Added detail is required with the format used in this book, but the basics of the four-step lesson are still present.

THE LESSON PRESENTATION

CHECK SHEET FOR LESSON PRESENTATION

The content presented in Figure 9-2 is taken from the same source as Figure 9-1 with some basic modifications. Such a check sheet could be used by a college supervisor who is assigned to assist you in student teaching. You may find it helpful for your own use as a self-evaluation technique, especially if you take time to video tape or audio tape your lessons.

APPLICATION AND FOLLOW-UP

Each presentation should be followed by hands-on or practical application of the lesson content especially after demonstration-type lessons. The teacher should move about the shop giving individual assistance, as needed.

Theory lessons should also require application in the form of added reading or written assignments. Teacher follow-up is essential. The teacher should review Monday's presentation before starting the presentation for Tuesday.

SUMMARY

This chapter was concerned with the actual lesson presentation. It should flow from the course of study (Chapter 5) and the lesson plan (Chapter 7) and be based on preplanning (Chapter 6). The importance of the lesson presentation and setting the learning environment was stressed. Operational details taken from the lesson plan format were presented, and relate directly to the lesson plan format that has been used in this book. The chapter concludes with a review of the four-step lesson approach and a check sheet for lesson presentations. The teacher who is either student teaching or in a supervised teaching situation may want to obtain a copy of the evaluation device the college supervisor will be using. In addition, it would be informative to see a copy of the teacher evaluation form used in the school you are teaching in. This is the form the principal or supervisor will use when he or she observes you in class.

The FOUR-STEP LESSON

STEP I

PREPARATION OR
INTRODUCTION STEP

STEP II

PRESENTATION STEP

STEP III

APPLICATION OR
TRY OUT STEP

STEP IV

CHECKING TESTING
and FOLLOW-UP STEP

The four-step plan is used for both individual and group instruction.

**HOW TO GET READY
TO INSTRUCT**

Have a Timetable

Include how much skill you expect him
to have and by what date.

Break Down the Job

List important steps.
Pick out key points. (Safety is always
a key point.)

Have Everything Ready

Have the right equipment, materials,
and supplies.

Have the Workplace Properly Arranged

Arrange workplace just as the worker
will be expected to keep it.

Name of
Sponsoring School
Here

Keep This Card Handy

HOW TO INSTRUCT

Step I: Prepare the Worker
Put him at ease.
State the job and find out what he already
knows about it.
Get him interested in learning job.
Place in correct position.

Step II: Present the Operation
Demonstrate and explain one IMPORTANT
STEP at a time.
Stress each KEY POINT.
Instruct clearly, completely, and patiently,
but no more than he can master.

Step III: Application or Try-Out Performance
Have him do the job--correct errors.
Have him explain each KEY POINT to you
as he does the job again.
Make sure he understands.
Continue until YOU know HE knows.

Step IV: Follow Up or Test
Test to determine if he has learned the
skill or information.
Put him on his own. Designate to whom he
goes for help.
Check frequently. Encourage questions.
Taper off extra coaching and close follow-up.

**If Worker Hasn't Learned,
The Instructor Hasn't Taught**

This illustration is the front and back of a reminder card used by many successful
vocational instructors. It tells how to use the four steps when teaching a skill.

27

FIGURE 9-1.   The Four-Step Lesson

Name of LESSON_____

AIM_____

INSTRUCTOR_____

Points To Check	Yes	No	Remarks
A. GET READY POINTS			
1. Did he appear to have everything planned? Did he know what he was doing?			
2. Were tools, equipment, and materials all in readiness (no fumbles)? Did he forget anything?			
3. Was his desk or workplace in order?			
4. Did he have a lesson plan?			
B. THE FOUR STEPS **STEP I, PREPARATION**			
1. Was the learner or group put at ease?			
2. Did instructor find out what learner or group knew about the lesson at hand?			
3. Did he tell learner or group enough about the lesson to make it genuinely interesting, yet keep the explanation brief?			
4. Did he place the learner or group in proper position for correct instruction?			
STEP II, PRESENTATION			
1. Did he demonstrate and explain one important step at a time? Could you follow the steps?			
2. Were the key points really stressed? Could you catch them?			
3. Did he instruct clearly, completely, and patiently?			

FIGURE 9-2. *Check Sheet for Teaching*

Points To Check	Yes	No	Remarks
STEP III, APPLICATION			
1. Did he have learner do the job?			
2. Did he correct errors?			
3. Did he provide enough time for practice?			
4. Did he have learner explain each key point as the learner did the job again?			
5. Did he really make sure the job or the information was learned?			
STEP IV, TEST			
1. Did the test cover what has been taught in the lesson?			
2. On completion, could the learners do the job unaided? Did the learners possess the essential knowledge?			
3. Were checks made of their performance or did he indicate such checks would be made?			
C. ORAL QUESTIONS			
1. Did he use questions to motivate learners?			
2. Did he find out what learners already knew?			
3. Did he encourage active participation by use of questions?			
4. Did he spot-check instruction with questions?			
5. Did he use questioning to clarify points learners had not understood?			
6. Did he use questioning to stress important points?			
7. Did questions help hold the attention of the learner or learners?			
8. Were questions used to review material?			

FIGURE 9-2 continued

Points To Check	Yes	No	Remarks
9. Were questions brief and easily understood?			
10. Did questions require thought?			
11. Was each question limited to one main thought?			
12. Did each question have a specific purpose related to the subject under discussion?			
13. Did the instructor ask the question, then name a person to answer it?			
D. SIX RECOMMENDATIONS			
Did the instructor: 1. Have a long-range goal, in addition to the immediate aims?			
2. Teach from the known to the unknown?			
3. Tie knowledge and skill together?			
4. Proceed from simple to complex, from easy to difficult?			
5. Reward success?			
6. Provide for practice or drill?			
E. RELATED INFORMATION LESSONS			
1. Did the instructor explain why the information should be learned?			
2. Did he make use of audio-visual aids when they were needed?			
3. Were actual trade situations the basis for explanations of how the information could be used?			
4. In Step III, were learners required to carry out an assignment related to the trade?			
5. Was a written test prepared for use in Step IV?			

SOURCE: *The Preparation of Occupational Instructors.* Washington, D. C.: Superintendent of Documents, 1966, pp. 45–47.

FIGURE 9-2 continued

159

SOURCE MATERIALS

Larson, Milton E. *Teaching Related Subjects in Trade and Industrial and Technical Education.* Columbus, Ohio: Merrill, 1972.

Leighbody, Gerald B. and Kidd, Donald M. *Methods of Teaching Shop and Technical Subjects.* Albany, N.Y.: Delmar, 1966.

Pucel, David J. and Knaak, William C. *Individualizing Vocational and Technical Instruction.* Columbus, Ohio: Merrill, 1975.

U.S. Department of Health, Education, and Welfare. *The Preparation of Occupational Instructors.* Washington, D.C.: U.S. Government Printing Office, 1966.

10

INDIVIDUALIZATION
OF INSTRUCTION

In Chapter 3, considerable stress was placed on differences between individual students. If you agree that individuals vary in their abilities, desires, and attitudes toward learning, it should make sense that no one technique will meet the individual needs of all the students in your shop or laboratory.

Being aware of the differences between students in his class, the teacher should try to individualize his instruction by providing the necessary materials to allow each student to progress at his own rate. This procedure is referred to as self-pacing. Many shop and laboratory teachers individualize their teaching by varying activities in their classrooms. An observer seldom walks into a shop and finds all the students doing exactly the same thing.

DEFINITION

Two examples come to mind as illustrations of individualized instruction. One is the driver education instructor teaching the driving phase of his course. His concern is the one student behind the wheel. This is a one-to-one relationship between student and teacher. Another example is the flight instructor working with the student pilot.

Situations that are essential for driver education and flight training are impractical and much too costly for other areas of instruction. The teacher can attempt to individualize instruction within the group. It is something that the teacher must want to do and work at to be successful. It takes a high level of instructional skill on the part of the teacher and the cooperation of the students to make the most of this technique.

Individualized instruction is not a new concept. It is a technique that was suggested and used many years ago. The technique is especially useful to the shop or laboratory teacher due to the "hands on" nature of the subject. Improved instructional materials such as audiovisual aids make individualized instruction a more useful technique than it was in the past.

In individualized instruction, you are basically attempting to tailor the learning experience to each student in the class. Some students will progress faster and further than others. But this is as it should be. It is your responsibility to encourage each student to progress as far as he is able.

GROUP VERSUS INDIVIDUAL INSTRUCTION

Group instruction can be used for information lessons or, if the group is small enough, for demonstrations. The following are some of the advantages of group instruction:

1. *Saves time:* More students are reached simultaneously, and more material can be covered.
2. *Provides uniform instruction:* The teacher presents the same material to all the students. All learners receive identical information.
3. *Develops team spirit:* Students learn to work together.
4. *Motivates individuals:* Learners with common aims support each other's determination to succeed.
5. *Develops leadership:* Provides opportunities for individuals within the group to demonstrate their leadership abilities.
6. *Teaches basic principles:* Is useful for teaching elementary principles and is a good starter for teaching common elements.
7. *Learners may assist:* Learners may assist other class members who have not understood a certain point during the lesson.

Because of differences between people, there are times when it is advisable to teach them individually or to give them supervision while they learn independently. The following are some of the advantages of individual instruction:

INDIVIDUALIZATION OF INSTRUCTION

1. *More thorough:* Makes the teaching-learning process more thorough, even though at times it is slower.
2. *Self-pacing:* Instruction is geared to the learning speed of one person.
3. *Easier:* Makes instruction easier since the teacher is concerned at the moment with one learner rather than a total group.
4. *Personalized instruction:* Gives opportunities for remedial work or more advanced work, making it easier to review, correct, and prescribe future activities.
5. *Varied instructional techniques:* Makes it easier to use varied instructional techniques that meet the needs of each person.

Most vocational teachers will combine the two methods described above. A common procedure is for the lesson plan to provide for both group and individual instruction. The lesson is presented to the group and activities after the formal lesson individualize the process. This seems to be a typical and successful way for vocational teachers to direct the instructional process.

SELF–PACING

The shop or laboratory teacher who has made use of the progress chart has in a way been using a form of individual or self-pacing instruction. Self-pacing is basically a technique that allows and encourages each student to advance at his own rate. It takes into consideration the factor of individual differences. Correspondence courses are probably one of the best examples of self-pacing. The student can move as fast or slow as he desires to complete the course. Much, no doubt, depends on the student's motivation and time available to work on the lesson.

The teacher can provide a learning situation that encourages such self-pacing. The concept is compatible with the course of study design and behavioral objectives discussed in earlier chapters. The unit system places the subject content in procedural order and opens the door to self-pacing in the shop or laboratory.

Self-pacing instruction gives the student a clear picture of his rate of progress. It allows each student to progress at his own rate and even, perhaps, complete a three-year program in two years or less. If early completion is not possible, due to administrative red tape, the student could go into still more advanced work in his specialization. Likewise, the slow student might take four years to complete the requirements that normally take three years. But this is not objectionable as long as his level of performance and skill are developed to make him employable.

PRESENTATION

A minimum amount of time is spent in lectures and a maximum amount of time in individual instruction in this structure. The teacher is a resource person and manager of the instructional facility. His importance is just as great as, but his role somewhat different than, the traditional teacher.

SUGGESTED TECHNIQUES

The following activities may be useful in your teaching assignment. They can be used in various ways to individualize instruction.

COURSE OF STUDY. When behavioral or performance objectives are used, and students are evaluated in terms of the stated objectives, the individual approach to teaching has been used. Each student is evaluated in terms of the objectives he is able to master and not in terms of the performance of his fellow students.

Self-pacing can also function if the teacher is willing to allow and encourage students to advance at their own rates. If a student completes Unit X, he should be allowed immediately to start the next unit and not have to wait until the rest of the class completes Unit X. A teacher may very well have students working on four or five different units at the same time, but this is to be expected with individual abilities and levels of motivation.

THE PROJECT. An important and helpful way of individualizing instruction is the project method. The project in a machine shop course might be to construct a C clamp to meet certain assigned specifications. The project is not the end product but is only a means to an end. The main purpose should be practicing performance objectives that a student must meet in order to end up with a properly machined and constructed C clamp. The selection of projects should be closely coordinated with the performance objectives.

Project work makes it necessary for the teacher to move from student to student and work with each student individually. At times, it will be necessary to call the entire class together for a lesson or demonstration. At other times, you may want to work with a small group of students on a particular problem that is of interest to them all. The chart presented in Figure 10-1 is an example of a progress chart that can be used to record the individual progress of students in a class.

LIVE WORK. Automotive mechanics, cosmetology, food service, television repair, and other specializations are able to use "live" work in the instructional program. Many automotive mechanics teachers will operate their shop

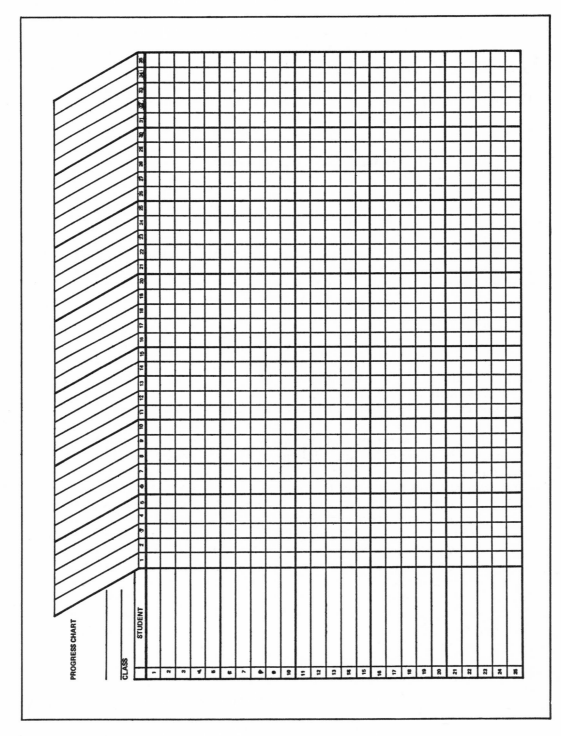

FIGURE 10-1. Progress Chart

just like a shop in an automobile agency. The teacher is like the service manager in an agency and is accountable for the work turned out.

Before taking on live work, be sure you check out any state or local regulations that might apply. Use special care in determining legal liability in the event of damage to property or injury to an individual. Most boards of education have established policies regarding live work in the shops and laboratories.

Some schools operate walk-in tea shops which are used as teaching situations for food service students. Walk-in school barber shops, bakeries, and beauty parlors are not uncommon in vocational education programs.

Such activities do individualize instruction as well as create real learning situations for students. Students repair, replace, locate trouble, or provide some form of service rather than end up with a finished product as in the project method.

Some specializations can and should use a combination of live work and project work. It would be best for the beginning automotive mechanics student to first do some project work on "dead" jobs (perhaps school-owned vehicles, obtained especially for this purpose) before doing any live work. The same would apply to the barbering, cosmetology, and television repair students.

EXPERIMENTATION. The experiment approach can be a suitable alternative to project or live work in some areas of instruction. Electronics is one subject in which a series of experiments designed to take a student from one level to another can be used with a high degree of success. Behavioral or performance objectives can and should be built into the experimental approach.

Teacher-made experiments are more relevant to the local situation than some purchased book of experiments. Each student or students, in groups of two to four, can work on the experiments and progress from one experiment to the next at their own rate.

With more advanced students, the "experiment in reverse" might be effective. The student or group of students is charged with the responsibility for developing an experiment. In other words, they set out to prove a concept or law by writing an experiment, rather than just being handed an experiment to complete.

PROGRAMMED INSTRUCTION. As more and more programmed instruction books and materials are published, teachers should be aware of what is available in their teaching area. Such materials can help in remedial as well as in supplemental instruction in the shop or laboratory.

Programmed materials appropriate to the objectives of the course can help to individualize the instructional process. They have the advantage of allowing students to progress at their own rate while periodically testing them on past information. With supportive hardware devices, the instructional system can even be a hands-on experience for the students, much like that found in correspondence courses in electronics and other areas. A teacher who has received some basic instruction in programmed learning techniques can write his own programmed materials to suit the goals of a particular course.

INDEPENDENT STUDY. Individual independent study projects or assignments can be arranged between the teacher and the student. The special interests of the student can result in some particular type of project or research effort on his part. Each student selects his own topic and then carries out the project. He consults with the teacher when it is necessary.

The independent study topic is decided on as a result of pupil-teacher planning and should have some stated objective. In this situation, some form of contract should exist between both parties so that each knows what is expected of the other.

ROLE PLAYING. Role playing can be an excellent technique for understanding ourselves and others in the roles we play and for practicing interpersonal group skills. The technique places the student in the position of a person who is very different from the student.

The role playing technique can be of special value in shop and laboratory teaching in discussing employer-employee relations. The employment interview, on-the-job relations with other employees, and special other uses can be suitable to the technique.

The role playing is directed by the teacher, and the scene resulting might be in response to something that happened in the shop. Perhaps a violation of a shop safety rule occurred. The implications could be used in a role playing situation to see how the matter would have been resolved had it occurred in industry rather than school.

SMALL GROUP INSTRUCTION. As indicated earlier, it is not essential to always have a one-to-one ratio for individual instruction. Every time the instructor calls together a small group of students for a demonstration or discussion, individualization of instruction is taking place.

Project work, live work, and experiments can all be used in the small group process. The teacher must use care in the selection of group members. The more advanced students might function as group leaders and be of real assistance to the slower members. As a teacher gets to know the students in his class, he will soon find out which students can best work together and which ones cannot.

VIDEO TAPE RECORDER (VTR). If closed circuit television equipment (CCTV) and/or video tape recording equipment (VTR) are available, both can be useful to the teacher attempting to individualize instruction. Demonstration lessons can be video taped by the instructor and made available for student viewings. If a student was absent on the day the lesson was given, or just wanted to review the lesson, it could be played back for him at a convenient time. More and more schools are being equipped with CCTV and VTR equipment.

COMPUTER–ASSISTED INSTRUCTION. Considerable time and money are being spent on electronic computers that provide for various kinds of feedback and branching based on the student's immediate and earlier replies and other data. Different models use electronic typewriters and push buttons which make it possible to hold a question until the student gets it right. Computer-assisted instruction is a very advanced form of programmed instruction with many unique advantages. Properly prepared programs can help to individualize the instructional process especially in related theory.

SINGLE CONCEPT FILMS. As the name implies, each film is concerned with one concept. They seem to be of particular value in demonstration lessons where a student is required to develop a certain level of manual skill. The continuous film can be reviewed over and over again, until the student masters the subject matter.

The teacher who so desires can make his own films if he takes the time. Some commercial single concept films can also be purchased.

PROBLEM SOLVING. The problem-solving technique can be used in the shop to encourage creativity as well as individualize the instructional process. The teacher can have students form groups, each group working on the same or a different problem. The problems might concern labor-management questions, design of some product, redesign of an existing product, current labor problems, etc.

This is an ideal situation because the teacher is working with each student in the class, recognizing individual differences and encouraging each student to advance to his maximum potential.

SUMMARY

By the nature of the subject matter, the vocational teacher spends most of his time in individualized instruction with his students. This chapter has presented a variety of ideas which should help the vocational teacher understand what is meant by the individualization of instruction.

EXHIBIT 10-1

THE ASSIGNMENT SHEET

Assignment sheets can be used to:

1. Present new related information by having the learner study it in references.
2. Help learner apply information that he is learning. Such sheets provide the element of repetition so essential in the development of judgment and the ability to use information. In general, assignment sheets are most effective when they are used soon after presentation of information.

Examples of assignments in several representative occupations are:

Auto mechanics: Take specific gravity and voltage readings of several storage batteries and describe the condition of each from the data obtained.

Electrical installation: Solve the assigned problems by means of Ohm's Law.

Commercial art: Collect several samples of printing that illustrate the difference between the optical and the geometrical center of the page.

Foundry work: Calculate the estimated weights of the iron castings which are to be made from the accompanying drawings.

Printing: Figure the cost of the stock for the jobs described.

Dressmaking: Examine the samples of textiles furnished and fill out the data requested in the space provided.

Assignment sheets may involve:

1. New concepts to be learned
2. A series of questions to be answered
3. An experiment to be performed
4. Some problems to work out
5. Bills of material to make up
6. Drawings to analyze
7. Data to study and interpret
8. Procedures to plan
9. An observation or investigation to be made and data to be recorded

An assignment sheet should provide examples or other guidance to help the learner succeed. For example, if there are several problems, at least one of them should be solved with the correct approach clearly shown.

The purpose of an assignment sheet is to get a learner to do something. For that reason it is important for such a sheet to motivate the learner, convincing him that he will benefit by completing the assignment.

SOURCE: *The Preparation of Occupational Instructors.* Washington, D. C.: Superintendent of Documents, 1966, p. 97.

EXHIBIT 10-2

ASSIGNMENT SHEET

School _____   Assignment Sheet No. _____

Use same No. as in course of study.

Insert title of assignment

INTRODUCTORY INFORMATION: *Short, concise statement to motivate the [student] to complete the assignment.*

ASSIGNED READINGS: *Listing of all printed matter and other resources to be used by the [student] in completing the assignment.*

List the facts of publication: author, title, publisher, date, and page numbers covering assignments.

QUESTIONS, PROBLEMS,   or   *The assignment should adequately cover the specific subject in this*
ACTIVITY: *assignment sheet.*

Questions and problems should be stated clearly and concisely.

The [student] should clearly understand what he is to do.

SOURCE: *The Preparation of Occupational Instructors.* Washington, D. C.: Superintendent of Documents, 1966, p. 98.

EXHIBIT 10-3

THE INFORMATION SHEET

Information sheets are intended to supply information which is not available to the learner in any other suitable form. Some representative information sheets from various occupations are:

Occupation	Information
Auto mechanics	The principle of the differential in an automobile
Electrical	The principle of the transformer
Plumbing	Cast iron pipe — types, sizes, and uses
Printing	The point system of measurement
Commercial food preparation	The action of yeast in bread dough
Cosmetology	The purpose and use of astringents
Dressmaking	Linen — what it is and where to use it

Because information sheets are to be studied rather than used to direct activity of a [student], their format is not as formal as that of assignment sheets. An information sheet should be easy to read, clear, and concise. It should also be interesting to read and hold the [student's] attention.

An instructor may prepare and use an information sheet if any of the following conditions exists:

1. The information is in a reference book of which he has only one copy.
2. Up-to-date information is not included in the references used in the course.
3. Information in the reference does not cover the subject completely.
4. Material in a reference is too long.
5. Material in a reference is too difficult to understand.
6. Material from several sources should be consolidated in one place.

SOURCE: *The Preparation of Occupational Instructors.* Washington, D. C.: Superintendent of Documents, 1966, p. 99.

EXHIBIT 10–4

INFORMATION SHEET

School _____   Information Sheet No. _____
Use same No. as in course of study.

Insert title of information to be presented

INFORMATION: *Written to suit level of* [student].

Sentences and paragraphs should be concise.

Illustrations should be used where they will assist in clarifying the information.

Material should be organized and presented in a logical sequence.

Material should be of sufficient length and complexity to challenge the [student].

SOURCE: *The Preparation of Occupational Instructors.* Washington, D. C.:
Superintendent of Documents, 1966, p. 100.

EXHIBIT 10-5

THE JOB SHEET

In vocational education, learners are usually assigned actual jobs to perform under varying degrees of supervision. To help ensure success and high standards the *instructor prepares a job sheet* for each such job. Job sheets are particularly useful in classes where different levels of instruction are being given at the same time.

Some typical jobs for which a learner would need a job sheet are:

Occupation	*Job*
Auto mechanics	Reline and adjust the brakes on a car.
Electrical	Install an extra convenience outlet.
Commercial food preparation	Make an order of cupcakes.
Plumbing	Run in a roof vent.
Printing	Print a wedding invitation.
Machine shop	Make a flanged bushing.
Sheetmetal	Make a section of sheetmetal cornices.
Cosmetology	Make a pin curl.

As used in the occupation itself, a job sheet may be quite simple, containing a blueprint or sketch and providing only the minimum information needed for the job. In a sense, the tickets, shop blueprint, work orders, and similar items used in an occupation are job sheets.

However, the learner in his early training needs more information than the experienced worker. For that reason the job sheets used in training are designed to help the [student] learn *how* to do the job, as well as to serve as a job assignment. Job sheets used for instructional purposes usually contain:

1. A statement of the job to be done.
2. A list of materials and equipment needed.
3. A procedure outline.
4. Directions for checking the finished work.
5. Pictures, diagrams, working drawings, and sketches to show what is wanted.
6. Pictures, diagrams, and sketches to clarify any anticipated difficulties the learner may have.

Gradually, the job sheets given a learner should become more like the job ticket, work order, or blueprints he will use in the occupation.

Some job form or job sheet should be prepared for each job that will be taught in a course.

SOURCE: *The Preparation of Occupational Instructors.* Washington, D. C.: Superintendent of Documents, 1966, p. 101.

EXHIBIT 10–6

JOB SHEET

School _____   Job No. _____

Use same No. as in course of study.

_____

Insert name of job

_____

SKETCH OR DRAWING: *Provide drawing or make sketch if instructor deems necessary.*

MATERIALS: *List materials needed to perform job.*

TOOLS AND EQUIPMENT: *List tools and equipment needed to perform job.*

PROCEDURE: *State each operation or step in the job. Operations should be stated clearly and concisely.*

List operations in proper sequence.

Number operations consecutively.

Safety and key points should be listed with the operations where they apply.

Double-space between each operation.

CHECK POINT: *A check point may occur at any operation in the procedure where the instructor desires to check the [student] before allowing him to proceed.*

There may be more than one checkpoint in the job.

Place the words <u>check point</u> in the left margin at the point in the procedure where the [student] is to be checked by the instructor before the [student] is to proceed with the next operation.

SOURCE: *The Preparation of Occupational Instructors.* Washington, D. C.: Superintendent of Documents, 1966, p. 102.

EXHIBIT 10-7

THE JOB PLAN SHEET

As a [student] gains knowledge and skill in an occupation, the amount and kind of planning expected from him change. The *job plan sheet is prepared by the* [*student*] when he has enough ability to begin to plan his own work.

The amount of detailed planning shown on a job plan sheet should vary with the needs of the individual [student]. To begin with, he should be required to provide considerable detail. In time, a [student's] job plan sheet should become like the typical work order of the occupation....

This information is provided on the job plan sheet which a [student] prepares:

1. A bill of material listing the amount, kind, and size of material required.
2. A list of operations in their proper sequence.
3. A list of tools and equipment needed.
4. An estimate of the time required to do the job.
5. The necessary mathematical computations.
6. The freehand sketches required.
7. A list of the assignment sheets relating to the job.

Advantages to be gained from using the job plan sheet are:

1. The learner gains experience in planning a job.
2. The learner knows the proper sequence of operations before he begins work.
3. The learner becomes acquainted with the necessary technology of the job.
4. The learner is required to solve practical problems for a job.
5. Both the learner and the instructor save shop time.
6. The job plan sheet serves as a record of work experience.
7. The job plan sheet provides a basis for later assignments.
8. Shop and related instruction can be coordinated more easily.

SOURCE: *The Preparation of Occupational Instructors.* Washington, D.C.: Superintendent of Documents, 1966, p. 103.

EXHIBIT 10–8
JOB PLAN SHEET

[Student's] Name _____

School _____ Job Plan No. _____
Use same No. as on progress chart.

Insert name of job

SKETCH OR DRAWING: *If instructor deems necessary, [student] makes sketch or drawing as directed.*

MATERIALS: *List materials needed to perform job.*

TOOLS AND EQUIPMENT: *List tools and equipment needed to perform job.*

PROCEDURE: *State each operation or step in the job.*

Operations should be stated clearly and concisely.

List operations in proper sequence.

Number operations consecutively.

Safety and key points should be listed with operations where they apply.

CHECK POINT: *A check point may occur at any operation in the procedure where the instructor desires to check the [student] before allowing him to proceed.*

There may be more than one checkpoint in the job.

Instructor draws a red line in the left margin at the point in the procedure where the [student] is to be checked by the instructor before the student is to proceed with the next operation.

Estimated time _____ hrs.
(Determined by [student], subject to instructor's approval)

Actual time _____ hrs. _____
(Actual hours to complete job) **Approved by instructor**

(Initialed or signed before work is started)

SOURCE: *The Preparation of Occupational Instructors.* Washington, D. C.: Superintendent of Documents, 1966, p. 104.

EXHIBIT 10-9

THE OPERATION SHEET

An operation is one step in the process of doing a job. To print a poster is a job. To ink the printing press used for that job is an operation. An *operation sheet* provides the information required by a [student] in performing the operation. Operation sheets are prepared by the instructor.

Some representative operations which might be the subject of operation sheets are:

Occupation	Operation
Auto mechanics	Make a compression test on a motor.
Electrical	Thread a piece of conduit.
Machine shop	Sharpen a drill.
Plumbing	Cut pipe with a pipe cutter.
Printing	Ink a press.
Sheetmetal	Wire an edge.
Cosmetology	File fingernails.
Dressmaking	Make a mitered corner in a hem.

An operation sheet tells how to do something, just as the instructions that accompany a game tell how to play the game.

A good operation sheet must:

1. Be written in simple, clear, and concise language.
2. Be well illustrated, picturing each step or point that may cause difficulty.
3. Be arranged in good learning order just as the lesson itself is.
4. Emphasize safety and precautions at points where they apply.
5. Explain and, if possible, illustrate all new terms and names.

An operation sheet should be detailed enough and clear enough so that a capable [student] with the required experience can succeed by using just the sheet for guidance.

The operation sheet is a *supplement* to the instructor's demonstrations and instruction. It helps the normal learner to help himself after a demonstration has been given. It may serve as initial instruction for the brighter [students] who are capable of moving ahead of the others in the group. It helps the slow [student] by providing a means of reviewing the instructions previously given by the instructor.

SOURCE: *The Preparation of Occupational Instructors.* Washington, D.C.: Superintendent of Documents, 1966, p. 105.

EXHIBIT 10–10

OPERATION SHEET

School _____ Operation No._____

Use same No. as in course of study.

Insert name of operation

SKETCH OR DRAWING: *Provide drawing or make sketch if necessary.*

MATERIALS: *List materials needed to perform operation.*

TOOLS AND EQUIPMENT: *List tools and equipment needed to perform job.*

PROCEDURE: *State each step in the operation.*

Steps should be stated clearly and concisely in occupational terms.

List steps in proper sequence.

Number steps consecutively.

Safety and key points should be listed with steps where they apply.

Double-space between each step.

CHECK POINT: *A check point may occur at any step in the procedure where the instructor desires to check the [student] before allowing him to proceed.*

There may be more than one checkpoint in the operation.

Place the words <u>check point</u> in the left margin at the point in the procedure where the [student] is to be checked by the instructor before the [student] is to proceed with the next step.

SOURCE: *The Preparation of Occupational Instructors.* Washington, D.C.: Superintendent of Documents, 1966, p. 106.

A number of suggested techniques were presented, most of which teachers will find of value in their area of specialization. The use of a variety of techniques should make the instructional process more interesting and challenging to the teacher as well as the students.

The chapter concludes with a number of exhibits showing such useful forms as assignments sheets and information sheets, to mention only two. These forms help to individualize instruction.

As teachers develop their own "bags of tricks," learning should become a much more rewarding experience for the pupils.

ACTIVITIES

1. Keep a log of your time for one week indicating how your time is spent in the instructional process. Use the following chart or another as you see fit.

Total time in minutes	Mon	Tues	Wed	Thurs	Fri	% of total
Lecturing						
Large group instruction						
Small group instruction						
Individual instruction						

SOURCE MATERIALS

Alexander, William M. and Hines, Vynce A. *Independent Study in Secondary Schools.* New York: Holt, Rinehart & Winston, 1967.

Harnack, Robert S. *The Teacher: Decision Maker and Curriculum Planner.* Scranton: International Textbook, 1968.

Macdonald, James B. and Zaret, Esther. *Schools in Search of Meaning.* Washington: Association for Supervision and Curriculum Development, 1975.

Pucel, David J. and Knaak, William C. *Individualizing Vocational and Technical Instruction.* Columbus, Ohio: Merrill, 1975.

PRESENTATION

11

INSTRUCTIONAL
AIDS

DEFINITION

Instructional aids are devices of one nature or another that can be used by the teacher to make lessons or demonstrations more interesting to the students. It is much easier to demonstrate how to use a cross-cut saw than to tell a class how to use one. The cross-cut saw and lumber to be cut are therefore instructional aids. Training aids have been used for many years and perhaps date to the time the first caveman drew pictures on cave walls.

Instructional aids include such things as information sheets, working models, overhead projectors, electronic teaching devices, and simulators such as used in driver training or flight instruction. Chalkboards, flannel boards, closed circuit television, and films are also considered instructional aids.

This chapter will cover a wide range of instructional aids that may be of value to shop and laboratory teachers. Operational details will not be discussed since such information can be found in instruction manuals and books dealing with the particular aid in question. This chapter is included to give an overview of the types of instructional aids that are available and how they can be used in the instructional process.

WHY USE INSTRUCTIONAL AIDS?

A good teacher will not use instructional aids to replace good teaching methods, but to supplement his teaching skill and aid the student in grasping and utilizing the material. Instructional aids should only be used if they are suitable to the needs of the teacher and learner and improve the teaching-learning situation.

Much research has been conducted dealing with various types of instructional materials and media (training aids). Almost any subject can be enhanced through the teaching media available to us today. There is a wide range of both hardware and software devices on the market today. However, the individual teacher must use care in selecting what will best meet the needs of the class.

An instructional aid will not necessarily make teaching any easier. However, the instructional aid may help the teacher teach a particular lesson more effectively or solve a particular problem. Instructional aids, if properly selected by the teacher, have the following advantages:

1. They can be used for all ability and age groups.
2. They hold the attention of almost all learners.
3. They can induce greater acquisition and longer retention of factual information.
4. They can show otherwise unavailable processes, materials, and events.
5. They can illustrate and help clarify nonverbal symbols and images.
6. They can illustrate and help clarify specific details.
7. They can bring modern industrial practices into the shop or classroom.

SELECTION OF INSTRUCTIONAL AIDS

The selection of instructional aids depends on a number of factors.

Subject matter

Student interests and tastes

Lesson or course objectives

Physical location—lighting, seating, etc.

Class size

Budget

PRESENTATION

You should be able to find a number of instructional aids to meet your needs and stay within your budget. The availability of the hardware associated with instructional aids is a major factor to be considered by the teacher. It makes little sense to order transparencies for an overhead projector unless an overhead projector is available for classroom use.

In selecting instructional aids, ask yourself the following questions.

1. Does the aid deal with the important curriculum content?
2. Is the aid the best one on the market on a dollar-for-dollar basis?
3. Is the aid suited for students of the age level with whom you are planning to use it?
4. Is the item up to date and accurate?
5. Is the aid suitable for individual, small-group, or large-group instruction?
6. Is it worth the money it costs and the time required to use it?
7. Has the manufacturer run any studies to determine the relative advantages of the instructional aid? What has research found?
8. Is the aid technically satisfactory?
9. If it is possible, try out the item before purchasing it. Has student reaction been obtained and recorded?
10. Is the item the best available and the best way to present the subject matter to the students?

On the basis of these questions, you should be able to select the most suitable instructional aid for your purposes. Do not be afraid to ask your administrator to purchase both equipment and supplies of an instructional nature, but be prepared to demonstrate their need. If your first request is not approved, continue to resubmit it if you can justify its use. The surest way not to get what you want is not to resubmit a requisition.

Many vocational schools are sadly lacking in audiovisual aids, while others are well equipped. Teachers must make their needs known, and when the equipment is available, make sure it is used well in the classroom.

CLASSIFICATION OF INSTRUCTIONAL AIDS

Instructional aids generally can be classified into four groups.

VISUAL INSTRUCTIONAL AIDS. This group consists of demonstration boards, chalkboards, flip charts, bulletin boards, models, silent films, single-concept films, slides, projected material, and filmstrips.

AUDITORY INSTRUCTIONAL AIDS. AM and FM radio, all types of tape recordings, and records can be classified as audio instructional aids.

AUDIOVISUAL INSTRUCTIONAL AIDS. This area includes sound motion pictures, television, combination record with filmstrip, or tape with slide series or filmstrip. Such aids include sound with a visual display of one sort or another.

SIMULATION INSTRUCTIONAL AIDS. Classroom driver trainers and aircraft simulators are two primary examples of simulation-type instructional aids. This category includes all instructional devices used to simulate a real-life situation.

VARIOUS INSTRUCTIONAL AIDS

This review of instructional aids is intended only to give a brief overview. Additional information and operational details can be found in books and manufacturers' materials that describe the aids in greater detail. No attempt has been made to place them in any sequence.

THE CHALKBOARD. The chalkboard is, for many teachers, the most frequently used instructional aid. The chalkboard is only as good an instructional aid as the person who uses it. The instructor only needs some simple drawing skills and some imagination to make effective use of the board. Chalkboards now come in a variety of colors, including white. With the white it is possible to use a felt-tip marking pen to write on the board. A white board can also be used as a screen for projected materials.

The instructor's technique in the use of the chalkboard is very important. It is easy to find yourself talking to the chalkboard rather than the class. Simply watch yourself and your chalkboard technique.

DEMONSTRATION BOARDS. Demonstration boards come in a variety of types, including flannel and magnetic. They can be effectively used to progressively build elements of a presentation (schematic diagram, systems technique, etc.). All require the speaker to physically handle the material, adding interest to a relatively static presentation. It is necessary to prepare in advance the material to be used with the various demonstration boards. The boards can be used very effectively for lessons that are video taped.

POSTER-TYPE DISPLAYS. These include charts, diagrams, maps, illustrations, bulletin board displays, and other materials large enough for the class to see. Most schools already have some of these. Manufacturers and sales organizations also have many available, often free to schools. Investigate poster possibilities through your school and trade connections. These types of materials can be quite beneficial in complementing the presentation of the instructor.

FLIP CHARTS. Flip charts include flipovers, easel cards, dropdowns, and portfolios. Bound presentations are used when a rigid, prescribed sequence is desired. The more flexible, loose-card forms are desirable when a personalized approach necessitates adding, deleting, or changing the order of the cards. The size of the flip chart limits the size of the group with which it may be effectively used. The charts and presentation must be set up in advance. Types of presentations are limited only by the imagination.

INFORMATION OR INSTRUCTIONAL SHEETS. This group includes any instructional aid containing factual information about nomenclature, materials, tools, equipment, processes, and theory. This category can include such things as assignment sheets, operation sheets, and job sheets.

The sheets are usually teacher made, run off on a ditto, mimeograph, or other type of duplicating process, and given to the students. Additional information can be given as needed and the sheets kept in the students' notebooks.

Assignment sheets are used to give the learner definite work to do for the application or practice step of a lesson. They should be very specific, adding detailed explanation when necessary.

An operation sheet usually gives detailed step-by-step instructions for performing a single operation or acquiring a skill.

A job sheet usually lists the major operations, in order of performance, that are required to do a complete job that involves a number of separate operations. Such sheets should supplement the instructional procedure and not duplicate material readily available in textbooks.

TEXTBOOKS/REFERENCE LIBRARY. Books, magazines, pamphlets, and manufacturers' catalogs are all instructional aids. For the instructor's own use, every kind and form of printed material that may be useful for his teaching should be investigated. The teacher should use a high degree of selectivity in picking out the textbooks for the class. He should pick the one that best suits the needs and stated objectives of his course. All too often, the greatest influence on curriculum has been the textbooks available. Your course of study is the key, not the textbook. Pick out the book which most completely covers the material in your course of study. Do not let the book set the direction the course will follow.

MOTION PICTURE FILMS. One of the most effective instructional aids is the motion picture film. The motion picture is the nearest thing to personal experience and is the most professional of the completely packaged presentations. No other audiovisual aid combines the versatility, clarity, and dramatic impact of motion pictures. The fluidity of motion pictures enhances many stories. Use it when a more dramatic program is in order, when no sequence changes are needed, and when you can afford it.

From an instructional standpoint, the motion picture offers many advantages not found in other audiovisual aids. Motion picture photography makes it possible to speed up slow processes or slow down fast action.

Many films are available on a cost-free basis and others on a rental basis. Your school should have catalogs which list what films are available to suit your needs.

Always preview any film you plan to use before showing it to a class. This procedure, although it takes your time, might save valuable instructional time. The film might not be suited to the needs of your class, and be of limited value. The film might have breaks in it that require repair. Always make sure that the film and projector are both in good operating condition.

FILMSTRIPS. A filmstrip is a series of still images that are photographed in sequence on a roll of film. Some filmstrips are available with synchronized sound on record or tape. Projectors are available that include a record player. Other filmstrips are available with a booklet that can be used by the instructor to explain the various slides.

The projector itself consists of a reflective mechanism which conveys the film to the student by use of a screen. It is lightweight and relatively inexpensive. It is easily carried from room to room. Prepared filmstrips can be purchased in various subject areas.

SLIDE PROJECTOR. The slide projector is similar in its function to the previously discussed filmstrip projector. It is lightweight, adaptable, easy to operate and flexible. It is more flexible than the filmstrip, as material can be rearranged, deleted, or changed.

Instructor-prepared materials are also a possibility with the slide projector. The machine uses slides made from 35 mm film which is very commonly used by amateur photographers.

In recent years, great improvements have been made in slide projectors. With the proper equipment, sound on tape can be automatically synchronized to the slide. It is best to review the catalogs of the various projector companies before making a purchase.

OPAQUE PROJECTOR. This type of projector shows on a screen the image from a book page or similar source. Thus, material not on slides or films can be projected on a screen in the room.

An open form of opaque projector permits the instructor to write or draw on a transparent sheet in the machine. Thus, the enlarged picture grows on the screen as the lesson proceeds. Copy for opaque projection can be prepared by the instructor.

A third variation of the opaque projector will project an enlarged silhouette of a solid object on the screen. This can be an aid in inspection and instruction especially for details or small tolerances not readily seen without enlargement.

OVERHEAD PROJECTOR. The overhead projector transmits a strong beam of light through a transparent material onto a screen behind the instructor at the front of the room. The instructor, facing the class and to the side of the projector, can point, write or draw on the transparency, and the material is projected on the screen as he does so.

Overhead projectors are designed for speaker operation. By adding overlays or removing opaque flaps, the speaker can exploit the dramatic qualities of progressive disclosure.

Transparencies can be purchased from several companies in a wide number of subject areas. Transparencies can be prepared in black and white, single colors, or any number of colors. This can be done photographically, manually (grease pencil), or on some type of office copying machine.

Each and every classroom or shop should have an overhead projector. It is, of course, essential that the school provide the necessary supplies to assist the teacher in making transparencies.

SINGLE CONCEPT FILMS. Single concept films are usually three or four minutes in length. Each film is contained in its own plastic cartridge, which slides conveniently into the single concept projector. This eliminates problems in threading or rewinding, since the film is continuous and the cartridge can be placed or removed from the projector at any time.

Single concept films focus their attention on individual segments of subject matter. They are especially of value for individual or small group instruction.

A number of companies produce single concept films that are suitable for various vocational programs. It is also possible to produce your own 8 mm film and have it packaged in the plastic cartridge.

Single concept films can free the teacher from the tedious task of repeating demonstrations and permit the addition of a creative dimension in teaching. They are especially valuable to the teacher who is attempting to individualize the instructional process.

MOCK–UPS. These are simplified arrangements of real parts, usually mounted on boards or stands so that the essential parts work together normally. The teaching advantage is that nonessential parts do not distract from the specific topics being studied. Mock-ups may sometimes be brought into a classroom when it would not be possible to show the actual parts of assemblies.

MODELS. Models are imitations of real objects. They may be enlargements of the real object or made to smaller scale. Scale models can be used effectively to show the relationship of one part to another. Working models can show relationships and movement of parts. Caricature models can be used to identify and give extra emphasis to important details. Such models attract special attention by exaggeration.

Three-dimensional aids may also be available through school and trade contacts. In many cases, it is necessary to make them.

CLOSED CIRCUIT TELEVISION (CCTV). The simplest television circuit connects a camera with a single receiver. Closed circuit television by cable may reach a number of locations in nearby rooms and buildings or at even greater distances. In recent years, many schools have built in the necessary wiring for closed circuit television capabilities. CCTV programs can be devoted not only to direct instruction of students, but also to system-wide teachers' meetings, to previewing new instructional materials, and to in-service teacher education programs.

If your school is equipped with CCTV equipment, it will pay you to find out what services and facilities are available for your use. Additional study on your part is essential for you to understand the many uses of CCTV. This study should benefit your class and improve the teaching-learning situation.

VIDEO TAPE RECORDERS (VTR). Video tape recording equipment in its simplest form consists of a camera, receiver, and video tape recorder. It allows you to tape and play back material as needed. Portable, light weight video tape recorders are now available for a cost well within the budget of most schools. The equipment is easy to operate and can be moved from room to room as needed.

The VTR has many uses and can be of value to the shop or laboratory teacher. Industrial visits or processes can be video taped for viewing in the school shop or laboratory. A teacher can video tape a lesson and then replay it as many times as needed by the students. The taped rerun can also be helpful in evaluating your own teaching style. Self-evaluation is essential for all engaged in the teaching profession.

COMPUTER–ASSISTED INSTRUCTION (CAI). If your school has the facilities for computer-assisted instruction (CAI), try to work up an instructional program for your students. The computer is intended not to replace but to assist the teacher. The computer can respond only in ways it has been programmed. The computer can supplement your instruction and relieve you of many routine teaching tasks. Additional study on your part is essential if you have CAI equipment in your school.

AUDITORY TRAINING AIDS. Radio, phonograph records, and audio tape are considered audio training aids. Without any picture, slide, or video presentation, they are limited for use in the shop and laboratory.

ORDERING INSTRUCTIONAL AIDS

The ordering policies of schools vary, depending on the type of audiovisual services available. Equipment can usually be requested within a fairly short period of time, say twenty-four hours' advance notice. However, if the amount of equipment is in short supply and many teachers are requesting it, a longer lead time may be necessary. Inquire early about your school's policy.

Teaching aids that have to be rented from a commercial supplier will require a longer period of time to obtain. Films that need to be requested from certain suppliers or companies may require six months' advance notice.

If you are aware of what is available and what you plan to use, it is a good idea to order all your films well in advance. Many experienced teachers will order aids from commercial suppliers for the whole school term. In the public schools, it is not uncommon to prepare your audiovisual aids list in May for use during the next academic school year. Rental aids are usually available for your use for a period of three to five days.

SUMMARY

This chapter gives the vocational teacher an overview of a variety of instructional aids that may be helpful in the teaching-learning situation. No attempt was made to explain the operation of the various pieces of audiovisual equipment or how materials may be made by the teacher.

Many vocational schools have a variety of equipment and aids available to the staff. Larger schools may have a full-time media specialist to advise teachers new to the school. Make sure you seek out this person early in your career so you will know what is available.

Every vocational teacher should have some form of index file listing

EXHIBIT 11-1

USING TEACHING AIDS, A FEW RECOMMENDATIONS

Before the class meets:

1. Know what you want to accomplish. When using films or other aids you did not design, preview each one carefully to determine what to emphasize and what to ignore. You may find out you wish to show only a part of the film.

2. Rehearse the use of the teaching aid and plan comments.

3. Have everything ready so you will not have to waste group time fumbling around. For films, check projection equipment, have a spare bulb, arrange seats and screen for best viewing.

4. If chalkboard drawings are complicated, draw them ahead of time or have very light pattern on the chalkboard which you can follow.

5. Cover or hide display and three-dimensional aids so they will not distract the learners.

During the class session:

1. Don't let the aid be a substitute for the instructor. Use them, don't just show them. Make explanations; ask questions.

2. Show each aid at the proper time in the lesson, but keep it covered or hidden when it is not in use.

3. Speak to the group, not the teaching aid.

4. If models are used, do not pass them around while they are being discussed. This can be distracting, and learners can handle them later.

5. For a motion picture or filmstrip, make certain the learners know before the showing exactly what they are to look for. Otherwise, they may miss the important points, emphasize unimportant information, or consider the whole thing just a form of entertainment.

6. Reshow any film or other teaching aid if necessary to teach a point that has been missed.

SOURCE: *The Preparation of Occupational Instructors.* Washington, D. C.: Superintendent of Documents, 1966, p. 117.

EXHIBIT 11-2

HOW TO USE THE CHALKBOARD

Chalkboard work should be simple and brief. Copying lengthy outlines or lists of subject matter is a waste of time to instructor. If it is important for the [student] to have a copy of this material, it should be duplicated and distributed.

The chalkboard is similar to a store window. Everyone knows that an overcrowded, dirty, and untidy window display has little "stopping" value as compared to one that is clean and neat and displays a few well-chosen items.

The following rules for using the chalkboard should definitely increase its effectiveness as a visual aid:

1. Don't crowd the chalkboard. A few important points make a vivid impression.

2. Make the material simple. Brief, concise statements are more effective than lengthy ones.

3. Plan chalkboards ahead. Keep the layouts in your training plan folder.

4. Gather everything you need for the chalkboard before the group meets — chalk, ruler, eraser, and other items.

5. Check lighting. Avoid chalkboard glare. Sometimes it will be necessary to lower a shade and turn on the room light.

6. Use color for emphasis. Chrome yellow and pale green chalk are more effective than white chalk.

7. Print all captions and drawings on a large scale. The material must be clearly visible to each [student].

8. Erase all unrelated material. Other work on the chalkboard distracts attention. Use a board eraser or cloth, and not your fingers.

9. Keep the chalkboard clean. A dirty chalkboard has the same effect as a dirty window.

10. Prepare complicated chalkboard layouts before the group meets.

[11. When using the chalkboard, be careful not to talk to it with your back to the class. This is a common fault of teachers and weathermen on television.]

SOURCE: *The Preparation of Occupational Instructors.* Washington, D. C.: Superintendent of Documents, 1966, p. 123.

EXHIBIT 11-3

CHARACTERISTICS OF A GOOD VISUAL AID

A visual aid is a specifically prepared drawing, model, or device that will expedite learning through the visual sense. When selecting or making a visual aid, the following points should be considered.

1. It should explain an abstract idea, show a relationship, or present a sequence or procedure that cannot be clarified without it.

2. It should be large enough to be clearly visible to everybody in the group. An aid is not an aid if part of the group cannot see it.

3. The lettering should be large and bold to avoid eyestrain from any point in the room. Avoid decoration and prevent distraction.

4. The wording should be easy for the learners to understand. Terms should be acceptable and in common use in the occupation itself.

5. The important parts should be accentuated by the use of bright color.

6. It should be made to scale, whether reduced or enlarged. The essential parts should be in proper proportions. Otherwise, the learner may be confused.

7. It should be constructed of good materials, so it can stand frequent use.

8. It should show evidence of good workmanship and be carefully finished in good taste.

9. It should be portable to permit its use in more than one location.

10. It should be protected with paint, shellac, glass, cellophane, or other protective materials.

SOURCE: *The Preparation of Occupational Instructors.* Washington, D. C.: Superintendent of Documents, 1966, p. 121.

EXHIBIT 11-4

SOURCES OF TEACHING AIDS

For most major trades and occupational areas, there is a large and readily available supply of teaching aids of one type or another. When planning a course or a lesson, contact the possible sources listed. If they do not have the actual aids, they may be able to direct you to an organization that does.

Local industries and employers

Employment offices

Libraries and museums

The vocational division of your State Department of Education

Local school authorities

Vocational curriculum laboratories at universities

Manufacturers of equipment

Supply houses

Agencies of the U. S. Government, particularly, the Office of Education, U. S. Department of Health, Education, and Welfare, and the Government Printing Office.

SOURCE: *The Preparation of Occupational Instructors.* Washington, D. C.: Superintendent of Documents, 1966, p. 119.

various instructional aids that are suitable to his or her area of specialization. This would include the source of the item, its cost or rental charge, and a brief description of its contents and how it fits into the instructional program.

ACTIVITIES

1.   Conduct an inventory of the instructional aids available in your school. For purposes of this question, only concern yourself with hardware such as movie projectors, VTR, tape recorders, etc. The inventory should include the number of each item and its manufacturer.

2.   Conduct an inventory of the instructional aids, both hardware and software, available in your shop or laboratory. This inventory should include charts, models, films, records, etc.

3.   Using one of the various audiovisual equipment directories, make a list of at least twenty items suitable for your teaching specialization.

4.   Using your most current course outline or course of study, list the various instructional aids on a unit-by-unit basis that would be suitable for use in each unit of instruction.

SOURCE MATERIALS

Audiovisual Equipment Directory. Fairfax, Va.: National Audiovisual Association.

Educational Films. East Lansing: Michigan State University.

Educational Motion Pictures. Bloomington: Audiovisual Center, Indiana University.

McGraw-Hill Films, 8mm. Film Loops, Records, Transparencies. New York: McGraw-Hill Films.

Multi-Media Instructional Material. New York: Universal Education and Visual Arts.

Saterstrom, Mary H., ed. *Educators Guide to Free Science Materials.* Randolph, Wis.: Educators Progress Service. Revised annually.

Wittich, Walter A., ed. *Educators Guide to Free Tapes, Scripts, and Transcriptions.* Randolph, Wis.: Educators Progress Service. Revised annually.

PRESENTATION

EVALUATION

Part IV

12

CLASS RECORDS

DEFINITION

Class records vary from school system to school system. There are no standard record forms which meet the needs of all schools. It is essential that you be aware of the required class records for your school. Most shop instructors will find that two general classes of records are needed for the well-organized and managed shop, those records required by national, state, or local regulations, and those needed by the teacher for the efficient management of the shop, laboratory, or classroom. Class records, therefore, are those required or helpful records which make for the successful operation of the teaching-learning situation. The class records discussed in this chapter deal in the main with student progress and evaluation. Not of concern in this chapter are such things as staff-personnel records, financial records and materials, and equipment records or shop safety records.

You will have little control over school-required records. It is to your advantage to understand the forms used and regiment yourself to the record keeping required by the system. This does not mean that after you are accustomed to the required record keeping system you must be content with it. Most school administrators are willing to consider suitable alternatives. Record keeping time should be kept to a minimum and instructional time to a maximum.

THE IMPORTANCE OF RECORD KEEPING

Record keeping concerned with student performance and evaluation should be taken very seriously. After hundreds of students pass through your shop and graduate, it becomes difficult to keep a mental picture of each one. You will be called on by prospective and present employers of your students to verify attendance, shop attitude, and shop skills they exhibited while studying with you.

Good record keeping is essential to give a fair and honest appraisal of a student's performance in your shop. Such records and evaluation criteria should be consistent with the stated objectives of your school, department, and course. The evaluation criteria and associated records should be well understood by the students in the class.

If you are attempting to individualize the instructional process and make use of performance objectives, it is especially important that your record keeping system be consistent with your instructional strategy. The importance of accurate record keeping should be obvious. If performance objectives are used, the student will know when he moves from one objective to the next, and the class records should accurately reflect the movement. In many cases, you will have to design your own shop record keeping system to suit your needs and those of your students.

The report card is the most common way of reporting progress to parents as well as students. In the case of vocational students, the reporting system must be clearly understood by the students, their parents, and employers. Any number or variety of reporting systems exist. Figures 12-1, 12-2, 12-3, and 12-4 are four rather different reporting forms. You should review these forms in detail before continuing with this chapter.

THE TEACHER'S RESPONSIBILITY

The principal has the major responsibility for record keeping. He, then, will delegate various record keeping responsibilities to the administrative and teaching staff of the school. The teachers should be well informed at a yearly orientation session as to what records are required, how they should be maintained, and any due dates essential to an orderly process. Operational procedures for record keeping should be spelled out and clearly understood by the staff.

Since wide variations exist in required records from one school to another, it would make little sense to review record keeping in detail in this

STUDENT NAME:

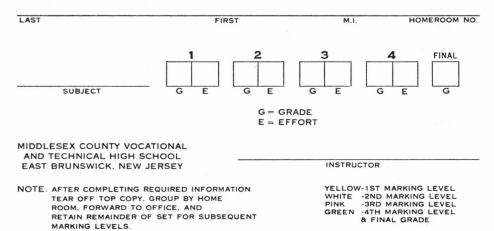

FIGURE 12-1. Typical Reporting System

book. It is your responsibility to find out early in the school year all you can about your record keeping responsibilities.

Whatever other records, other than those required, you find necessary for the operation of the shop are up to you. But use care, it is easy to design a record or record system, but it is time consuming to record data. Maintain only those records that are essential to the smooth operation of your teaching-learning situation.

STUDENT INVOLVEMENT IN RECORD KEEPING

Many administrators insist that all records of a personal nature be kept by the teacher or office clerks. This would include personal records, report cards, health records, etc. In other schools, the policy might apply to only those records which are central office records. Still other administrators might require that all records, including central office and classroom records, be maintained by the teacher without any assistance from the students.

Before you involve students in record keeping, check out the school policy. If students can have some involvement in the record keeping procedure, you might design some procedures to be used in your shop. This does

CLASS RECORDS

MARKING SYSTEM

ACHIEVEMENT		EFFORT	
Letter Grade	Numerical Equivalent		Numerical Grade
A = Excellent	90 - 100		1 = Outstanding
B = Very Good	80 - 89		2 = Satisfactory
C = Satisfactory	70 - 79		3 = Poor
D = Poor	60 - 69		
E = Failure	Below 60		

EXPLANATIONS

1. "D" is a passing grade but indicates unsatisfactory work; close to failure and not worthy of recommendation.

2. "E" for a final grade requires that the subject be repeated if credit toward graduation is desired.

3. "ab" indicates the pupil was absent for more than half of the checking level.

4. A checking level covers approximately 45 school days.

PARENT'S SIGNATURE

1. _____

2. _____

3. _____

4. _____

No. ....

Name. .... Year Ending. .... 19 .... Shop. ....

Report Card
Middlesex County Vocational and
Technical High Schools

.... New Brunswick .... Perth Amboy .... Woodbridge .... East Brunswick

SUBJECT	COURSE	CHECKING LEVEL								FINAL
		1		2		3		4		
		Achievement	Effort	Achievement	Effort	Achievement	Effort	Achievement	Effort	Achievement
Shop										
Mathematics										
Science										
Drawing										
English										
History										
Health										
Physical Education										
Days Absent										
Times Tardy										

FIGURE 12-2. Typical Report Card

EMPLOYABILITY PROFILE
OSWEGO COUNTY BOARD OF COOPERATIVE EDUCATIONAL SERVICES
MEXICO, NEW YORK 13114
PHONE: 315-963-7251
1974 - 1975

Name _____ Home School _____ Grade _____

Course _____ HEAVY EQUIPMENT OPERATION _____ Date _____ Quarter 1st__ 2nd__ 3rd__ Final__

The following is a list of operations and skills that the above student has been exposed to, and instructor's appraisal of his/her entry level employ-ability in these areas. These operations have been accompanied by a significant amount of classroom work in related theory.

GENERAL SKILLS
- ☐ Proper Attire for work
- ☐ Participation in VICA
- ☐ Safety & O.S.H.A. training
- ☐ Preventive maintenance supervision
- ☐ Job-site supervision
- ☐ General supervision of student personnel
- ☐ Service manual interpretation
- ☐ Parts book interpretation
- ☐ Shop math
- ☐ Metric measurements & interpretation
- ☐ Precision measuring tool utilization
- ☐ Steam cleaning operation
- ☐ Chemical cleaning operation
- ☐ Jacking & blocking operations

EQUIPMENT MAINTENANCE
- ☐ Daily Maintenance
- ☐ Schedule Maintenance
- ☐ Hand Lubricating
- ☐ Power Lubricating
- ☐ Oil & Filter Change
- ☐ Air Cleaner Service
- ☐ Fuel System Service
- ☐ Hydraulic System Service
- ☐ Cable Lubrication
- ☐ Cable Cutting

RECONDITIONING
- ☐ Cleaning
- ☐ Inspection
- ☐ Estimating repair costs
- ☐ Remove dents
- ☐ Straightening
- ☐ Fill dents & holes
- ☐ Fabricate pants
- ☐ Stripping
- ☐ Sanding
- ☐ Masking
- ☐ Priming
- ☐ Painting

HYDRAULICS,
- ☐ Basic Principles
- ☐ Hydraulic Terms
- ☐ Symbols & Circuit Interpretations
- ☐ Check hydraulic pressures
- ☐ Utilize flow & pressure tester
- ☐ Change hydraulic filters
- ☐ Cutting & flaring tubings
- ☐ Install hydraulic hoses & tubing
- ☐ Check, locate, & repair leaks
- ☐ Replace 'O-Rings'
- ☐ Inspect & Service value assemblies
- ☐ Replace Packings & Seals
- ☐ Test & adjust relief values
- ☐ Inspect pumps
- ☐ Test pumps
- ☐ Test cylinders
- ☐ Troubleshoot hydraulic system problems

BASIC SURVEYING
- ☐ Telescopic level set-up
- ☐ Interpretation of measurements
- ☐ Planning & layout with instruments
- ☐ Grade stake locations & interpretations
- ☐ Leveling to a specified grade
- ☐ Ditching to a specified grade

TRACKS & UNDERCARRIAGE
- ☐ Cleaning & Inspection
- ☐ Lubrication
- ☐ Adjust tracks
- ☐ Remove tracks
- ☐ Install tracks
- ☐ Remove rollers
- ☐ Install rollers
- ☐ Remove sprockets
- ☐ Install sprockets

WELDING
- ☐ Safety
- ☐ Gas Welding
- ☐ Cutting
- ☐ Brazing
- ☐ Soldering
- ☐ Arc Welding, horizontal
- ☐ Arc Welding, vertical
- ☐ Hand surfacing

EQUIPMENT SAFETY OSHA. OPERATIONS, & MAINTENANCE LIGHT VEHICLES
- ☐ Trucks, 2x4
- ☐ Trucks, 4x4
- ☐ Trucks, 4x6
- ☐ Trucks, 6x6
- ☐ Tractor-Trailer Combinations
- ☐ Tractor-Trailer Combinations
- ☐ Learner's permit
- ☐ Class 3 license
- ☐ Class 1 license
- ☐ Forklifts
- ☐ Backhoes
- ☐ Digging holes
- ☐ Digging square holes
- ☐ Digging flat-bottom trench
- ☐ Digging trenchs to grade
- ☐ Tractor loaders
- ☐ Skid-steer loaders, friction drive
- ☐ Skid-steer loaders, hydrostatic
- ☐ 4 Wheel drive loaders, straight frame
- ☐ 4 wheel drive loaders, articulated
- ☐ Crawler-type loaders
- ☐ Bulldozers, hydraulic blade
- ☐ Bulldozers, hydraulic 6 way blade
- ☐ Bulldozers, cable controlled blade
- ☐ Hydraulic Excavators
- ☐ Gradalls
- ☐ Drag line
- ☐ Clam buckets
- ☐ Lifting crane
- ☐ Graders, straight frame
- ☐ Graders, articulated
- ☐ Scrapers
- ☐ Rollers
- ☐ Industrial tractors & attachments
- ☐
- ☐
- ☐
- ☐
- ☐
- ☐

WORK HABITS	IGNORES DIRECTIONS	FOLLOWS SOME DIRECTIONS, WORKS INEFFICIENTLY	FOLLOWS DIRECTIONS AND WORKS SATISFACTORILY	STEADY CONSCIENTIOUS WORKER	VERY ACCURATE RESOURCEFUL AND EFFICIENT	MOTIVATION	APATHETIC	SPORADICALLY MOTIVATED	GENERALLY MOTIVATED	INTERESTED IN EXCELLING	HIGHLY INVOLVED AND MOTIVATED
SAFETY HABITS	SLOPPY AND HAZARDOUS	FAIR, NEEDS IMPROVEMENT	GENERALLY WORKS SAFELY	MEETS REQUIRED SAFETY STANDARDS	NEAT, CONSCIENTIOUS AND CAREFUL	INITIATIVE	REQUIRES CONSTANT PRESSURE	NEEDS OCCASIONAL PRODDING	DOES ASSIGNED WORK	OCCASIONALLY SEEKS EXTRA WORK	SEEKS AND RECOGNIZES WORK TO BE DONE
WORK AREA NEATNESS	VERY SLOPPY AND INCONSIDERATE	FORGETFUL AND UNCONSCIENTIOUS	ADEQUATE	THOROUGH	PRIDE IN OVERALL APPEARANCE OF FACILITIES	EFFORT	"QUITTER"	APPLIES MINIMAL EFFORT	SHOWS SATISFACTORY EFFORT	SHOWS GROWING DETERMINATION	DETERMINED PERSEVERING AND DILIGENT
WORK AREA ATTENDANCE	OFTEN NOT IN WORK AREA	MAKES EXCUSES TO LEAVE WORK AREA	GENERALLY IN WORK AREA	SELDOM LEAVES WORK AREA	ALWAYS WHERE ASSIGNED	PEER RELATIONS	UNCOOPERATIVE	SOMETIMES HARD TO WORK WITH	GENERALLY COOPERATIVE	WORKS VERY WELL WITH OTHERS	OUTGOING WARM AND COOPERATIVE
SELF-ESTEEM	NO SELF-CONFIDENCE	INSECURE, SELF-CONSCIOUS DEFENSIVE	BALANCED ATTITUDE	POSITIVE SELF-EVALUATION	SELF-CONFIDENT AND SECURE	LEADERSHIP	UNABLE TO LEAD	RESIGNS TO FOLLOW	SHOWS LEADERSHIP WHEN REQUESTED	VOLUNTARILY DISPLAYS LEADERSHIP	MAKES THINGS GO
INTEGRITY	NOT TRUSTWORTHY	ERRATIC	SINCERE	RELIABLE AND DEPENDABLE	EXCEPTIONALLY TRUSTWORTHY	REACTION TO AUTHORITY	HOSTILE	INDIFFERENT	ACCEPTING	GENERALLY COOPERATIVE	EXCEPTIONALLY COOPERATIVE
RESPONSIBILITY	UNRELIABLE	SOMETIMES RELIABLE	USUALLY RELIABLE	CONSCIENTIOUS	ASSUMES RESPONSIBILITY VERY WELL	Total Days Absent			Excused		Unexcused

TEACHER'S COMMENTS _____

_____

_____

_____

_____

FIGURE 12-3. Employability Profile

FIGURE 12-4. Student Profile

HUNTERDON COUNTY
STUDENT
VOCATIONAL PROFILE

NAME ....

PHYSICAL ADDRESS ....
(street)

....
(city)   (zip code)

PHONE NO. ....
(area code)

SOCIAL SECURITY NUMBER ....

DATE OF GRADUATION ....

SCHOOL ....

VOCATIONAL HOME ECONOMICS

OFFERED AT

GUIDANCE COUNSELOR: ....

INSTRUCTOR(S): ....

....

P-10 VHE-1
(Jan. 1974)

LEARNING EXPERIENCE/ACHIEVEMENT

Place an "X" in the proper column

	EXCELLENT	GOOD	AVERAGE	FAIR	POOR	DOES NOT APPLY
Hand Sewing Skills						
Read & Interpret Labels						
Ability to Select Appropriate Patterns & Fabrics						
Math Skills						
Cash Register Skills						
Observes Job Skills						
Copes with Emergencies						
Bookkeeping Skills						
CHILD CARE						
Patience						
Dependability/Responsibility						
Honesty						
Abilities to Cope with Emergencies						
Knowledge of First-Aid						
Attitudes Toward Children						
Good Judgement						
Practices Good Safety Habits						
Selection/Preparation of Food for Children						
Planning Activities for Pre-School Children						
Ability to Recognize Abnormal Appearance or Behavior						
Understands Individual Differences						
Ability to Work With Exceptional Children						
Ability to Work With Others						
Knowledge of Appropriate Discipline						
Understands Emotional Development						

COOPERATIVE WORK EXPERIENCE

Date of Participation: From................ To................

Name of Training Station: ....

Address: ....

Phone No.: ....

Supervisor's Name: ....

Other Experiences: ....

Comments: ....

SCHOOL YEAR		FINAL GRADE
First Year	19 19	
Second Year	19 19	

There are four high schools in Hunterdon County; Delaware Valley, South Hunterdon, Hunterdon Central, and North Hunterdon Regional High Schools.

Hunterdon Central and North Hunterdon Regional High Schools have been designated as Area Vocational-Technical High Schools (A.V.T.S.) by the New Jersey State Department of Education.

Students in the 11th and 12th grades from the four high schools in the County are eligible to enroll for a half-day vocational major either at Hunterdon Central or North Hunterdon Regional High School. The student also spends half-day in his home high school taking academic courses leading to the high school diploma.

The Vocational Student Profile Project for Vocational Programs in Hunterdon County was accomplished through the cooperation and support of the New Jersey State Department of Education, Division of Vocational Education, Hunterdon County Department of Education, and the Hunterdon County Coordinating Council for Career Education. In addition, Hunterdon County vocational students, teachers, administrators, and employers also contributed many hours to develop the project.

PERSONAL CHARACTERISTICS

Please evaluate this student by placing an "X" in the proper column

Item	EXCELLENT	GOOD	AVERAGE	FAIR	POOR	DOES NOT APPLY
Personal Appearance and Cleanliness						
Speech						
Manners						
Relationship with Fellow Employees						
Attendance						
Willingness to Learn						
Care of Equipment						
Follows Good Safety Practices						
Salesmanship						
Ability to Communicate						
Ambition						
Customer Relations						
Utilization of Time						
Quality of Work						
Quantity of Work						

LEARNING EXPERIENCE/ACHIEVEMENT

Place an "X" in the proper column

Item	EXCELLENT	GOOD	AVERAGE	FAIR	POOR	DOES NOT APPLY
FOOD PREPARATION						
Appetizers						
Soup						
Salads						
Meat						
Seafood						
Vegetables						
Breads						
Pastries						
Beverages						
SHORT–ORDER COOKING						
SANDWICHES						
UNDERSTANDS KITCHEN EQUIPMENT						
FOOD PURCHASING SKILLS						
KITCHEN MANAGEMENT						
CAKE DECORATING						
PREPARES FOOD ATTRACTIVELY						
STORES FOOD PROPERLY						
FOLLOWS DIRECTIONS						
FOLLOWS SANITARY PROCEDURES						
MEASURES ACCURATELY						
SELECTION & USE OF TOOLS						
COPES WITH STRESS SITUATIONS						
TIME MANAGEMENT						
KITCHEN HELPER						
DISHWASHER						
ABILITY TO WORK WITH OTHERS						
JUDGEMENT IN FOOD QUANTITY						
FOOD SERVICE:						
Friendliness						
Courteous						
Honesty						

LEARNING EXPERIENCE/ACHIEVEMENT

Place an "X" in the proper column

Item	EXCELLENT	GOOD	AVERAGE	FAIR	POOR	DOES NOT APPLY
Patience						
Love of people						
Host/Hostess						
Waiter/Waitress						
Knowing Menu						
Ability to Cope with Crisis						
Sets Table Properly						
Understands Serving Techniques						
Ability to Communicate (Charisma)						
Follows Directions						
Respects Privacy of Others						
Realizes Limitations (Ability Potential)						
Uses Tools & Equipment Properly						
Accurate Mathematical Skills						
Show Concern for Customer						
Overall Health						
Meal Planning Skills						
Inventory Skills						
RETAILING						
HOUSEKEEPING:						
CLOTHING /TEXTILES						
Patience						
Dependability						
Self–reliance						
Neatness						
Aggressiveness						
Simple Clothing Repairs /Alterations						
Good Judgement						
Accuracy in Work						
Organization of Work Area						
Clothing Maintenance Skills						

FIGURE 12-4 continued

not imply that any one student becomes a record clerk and thereby neglects other assigned tasks.

Many jobs require some form of record keeping on the part of the employee. Certainly, students in particular specializations should be well acquainted with the typical paper work faced on the job. Record keeping responsibilities should be made as much a part of the total operation as possible.

At the minimum, consider assigning record keeping as one of the jobs of your shop personnel system. As clerk, the assigned student would be available ten or fifteen minutes each class session to assist with record keeping.

You, as the teacher, are accountable for the record keeping system. The work assigned to students must be thoroughly planned, well explained, and adequately supervised. You must constantly stress the importance of neat and accurate record keeping.

SCHOOL REQUIRED RECORDS

This chapter will focus on school records that involve student progress and evaluation. In most cases, you will have little control over the established procedures that are already in operation.

Attendance Records

Most schools have a well-established system for recording and reporting the attendance of students. The reporting procedure varies from state to state depending on the requirements and reporting procedures used. Many shop teachers are also asked to serve from time to time as homeroom teachers. As homeroom teacher, it usually is the teacher's responsibility to maintain an accurate record of the students assigned to his room. The procedures are usually well established, and it is the teacher's responsibility to learn the method used.

You should also maintain a record of attendance for students in your classes. Such records are of value if you are asked to comment on students' attendance and punctuality at a later time by an employer. Adequate records will yield the essential information. Usually the school will provide each teacher with a combination plan-attendance-grade book or other suitable materials for this type of record keeping.

Student Evaluation

The term *student evaluation* is used here for lack of a more suitable term. It is intended to refer to the day-to-day records that a teacher should maintain in order to accurately and fairly evaluate the performance of each student. In a sense, it relates to the grading and reporting system used by the school.

If you are structuring your course to meet individual students' needs, some problems might exist. If performance or behavioral objectives are being used, this will be a factor to be considered in the evaluation procedure. Your problem is to develop a record keeping system that is compatible with a system of individualized instruction and performance objectives and still usable within the school's reporting system.

It is difficult and perhaps impossible to use or illustrate one model that would be usable in more than one system. Whatever system is used, it should be very clearly explained to the students early in the school year and clearly understood by them. If the students do not understand the procedure, the system is worthless. It must also relate to and be compatible with the school's reporting system.

School-wide Grading System

Whatever evaluation system you use in your class, you must be able to convert grades from your class to the school-wide grading system. You may want to keep numerical grades and then convert them to letter grades. The marking periods and final averaging methods also vary widely from school to school.

SCHOOL A. This school uses a numerical grading system with 65 as the minimum passing average. Four ten-week marking periods are used to determine the final average.

10th week	20th week	30th week	40th week	final average

In such a grading system, it is possible for a student to pass during one marking period, fail the other three, and still pass the course on the basis of the final average. With ten-week grades of 80, 62, 62, and 62 the final average would be 66.5, which is passing. Likewise, a student could have a passing grade for three marking periods and a failing grade for one and fail the course on the final average. With ten-week grades of 66, 68, 70, and 50 the final average would be 63.5, which is failing.

In this system, the student who receives a very low grade during the first ten-week marking period, stands little chance of passing the course. Certain students might stop trying at all. Likewise, a student who receives a very high grade during the first marking period may be able to coast through the rest of the school year with a minimum amount of effort.

SCHOOL B. This school uses a numerical grading system with 65 as the minimum passing average. Four ten-week marking periods plus the final examination are used to determine the final average.

10th week	20th week	30th week	40th week	final exam	final average

As you will note, each marking period plus the final examination has a value of 20 per cent or one-fifth in determining the final average. If the final examination can be a performance type examination, the added advantage is a complete review of all the work covered during the school year. The system is subject to the same limitations as were discussed in the School *A* grading system.

SCHOOL C. This school uses a numerical grading system with 65 as the minimum passing average. Four ten-week marking periods are used in reporting student progress to the parents. A final examination is given which the student must pass to pass the course. In other words, no matter what the grades were for the four marking periods, the student must pass the final examination to pass the course. Such a system has some advantages and disadvantages. (a) The final examination must be valid and reliable. (b) A student who has done well all year may have a bad day and fail the examination. (c) The system provides some measure of final quality control, especially if performance objectives are used in the final examination.

SCHOOL D. The system is the same as School C, except that a student who has a failing average for the four marking periods can pass the course if he passes the final examination. Such a system places success within reach of every student including those who may have done poorly most of the year.

SCHOOL E. The system is the same as School *B,* but uses a letter grade system.

OUTSTANDING	A	100–91
ABOVE AVERAGE	B	90–81
AVERAGE	C	80–71
BELOW AVERAGE	D	70–65
FAILING	E	64–

In reporting grades by means of a letter grade system, the teacher must be careful to maintain the numerical grades from which the letter grade was converted. A "C" may be a 71 or an 80, and the nine-point spread may be significant in determining the final average.

SCHOOL F. This school uses the Employability Profile as found in Figure 12-3. It reports to the students, their parents, and employers what a student has done as part of the vocational program. It also has a section on work habits and attitudes as well as a place for teacher comments.

Review as completely as possible the system in your school. Make sure that you and your students have a full understanding of the system and how they will be evaluated.

CLASS RECORDS. Class records include both required records and any additional records that the teacher wants to use.

Each teacher will find it necessary to record the progress of each student in a class book. In this book, the teacher records the grades or progress of each student, and this information is used in reporting the student's progress on the report card. The class book may also be used to record attendance.

The teacher is accountable for maintaining accurate class records. If asked to justify why a student got a certain grade, the teacher is expected to produce suitable evidence to support the grade given. As indicated earlier, if grades are important, then the students must be kept fully informed of their progress in the course. Students must be told early in the school year how they will be evaluated. The evaluation system must be fully explained by the teacher and understood by the students.

In addition to required records, shop instructors may want to maintain additional records. One possibility is a simple type of progress chart. One example is shown in Figure 12-5. The chart can be used for projects, experiments, performance objectives, or any additional use the teacher has in mind. In most vocational education shops, you will find some type of progress chart in use.

If you are using performance objectives in your course, you would simply indicate the objectives in the upper columns and the names of students in the proper column. The objectives can be indicated by number and a full statement of the objectives written out in another chart or in a nearby notebook.

The progress chart, if properly used and maintained, can be very useful to the students and the teacher. It very simply reports the progress being made by each student in the class. You should find it useful no matter what instructional strategy you use.

In addition to the progress chart, you might find some form of student appraisal sheet useful in your shop. Figure 12-6 is one example of a student appraisal sheet. It represents a subjective judgment of the student by the teacher. Your evaluation system will have to reflect if such subjective evaluation will be reflected in the grading system. It is included here only as a form that may be useful to the teacher. It is the writer's belief that evaluation must be based on clearly stated objectives. Subjective evaluations might be nice to have, but many variables are involved that can limit the value of such evaluations.

THE PROGRESS CHART

Figure 12-5 is an example of a commonly used progress chart.

One must always be aware of the effect, if any, such a chart has on the slower students in the class. How would you like to have a record of your progress in a certain class on public display? A way around this might be to indicate students by assigned numbers on the chart rather than names. Such a system allows each student to be aware of his progress in relation to the class, but shields the identity of the individual.

Individual progress charts for each student can be maintained as a class record by the teacher. Such an individual progress chart can be made available to the students on an individual basis. Students should, in fact, have a copy of such a progress chart for their own information.

If you use behavioral or performance objectives in your course of study and your daily teaching, such a progress chart would be especially valuable. Each student should be encouraged to progress at his or her own rate. The individual or group progress chart will give a clear indication of the progress of each student in the class.

If your course of study was constructed using performance objectives as suggested in Chapter 4, the progress chart will give both students and

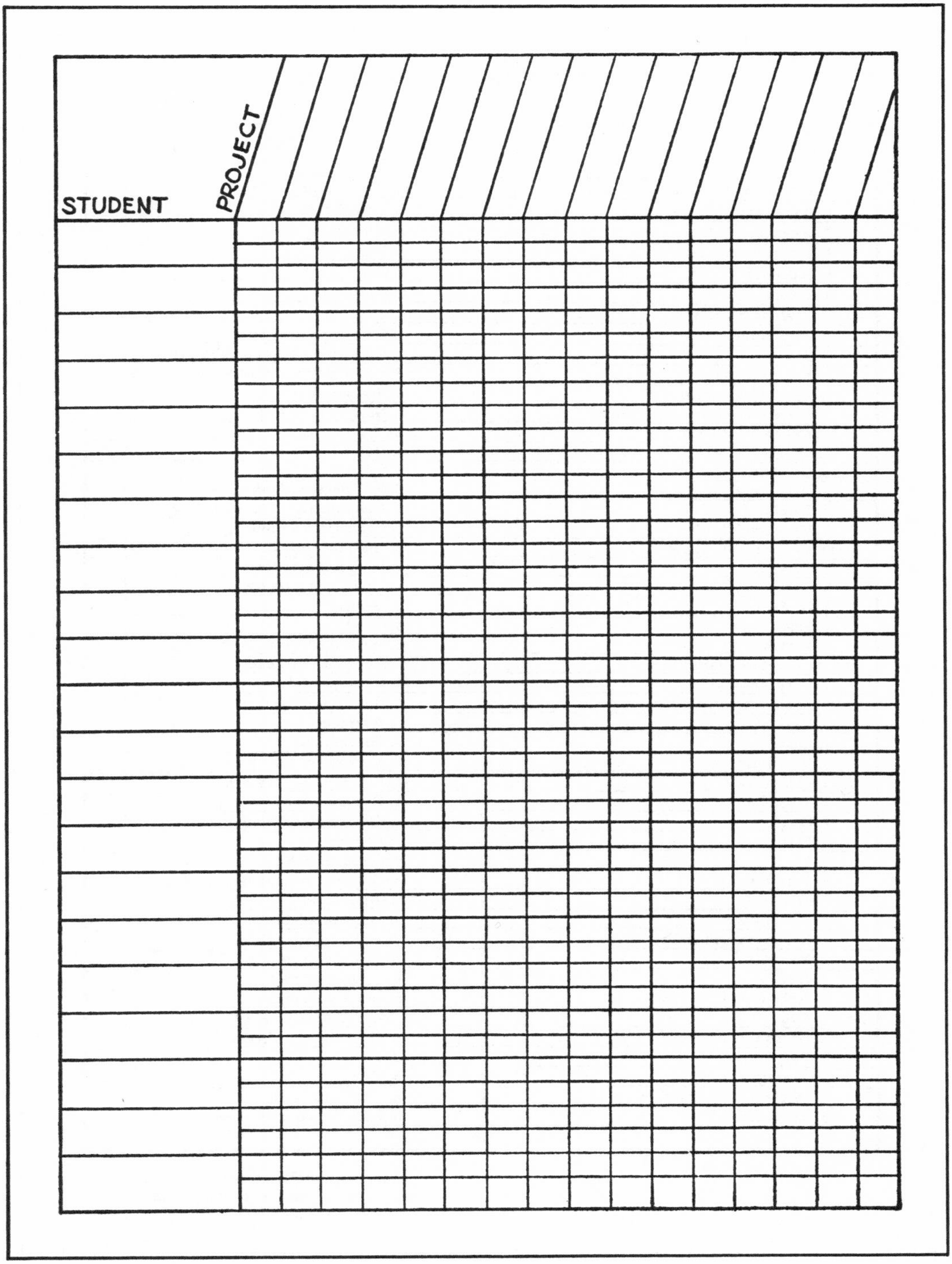

FIGURE 12-5. Progress Chart

STUDENT APPRAISAL SHEET

Name_____ Class_____ Date_____

Rated by_____ Score_____

ACCURACY OF SHOP AND CLASS WORK		ABILITY TO ACT AS A LEADER	
1. Makes many errors		1. Very dictatorial	
2. Is careless		2. Hinders	
3. Is fairly accurate		3. Fair	
4. Is careful		4. Good	
5. Is very accurate		5. Excellent	
CARE OF WORKING SPACE		ATTENDANCE	
1. Very untidy		1. Off a great deal no valid reason	
2. Careless		2. Off occasionally no valid reason	
3. Just passable		3. Off occasionally with valid reason	
4. Keeps space clean		4. Seldom off	
5. Space very clean and orderly		5. Never late or tardy	
HANDLING OF TOOLS AND EQUIPMENT		EXTRA ACTIVITIES	
1. Rough		1. Doesn't take part	
2. Careless		2. Seldom takes part	
3. Indifferent		3. Fair degree of participation	
4. Careful		4. Good degree of participation	
5. Very careful		5. Cooperates willingly, cheerfully	
SPEED IN SHOP AND CLASS		ATTITUDE TOWARDS CLASSMATES	
1. Very slow		1. Does not get along	
2. Slow		2. Looks down on them	
3. Ordinary		3. Neutral	
4. Fast		4. Good	
5. Very fast		5. Well liked, very cooperative	
USE OF WORKING TIME		ATTITUDE TOWARD TEACHERS	
1. Very wasteful		1. Disrespectful	
2. Loafs with others		2. Does not cooperate	
3. Passable		3. Average	
4. Busy		4. Cooperates	
5. Very busy		5. Very respectful, helpful	
USE OF MATERIALS		OBSERVANCE OF SAFETY RULES	
1. Wasteful		1. Disregards rules openly	
2. Careless		2. Disregards when not watched	
3. Fair		3. Average	
4. Good		4. Observes rules	
5. Very careful		5. Observes rules, has own rules too	
RESPONSIBILITY		ACCIDENT RECORD	
1. Buck passer		1. Many accidents thru carelessness	
2. Evades responsibility		2. Minor injuries thru carelessness	
3. Passable		3. Few minor injuries	
4. Likes it		4. Seldom injured	
5. Seeks it and handles it well		5. Never gets injured	
INITIATIVE		PERSONAL APPEARANCE, CLEANLINESS	
1. Doesn't exhibit any		1. Slovenly and dirty	
2. Very little		2. Untidy	
3. Average		3. Fair	
4. Offers many suggestions		4. Neat and clean	
5. Very original		5. Exceptionally pleasing	

Check only one item under each trait   Guidance and Placement Department
Middlesex County Vocational Schools

FIGURE 12-6. Student Appraisal Sheet

teacher a clear indication of progress towards the final measure of performance. Progress plotted and based on performance objectives will also prove of value to the future employer. It will be a clear indication of the types of performance the student successfully demonstrated in school. Such a record would mean much more to a prospective employer than a grade of A, B, or C. The progress chart used with a course of study based on performance objectives would tell what hands-on experiences the student has demonstrated in a specified period of time, and with what degree of success.

STUDENT NUMBERS

You might want to consider assigning each student a student number to be used in your class. This technique has been highly successful with some teachers.

Such a student number system is useful for a number of purposes. It can be used in connection with the student personnel system or on the progress chart. Rather than posting the names of the students in the class, a series of numbers known only to each student is recorded on the chart. It can be used in explaining how term grades were arrived at. Each student knows where he stands in relation to his fellow students.

SUMMARY

Part IV of this book deals with evaluation as it relates to the vocational program. The first chapter centered on the topic of the student and class records.

The vocational teacher is advised to keep adequate records of student performance in the vocational specialization. Remember that you as a teacher may be called upon at any time to justify the grade that appears on the student's report card. Such justification can be demanded by the student, his parents, or the administration of the school. In the case of borderline grades, justification can be very messy.

A variety of reporting forms and records has been displayed in this chapter. You may choose to use some of them in your program but take care that your system is compatible with the forms that your school requires, since these will be used in the final report.

EXHIBIT 12-1
CARPENTRY PROGRAM   CAMDEN COUNTY VOCATIONAL
STUDENT PROGRESS CHART

Student _____   Campus _____

	Date Completed	Instructor's Signature
I. Tool Room Attendant _____		
a. Safety	_____	_____
b. Hand Tools	_____	_____
c. Power Tools	_____	_____
d. Identification of Hardware	_____	_____
II. Carpenter Helper _____		
a. Safety	_____	_____
b. Hand Tools	_____	_____
c. Power Tools	_____	_____
d. Types & Identification of Lumber	_____	_____
e. Types & Identification of Hardware	_____	_____
f. Materials Handling	_____	_____
III. Layout Carpenter _____		
a. Footings and Foundations	_____	_____
b. Pre-Fabrication	_____	_____
IV. Carpenter Framing _____		
a. Floor Framing	_____	_____
b. Wall and Ceiling Framing	_____	_____
c. Roof Framing	_____	_____
V. Carpenter Roofer _____		
a. Roofing Materials	_____	_____
b. Shingling	_____	_____
VI. Dry Wall Applicator _____		
a. Thermal and Sound Insulation	_____	_____
b. Interior Wall Construction	_____	_____
VII. Carpenter Finish _____		
a. Completion of all prescribed units to Instructional Standards	_____	_____
VIII. Door Hanger _____		
a. Doors and Interior Trim	_____	_____
b. Interior Doors and Windows	_____	_____
c. Exterior Doors and Windows	_____	_____
d. Wood Joints	_____	_____
IX Stair Builders _____		
a. Stair Construction	_____	_____
b. Wood Joints	_____	_____
X. Siding Applicator _____		
a. Hand Tools	_____	_____
b. Power Tools	_____	_____
c. Exterior Wall Finish	_____	_____
XI. Hardwood Floor Layer _____		
a. Flooring	_____	_____
XII. Trim Setters _____		
a. Door and Interior Trim	_____	_____
XIII. Form Builder (Foundation) _____		
a. Form Building	_____	_____

EXHIBIT 12-2
INTERIM REPORT TO PARENTS

BOARD OF COOPERATIVE EDUCATIONAL SERVICES
OCCUPATIONAL EDUCATION DEPARTMENT
ERIE COUNTY

Date_____

Dear Parent:

Although you will be receiving regular grade reports from your Home School District which reflect your son's or daughter's progress in his vocational program at the Board of Cooperative Educational Services, we feel that it is important to keep you informed of any important factors concerning this program which may need your attention. The following report indicates that your son or daughter either is doing outstanding work or is having difficulty with work in his chosen field.

You are cordially invited to visit or call and discuss the work of your child with the Vocational Instructor or Guidance Counselor at _____.

Student's Name _____ Vocational Course_____

_____Student is doing exceptionally good work and should be complimented.

_____Improvement by the student is needed in the following categories:

CLASSROOM

_____Written
_____Practical

PERSONAL RELATIONS

_____Attitude toward classmates
_____Attitude toward teachers
_____Attitude toward regulations

RESPONSIBILITY

_____Attendance
_____Tardiness
_____Completion of work within
        assigned time

_____Care of tools and equipment
_____Work dress habits
_____Preparedness for work (uniforms,
        equipment, notebooks, etc.)

ADDITIONAL COMMENTS:

Home School _____   Instructor _____

cc: _____   Counselor _____

EXHIBIT 12-3
COSMETOLOGY RECORD

BOARD OF COOPERATIVE EDUCATIONAL SERVICES
First Supervisory District, Erie County

Kenton Center
Harkness Center
Potter Road

Name _____
Address _____ Phone _____

Date of Birth _____
Home School _____

Date of Admission _____
Date of Discharge _____
Reason for Discharge _____
Application for License _____ Date _____
State Board Exam Date _____ Passed _____ Failed _____

HOURS COMPLETED AND GRADES

Subject	Cosmetology I Possible	Cosmetology I Completed	Cosmetology II Possible	Cosmetology II Completed	Total Possible	Total Completed
Manicuring	35		40		75	
Permanent Waving	85		110		195	
Shampoo – Rinse – Scalp Treatment	50		50		100	
Finger Waving	160		60		220	
Facials & Make-up	50				50	
Color (Bleach-Tint)			100		100	
Hair Cutting	60		65		125	
Sanitation – Sterilization	30		20		50	
Shop Management	40		40		80	
Examinations & Tests	10		15		25	
Unassigned	20		40		60	
Total Hours	540		540		1080	
Final Grades						

INSTRUCTOR COMMENTS

Cosmetology I

Instructor _____

Cosmetology II

Instructor _____

THIS FORM IS TO BE CONSIDERED AN OFFICIAL TRANSCRIPT *ONLY WHEN SIGNED BY THE VOCATION DIRECTOR OR HIS OFFICIAL REPRESENTATIVE.*

Vocational Director _____

EXHIBIT 12-4
BURLINGTON COUNTY VOCATIONAL AND TECHNICAL HIGH SCHOOL
SELF EVALUATION GUIDE – EXPLORATORY PROGRAM

To The Student
This guide is for you. It is designed to assist you with your educational and occupational planning. Information obtained should be of value to you in making judgments about the occupational area(s) you plan to take in high school. The guide is to be completed at the end of each exploratory cycle. It will be conveniently located for you to use.

RATING CODE
VG-VERY GOOD   G-GOOD   F-FAIR   P-POOR   VP-VERY POOR

NAME (LAST) _____ (FIRST) _____

OCCUPATIONAL AREA

INSTRUCTOR

DATE

CHECK RATING (√)	VG	G	F	P	VP	VG	G	F	P	VP	VG	G	F	P	VP	VG	G	F	P	VP	VG	G	F	P	VP
1. My use of time																									
2. Use of tools and equipment																									
3. My interest was																									
4. Use of materials																									
5. My appearance																									
6. Observance of safety rules																									
7. Relationship with instructor																									
8. Relationship with students																									
9. My understanding of occupation																									
10. I would like to continue in this occupation next year	YES___ NO___ NOT SURE___					YES___ NO___ NOT SURE___					YES___ NO___ NOT SURE___					YES___ NO___ NOT SURE___					YES___ NO___ NOT SURE___				

COMMENTS

SOURCE MATERIALS

Larson, Milton E. *Teaching Related Subjects in Trade and Industrial and Technical Education.* Columbus, Ohio: Merrill, 1972.

Leighbody, Gerald B. and Kidd, Donald M. *Methods of Teaching Shop and Technical Subjects.* Albany, N.Y.: Delmar, 1966.

Silvius, G. Harold and Curry, Estele H. *Teaching Successfully in Industrial Education.* Bloomington, Ill.: McKnight & McKnight, 1967.

TESTING AND
TEST CONSTRUCTION

The testing and test construction phases of your teaching assignment are very important. Testing is important as one technique of student evaluation as well as a means of improving the instructional process.

THE PURPOSE OF TESTS

Teaching as well as learning is measured by testing. Poor test scores may indicate the need for improvement of the instructional process.

There are two main reasons we test or attempt to evaluate students: first, to evaluate student performance in order to provide learners with a more accurate assessment of themselves and their abilities, and second, to indicate to the teacher how he might improve his instructional technique and materials.

The testing procedure itself then leads to evaluation of student performance and reporting this evaluation to the student and his parents. Fair and accurate evaluation is not possible without a fair and suitable testing procedure. Both testing and evaluation should be based on some clearly stated objectives, otherwise the value of both are in doubt.

If tests are necessary, students have a right to know why. You, as the teacher, must be able to answer the following questions:

1. Why do I give tests?
2. Of what value are tests?
3. What type of test is best for my purposes?
4. Of what value are tests to my students?
5. When should I test?
6. How should I test?

EVALUATION BASED ON STATED OBJECTIVES

All meaningful evaluation must be based on clearly defined objectives. It makes little sense to construct, administer, grade, and return a test to students unless there was some purpose for it in the first place.

If you move from one state to another, you may be required to take another driver's test to obtain the proper driver's license. The test itself, at this point, is not important. The objective is the important thing. You must pass the test, be it written or performance, in order to get the license.

In our schools, we should attempt to make educational objectives just as clear as in the previous example, realizing of course that no two students are exactly alike. Perhaps not all students will meet *all* the stated objectives, but most will satisfy the essential objectives. Those of us in vocational education should, and can, lead the way in this type of situation.

Clearly stated objectives should be given to the students. They must know why they are required to take the test.

If you have attempted to construct your course of study along the procedure suggested in this book, you should, by this time, be aware of stating objectives. If the unit method of course construction is being used, some form of evaluation is essential before a student moves on to the next unit in the sequence. The evaluation device might be based upon some well-defined behavioral or performance objective, or some other criterion. In any event, some type of evaluation is essential. Some cases might lend themselves to a type of hands-on performance examination and others to a pencil-and-paper type of examination.

EVALUATION

EVALUATION BASED ON PERFORMANCE OBJECTIVES

In a course of study using units and performance objectives, one unit logically leads to the next. Unit one should be essential to unit two, unit two to unit three, and so on. Units based on performance objectives should be helpful to shop and laboratory instructors. Evaluation is built into well-written performance objectives. At times, it will still be desirable to construct an objective or essay type of test to supplement the other forms of evaluation. Such measures should still be consistent with the stated instructional objectives.

Some students might complete all of the performance objectives listed for the course you are teaching. Some level to identify satisfactory performance will have to be established to identify average or below average performance. However this is a matter of evaluation rather than test construction.

When the performance objectives are written, consideration must be given to how the objective will be measured. The details of this evaluation must now take place in the test construction phase. For example,

OBJECTIVE #15   The student, given five resistors and a (VTVM) vacuum tube voltmeter will be able to measure and record the resistance of each, within a tolerance of ±5 percent in five minutes.

To evaluate the student's performance on the objective, some procedure is called for. An accurate reading of the five resistors is essential. An accurate VTVM and someone to keep time with an accurate clock or watch is also essential. Some method of recording the information is also needed, as shown in Figure 13-1.

As indicated earlier, when writing the various objectives, you should have some idea of how you will evaluate performance. The example shown in Figure 13-1 is used for Performance Objective #15. You should probably have some method of recording the evaluation of each objective that is a part of your course of study. This recording method should be useful to the student being evaluated and to the teacher responsible for the evaluation. A student not meeting the performance criterion should know why he failed. After additional experience, he should be given the opportunity to retake the performance test.

TESTING AND TEST CONSTRUCTION

PERFORMANCE OBJECTIVE #15

Name _____

Time   start _____ stop _____ Total _____

Resistor	Actual Valve	Reading	% Variation
#1	_____	_____	_____
#2	_____	_____	_____
#3	_____	_____	_____
#4	_____	_____	_____
#5	_____	_____	_____

Student passed/failed the evaluation of Performance Objective #15.

Signed _____

FIGURE 13-1.   Recording Evaluation for a Performance Objective

PREPARING A TEST

The teacher and students must clearly understand the purpose of any test. Are you attempting to measure how well your students have mastered a certain unit of study? Are you attempting to rank your students to determine their individual strengths and weaknesses? Make sure that your students know why they are being tested.

Make an outline or plan for the test you plan to give. Is the plan consistent with the purpose of the test? This plan should indicate such things as:

1. Purpose (objective) of the test
2. Time for administration
3. Material to be included, consistent with the purposes
4. Types of questions (performance, objective, essay)
5. Number of questions

6. Method of evaluation
7. Student review or feedback

Many teachers find it helpful to write or type their questions on three-by-five-inch cards. The questions then can form a bank of questions for future use. Poor questions can be so noted or destroyed and replaced with new questions. After teaching the same course or subject a number of times, you will have developed a good number of test questions in your bank. You can then simply pull the number, type, and kind of question you need and give them to your typist for final typing. The two examples displayed in Figure 13-2 illustrate how the index system works.

Objective questions usually require a single word or number for an answer on a space provided near the question. Good objective tests can do a better testing job in less time than essay tests for many lessons or courses. As a rule, the objective test has more questions and requires a longer preparation time than the essay test.

Types of Test Items

The following examples show some of the types of questions that can be used in making out a test.

MULTIPLE CHOICE. The multiple choice test consists of an incomplete statement or question with several possible answers or completions listed below the question. The multiple-choice question measures knowledge more accurately than the true-false question since the probability of guessing correctly is reduced. The student marks or writes his choice from the four or five answers that are given. Test directions might read as follows:

> From each group of possible answers, choose the one you consider best for the statement. Place the letter that identifies the correct answer on the line before each question.

_____ The octane rating of gasoline tells us about its:
    a. color
    b. cost
    c. purity
    d. volatility
    e. anti-knock

_____ Three 10-ohm resistors are connected in parallel. What is their total resistance?
    a. 10 ohms
    b. 3⅓ ohms

COURSE NUMBER ___999___

TITLE _Electricity - basic_

UNIT _DC resistance_

PAGE & TEXT REFERENCE _Text, page 45._

In a parallel circuit, the voltage is always the
same across all the resistors.

a. <u>true</u>   b. false

UNIT _Parallel circuits_

REFERENCE SOURCE _Text, p. 101_

TYPE OF QUESTION _multiple choice_

The voltage forcing a current of 4 amperes
through a resistance of 40 ohms is

a. 10 volts
b. 160 volts (correct answer)
c. 0.1 volts
d. 16 volts

FIGURE 13-2. Example of a Card File System

      c.   30 ohms
      d.   5½ ohms
      e.   15 ohms

_____ What causes urine to move down the ureters?
      a.   blood pressure
      b.   peristalsis
      c.   gravity
      d.   diaphram contractions

_____ Cooking over or under direct heat is known as:
      a.   frying
      b.   broiling
      c.   braising
      d.   roasting
      e.   none of the above

_____ In T.I.G. welding, the electrode is used to
      a.   create the arc
      b.   fill the joint
      c.   transfer the gas
      d.   pass the electrical current

You should avoid including responses that are obviously wrong. Avoid establishing a pattern of correct answers associated with certain letters. Ending the lead statement with *a* or *an* can sometimes indicate the correct answer. Asking another faculty member to review your test questions may help you improve your writing ability.

TRUE-FALSE. In the most common form, the pupil makes a decision as to the most correct answer and writes *true* or *false* in the space provided. Test directions might read as follows:

_____ Current is measured by means of a voltmeter.
_____ There are 5280 feet in a mile.
_____ A filler rod is necessary to weld a corner joint.
_____ Of the two shielding gases, helium is heavier than argon.
_____ A small honey-colored seed with a toasted almond flavor is called a sesame seed.

Writing test questions takes time. In the true-false questions, by chance alone, a student could score 50 per cent. Avoid such words as "never," "always," "all," and "no" in writing true-false type questions. A wise student can often guess correctly that a statement using one of these words is false.

TESTING AND TEST CONSTRUCTION

COMPLETION OR FILL-IN. The student is required to write a word or number which completes the sense of the statement. This type of question is a recall item. Use this method only when it is essential to your needs and consistent with your testing objectives. Test directions for completion questions might read as follows:

> In the blank of each sentence write the word or number which best completes the sentence.
>
> The ignition is part of the _____ system of an automobile.
>
> The smallest division on a micrometer is _____ of an inch.
>
> To show the flow of gas in liters per minute or cubic feet per hour, a _____ is used.
>
> A disease caused by worms in infected pork is called _____.
>
> An abnormal constituent of urine, often found in the urine of diabetics, is _____.

The length of the line in the sentence should be the same in each item so as not to give any indication of the length of the missing word. It is easy, too easy, to copy sentences out of text books, remove one word, and use them as test items. Such a procedure is suitable only if one of your stated instructional objectives is to memorize the contents of a text book. Use caution in following such a practice.

MATCHING. A matching test has two lists. The student is required to check or mark the items on one list which are best related to the items in the other list. Only a code number or letter needs to be written. The two lists should have unequal numbers of items, but each item should have only one correct answer. Illustrations, charts, or photos can also be used and matched with statements which identify various features. Test directions for matching test items might read as follows:

> Place the letter from the list at the right in the proper space at the left to show which word best fits the statement.
>
> | | | |
> |---|---|---|
> | ( ) 1. Volt | A. | The unit of electrical power |
> | ( ) 2. Ampere | B. | The unit of electrical force |
> | ( ) 3. Ohm | | pressure |
> | ( ) 4. Watt | C. | The unit of electrical resistance |
> | ( ) 5. Coulomb | D. | The unit of current |

EVALUATION

MATCHING QUESTION
Match the following columns by placing the letter from in front of the term on the left in the appropriate blank beside the correct definition on the right.

A.	Anuria	–absence of urine	____
B.	Casts	–blood in the urine	____
C.	Dysuria	–difficult urination	____
D.	Glucosuria	–excessive urine	____
E.	Hematuria	–foreign to urine	____
F.	Oliguria	–normal component of urine	____
G.	Polyuria	–pus in the urine	____
H.	Pyuria	–retention of urine	____
I.	Urea	–scant amount of urine	____
		–sugar in the urine	____

Directions: Identify the various parts of the T.I.G. unit by using the correct letter.
Each answer is worth one point.

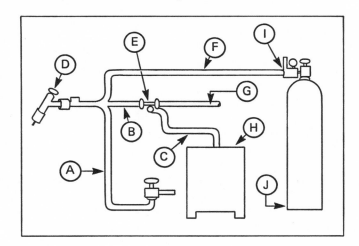

1.	torch	____
2.	power supply	____
3.	gas supply	____
4.	torch cable	____
5.	water supply	____
6.	gas hose	____
7.	welding cable	____
8.	gas regulating equipment	____
9.	fuse and hose assembly	____
10.	water outlet hose	____

TESTING AND TEST CONSTRUCTION

It takes times to construct good matching test questions. The basic question remains whether the matching test is the best type of test for the information you are attempting to sample.

ESSAY. Essay questions require students to express themselves in their own words. Such questions are evaluated on a more subjective than objective basis.

An objective test can usually cover a broad field of information in a given period of time. Essay questions take more time and usually cover only a limited field of knowledge. Essay questions are relatively easy to prepare but very time consuming to score.

Essay questions encourage pupils to organize their own ideas and express them clearly. If this is one of the stated objectives, you should find essay questions of value to you and your students.

Here are a few examples of essay questions:

Identify *five* different food service operations and give a brief explanation of the functions of each. Relate this information to an industry you know in the local area.

Explain the function of the kidney by means of its structural unit, the nephron, including the anatomical structures and physiological processes.

What are the specific advantages of gas-shielded arc processes?

The teacher's evaluation of an essay answer can end up being a very subjective review of the written response. The student may have the correct answer but not have expressed it in proper form. Students must be told if they are being evaluated on technical content only or on technical content and writing ability. The teacher should prepare some form of model answer for each essay type item and then compare the student's answer to the prepared model answer. This may help keep the evaluation more objective.

PERFORMANCE. Performance tests require students to use both their minds and hands in the solution of a problem. Performance tests are comparable to the criteria specified in well-written behavioral or performance objectives.

This type of test is the most valuable tool for the shop and laboratory teacher for evaluating the performance of his students. The teacher is able to observe and measure the individual's procedural techniques and the quality of the final product.

A well-constructed performance test will usually include directions for the person who will administer the test, directions for the student, a drawing or description of the job, a time limit, and a check list for evaluating the various phases of the job.

Performance testing is a time-consuming project, but of real value to both student and teacher. Performance tests are the best evaluation devices a shop or laboratory teacher can use to measure individual student achievement in terms of the stated course objectives.

TAKE-HOME EXAMINATION. You may find take-home examinations of value in your teaching situation. A take-home examination is, as its name implies, an examination that students take with them and complete on their own time. If the test items require research on the part of the student, a take-home examination may be the answer. It is expected that on such examinations students use whatever resources are available to them.

The success or failure of such an examination will depend to a large extent on the students in your class and how you prepare them for the evaluation. Do not let take-home examinations be the main type of your evaluation procedures. Use them only when their use is consistent with the stated course objectives.

A modified form of the take home examination is the open book examination. This type of examination is conducted in the school and encourages the student to use reference materials and text books in completing the examination. Since it is an in-school examination, some specified amount of time is usually given the students to complete it.

Answer Sheets

You may find the use of an answer sheet helpful on objective examinations. Rather than have students write the answers on the examination, a separate answer sheet is provided.

The use of answer sheets for objective tests usually makes the correction procedure much easier for the teacher. The answers to fifty or more questions can usually be put on one side of a standard-size piece of paper. Such a procedure eliminates going through five or ten pages of the normal examination.

The students should be allowed and encouraged to first place the answers on the question sheet. After they have answered all the questions, the final answers are marked on the answer sheet. The directions must state that the only answers to be considered will be those on the answer sheet.

Another advantage of using answer sheets is that the student may be permitted to keep the question part of the examination and hand in just the answer sheet. The teacher, time permitting, could immediately begin to

ANSWER SHEET

NAME _____ DATE _____

COURSE TITLE _____ UNIT _____

1. ____	26. ____	51. ____	76. ____
2. ____	27. ____	52. ____	77. ____
3. ____	28. ____	53. ____	78. ____
4. ____	29. ____	54. ____	79. ____
5. ____	30. ____	55. ____	80. ____
6. ____	31. ____	56. ____	81. ____
7. ____	32. ____	57. ____	82. ____
8. ____	33. ____	58. ____	83. ____
9. ____	34. ____	59. ____	84. ____
10. ____	35. ____	60. ____	85. ____
11. ____	36. ____	61. ____	86. ____
12. ____	37. ____	62. ____	87. ____
13. ____	38. ____	63. ____	88. ____
14. ____	39. ____	64. ____	89. ____
15. ____	40. ____	65. ____	90. ____
16. ____	41. ____	66. ____	91. ____
17. ____	42. ____	67. ____	92. ____
18. ____	43. ____	68. ____	93. ____
19. ____	44. ____	69. ____	94. ____
20. ____	45. ____	70. ____	95. ____
21. ____	46. ____	71. ____	96. ____
22. ____	47. ____	72. ____	97. ____
23. ____	48. ____	73. ____	98. ____
24. ____	49. ____	74. ____	99. ____
25. ____	50. ____	75. ____	100. ____

FIGURE 13-3. Model Answer Sheet

review the items on the examination. Students would then have immediate feedback as to how they did on the examination. If time did not permit an in-class review, the students could take the questions home and correct them on their own time. Figure 13-3 gives an example of one type of answer sheet.

Commercially prepared answer sheets are also available from a number of suppliers. Some are self-scoring. The student erases a block-out material that exposes a symbol that indicates if his choice was the correct answer. If his choice on a four-choice multiple choice type item was not correct, he goes on to make a second or even a third choice until he gets the correct answer.

RETURN AND EXPLANATION OF TESTS

If an examination is important enough to construct and administer, it seems essential that it be promptly corrected and returned to the students. Students are usually very interested in how well they did on the examination, and every effort should be made to review the results with them as soon as possible.

The correct answer for each item should be reviewed so that students will know where they went wrong. Part of the value of any examination is as a learning device. Learning should take place in the review of the test items.

The students should be encouraged to keep all returned papers, including examinations, for future reference and study.

Take time to review how the grades assigned to the students as a result of an examination fit into the total evaluation procedure. Explain the evaluation procedure used on the examination. It is easy to indicate the various raw scores, median, and mean score of the test. Each student will know his own score and be able to determine how well he did in relation to the other students in the class. This does not imply that the student who had the lowest score did not work to the best of his ability. All that is implied is a ranking of the test scores on one examination. The ability of each student must be considered in the final evaluation procedure.

SUMMARY

This chapter has presented basic material on testing and test construction which should be helpful to both beginning and experienced teachers. The teacher should explain to the class the purpose of the test and how the

EXHIBIT 13-1

CHECKLIST FOR REVIEWING LOCAL SCHOOL TESTS

This checklist covers the major test construction principles which teachers should observe in the preparation of local school tests. A negative answer to any question in the checklist indicates variation of local practice from accepted prinicples of test construction, suggesting that a reevaluation of local practice may be desirable with a view toward possible improvement of the test.

The items in the checklist cannot be added like the items of an examination to provide a "score" for a local school test. The questions are not of equal importance. Though a test may be satisfactory in all respects but one, that single deficiency may be sufficient to impair seriously the value of the test as a whole. The purpose of the checklist, rather, is diagnostic. It is designed to help insure that in the development of a local school test no important factor likely to influence the effectiveness of the test will be overlooked....

CLASSROOM TEST CHECKLIST

I. The Test Items
  A. Essay Questions
    1. Are essay questions restricted to measurement of objectives not readily measured by other item types?
    2. Are essay questions framed around specific problems, adequately delimited in scope?
    3. In general, is use made of a large number of brief essays rather than one or two extended essays?
    4. Does each essay question indicate clearly and accurately the desired extent and depth of the answer?
      a. Does the question indicate clearly how many reasons, examples, arguments, etc., are expected for full credit?
      b. Do the directions to "explain," "outline," "state," "compare," etc., indicate accurately the type of answer that will receive full credit?

  B. Completion Items
    1. Is each statement sufficiently unambiguous to limit the correct answer to one or two specific words or phrases?
    2. Is an excessive number of blank spaces avoided?
    3. Does the omitted part of each question come at the end or near the end of the statement?
    4. Are the items free from extraneous clues due to grammatical structure, length of blank space, etc.?
    5. Is use of the completion form generally avoided when items are essentially true-false in nature?
    6. Do computational problems indicate the expected degree of precision in the answer?
      a. Does the question indicate clearly the extent to which approximations or fractional answers are to be rounded?
      b. Does the question indicate clearly whether units (such as square yards or feet per second) are to be included by the pupil in his answer?

  C. True-False Items
    1. Is each item definite and unambiguous in meaning?
    2. Are the items based upon statements that are absolutely true or false, without qualifications or exceptions?
    3. Has the central point of each question been highlighted by placing it in a prominent position?
    4. Are the items free from double-barreled statements that are partly true and partly false?
    5. Are the items expressed as simply and directly as possible, without many qualifying clauses?

EXHIBIT 13-1, *continued*

6. Are trick questions avoided?
7. Is excessive "window dressing" in the items avoided?
8. Are negative questions avoided so far as possible?
9. Are the items free from specific determiners such as "always" and "usually"?
10. In the modified true-false type of item, is the word to be corrected clearly indicated by underlining or special type?

D. Multiple-Choice Items
1. Is use of the direct question or incomplete statement form consistent with the most effective presentation of the individual items?
2. Are the items presented in clear and simple language, with vocabulary kept as simple as possible?
3. Does each item have one and only one correct answer?
4. Is each item concerned with a single central problem?
5. Is the central problem of each item stated clearly and completely in the stem?
6. Does the stem, so far as possible, include all words repeated in the responses?
7. Are negative statements avoided?
8. Is excessive "window dressing" avoided?
9. Do the responses or choices come at the ends of the incomplete statements?
10. Are the responses grammatically consistent with the stem and parallel with one another in form?
11. Are all responses plausible and attractive to pupils who lack the information or ability tested by the item?
12. Are the responses, so far as possible, arranged in numerical or logical order?
13. Are the responses independent and mutually exclusive?
14. Are the items free from extraneous clues due to grammatical inconsistencies, rote verbal associations, length of response, etc.?
15. Is the "none-of-these" option used only when appropriate?

E. Matching Items
1. Do the premises and responses constitute homogeneous lists, each grouped around a single concept?
2. Are the lists of premises and responses relatively short?
3. Are the matching lists conveniently arranged?
   a. Are the longer, more complex statements used as premises and the shorter statements as responses?
   b. Wherever possible, are the responses arranged in some logical order to simplify matching?
4. Do the directions indicate clearly the basis upon which the lists are to be matched?
   a. If a single premise is to be matched with several responses, is the pupil advised that this is permissible?
   b. If a single response is to be matched with several premises, is the pupil advised that this is permissible?
5. Are the matching lists free from extraneous clues due to grammatical construction, rote verbal associations, etc.?
6. Is the list of responses longer than the list of premises to preclude guessing by elimination?

SOURCE: *Improving the Classroom Test*. Albany, N.Y.: University of the State of New York, 1975, pp. 51–53.

results of the test will be used. When both the teacher and the class know the purpose of the test, a common understanding of the value of the testing procedure will be appreciated by all parties.

A variety of test items were presented along with the examples of the most complex items. A good test takes time to design, prepare and evaluate. Used in the proper manner, it should serve as a learning experience for students. It will tell both the teacher and the student what is known and what more remains to be learned. It will point out to the teacher what items must be covered in more detail if all students are going to master the content of the course.

The next chapter will be concerned with the evaluation of student performance and test results.

ACTIVITIES

1. Prepare a forty-item test for your specialization. The test should consist of ten of each of the following:

   a) True-false items
   b) Multiple choice items
   c) Completion items
   d) Matching items

2. Write five performance objectives for students in your class. Develop an evaluation recording technique for each performance objective. (Use Figure 13-1 as an example.)

3. Specify your test construction criteria.

SOURCE MATERIALS

Armstrong, Robert, et al. *The Development and Evaluation of Behavioral Objectives*. Worthington, Ohio: Jones, 1970.

Green, John. *Teacher Made Tests*. New York: Harper & Row, 1963.

Katz, Martin, ed. *Making the Classroom Test: A Guide for Teachers*. Princeton: Educational Testing Service, 1961.

University of the State of New York. *Improving the Classroom Test: A Manual of Test Construction Procedures for the Classroom Teacher*. Albany, N.Y.: The University, 1975.

14

EVALUATION AND GRADING

DEFINITION

Evaluation is that procedure that leads to some type of grade on some type of grade reporting form. It may be subjective, objective, or a combination of both. The grade may be in the form of a written statement, numerical value, or letter grade. The evaluation system and standards of the person doing the evaluation can influence the grade. Two people evaluating an objective test would be expected to arrive at the same grade. However, two or more people evaluating an essay question may arrive at a number of different grades. The evaluation of essay questions, student work performance, and student behavior all tend to be subjective, and the grades may very well vary. The person doing the evaluation must be accountable to the person being evaluated and be able to explain and defend the procedure used to arrive at the grade in question. Every time a teacher posts a grade on a student's paper, report card, or record form, the teacher must be ready to defend the grade to the student, the student's parents, and the school administration.

This chapter presents the most important materials concerning evaluation and grading of vocational students.

232

THE PURPOSE OF EVALUATION

The purpose of evaluation is to assess the degree of success the learner had in mastering certain performance or instructional material that was presented to him. The person conducting or assessing the evaluation should keep in mind the individual abilities of the learners.

The practical side of evaluation in most school systems is to determine if a student passes or fails a course. Clearly stated objectives or criteria understood by the students will help make such evaluations easier.

As time goes on, perhaps schools will move closer to the self-pacing concept of instruction making the educational system a zero-reject system. The educational system should be geared to success, not failure. Your efforts to use the self-pacing system and performance objectives might be a step in the right direction.

Each teacher must give consideration to the purpose or purposes of evaluation. Why do you evaluate? Is it because you find yourself a member of an educational system that requires some type of evaluation system to measure student performance and a feedback system of information to the parents and students? The teacher must remember that a system designed to evaluate student performance is also a means of evaluating teacher effectiveness. In essence, every time a teacher evaluates a student, he is also evaluating his own effectiveness as a teacher. Continual poor results from the students may mean the instructional level is too high or that the teacher is not very effective in the role of teacher.

The teacher should make very clear to the learners the purpose of the evaluation system as well as how it will function. Better yet, the teacher should establish a system of evaluation and be able to explain it early in the course to the students. The system must be compatible with the school-wide system of evaluation and grade reporting.

A SYSTEM OF EVALUATION

The effective shop or laboratory teacher should establish and maintain a system of evaluation appropriate to the specialization being taught and to the school-wide system of evaluation and grading. The teacher must be able to explain the system so that students will know how they are being evaluated and, in turn, graded. The teacher can relate the standards applied in class to the industrial standards that the student will face in the world of work. Some minimum level of performance should be expected and allowances made for achievement above or below the expected level. The material displayed in Figure 12-3 is an example of an Employability Profile that is

EVALUATION

used in one vocational education program. You will note that the evaluation is based upon what experiences the student has been exposed to rather than just a final letter grade. This type of profile should make a lot more sense to a potential employer than a grade of, say, 80 per cent or a "B" in the subject of Dental Receptionist and Laboratory Assistant. However, it is but one system that is used. You must be able to work within the system of evaluation used in your school.

THE PURPOSE OF GRADES

The grades assigned to students on tests or for final evaluation usually indicate some degree of success or failure on the test or term work. The method or system used for grading in the school must be followed by all teachers.

   The grade given is the result of some evaluation technique used by the teacher. All the students must understand this technique if the grade is to be of any value to them.

   If a student received a 66 as his final grade in automotive mechanics, what does this really mean? If 65 is the minimum passing average, it means he passed the course. If 70 is the minimum passing average, it means he failed the course by 4 points. If a 66 is passing, does it mean the student mastered 66 per cent of the course work? Does it mean he is 66 per cent of an automotive mechanic? Does it mean he can do 66 per cent of the work normally expected of an automotive mechanic? Only the person responsible for the evaluation can answer these questions. The evaluator must also be able to explain the grade to a potential employer.

INDIVIDUAL DIFFERENCES

In arriving at a final evaluation for a class and, in turn, each student, always attempt to evaluate each individual in terms of his own abilities. The decision that you as the teacher must make concerning each student can have a positive or negative effect upon the student.

   Each student has strengths and weaknesses, and evaluation in a course should take these into consideration. You can, and will, find extreme situations, the high ability student who, for any number of reasons, fails to perform to the level of his ability versus the low ability student, who overperforms. In such situations, the teacher is truly a decision-maker, and must stand accountable for the decision.

   The Student Evaluation form in Figure 14-1 is a type of evaluation and

NAME _____ DEPARTMENT _____ DATE _____

Rate by checking appropriate column for each characteristic.

1. ACCURACY is the correctness of duties performed.

Makes frequent errors	Careless; makes recurrent errors	Usually accurate; makes only average number of mistakes	Requires little supervision; is exact and precise most of the time	Requires absolute minimum of supervision; is almost always accurate

2. QUANTITY OF WORK is the amount of work an individual does in a work day.

Does not meet minimum requirements	Does just enough to get by	Volume of work is satisfactory	Very industrious; does more than is required	Superior work production record

3. DEPENDABILITY is the ability to do required jobs well with a minimum of supervision.

Requires close supervision; is unreliable	Sometimes requires prompting	Usually takes care of necessary tasks and completes with reasonable promptness	Requires little supervision; is reliable	Requires absolute minimum of supervision

4. HOUSEKEEPING is the orderliness and cleanliness in which an individual keeps his work area.

Disorderly or untidy	Some tendency to be careless and untidy	Ordinarily keeps work area fairly neat	Quite conscientious about neatness and cleanliness	Usually neat, clean and orderly

FIGURE 14-1. Student Evaluation Form

STUDENT'S NAME _____   CLASS ASSIGNMENT _____

DATE _____   EVALUATOR _____

Evaluation Key: 10 — Superior;   9 — Above Average;   8 — Average;   7 — Below Average;
6.5 — Less than Minimum Acceptable Standards in this Instructional Area

WORK HABITS

	10	9	8	7	6.5
1. How well does the student *cooperate* with his instructor?					
2. How well does the student *get along* with fellow students?					
3. How good is the student's *initiative?*					
4. How well does he *keep his work area and equipment?*					
5. How would you describe the student's *grooming and hygiene?*					

Total Evaluation — Work Habits . . . . _____

WORK SKILLS

	10	9	8	7	6.5
6. How *productive* is the student as compared with other trainees for this occupation at this point in time?					
7. How good is the *quality* of his production when compared with the standards of quality one might expect of a trainee for this occupation at this point in time?					
8. How would you rate his *ability to learn* his currently assigned tasks?					
9. How does he *adjust* to new assignments?					
10. How well does he make *appropriate decisions?* (Judgment)					

Total Evaluation — Work Skills . . . . _____

TOTAL GRADE — WORK HABITS AND WORK SKILLS . . . . . . _____

FIGURE 14-1 *continued*

reporting form that deals with work habits and work skills. Many employers would be more interested in this type of evaluation than in a simple numerical or letter grade reported on a report card. However, this type of evaluation is a very subjective type of record based on the observations of the teacher. The person using this form has to be very careful in applying equal standards to all being evaluated.

Each of us has strengths and weaknesses and it is these things that we must look for in considering the individual students who enter our classes. It is our job as teachers to try and get as much out of each student as we can, but not push our students beyond their limits. The difficult part is determining the individual level of ability. There is no simple answer to this question.

DETERMINING GRADES FOR STUDENTS

The teacher working in a system that requires some form of letter grade or numerical marking system must determine very early in the school year the system of evaluation to be used. The system must be explained so that students will know how they are being evaluated.

It is essential for the teacher to review the course requirements on which a grade or grades could be based. Some of these may be:

1. Project work
2. Class experiments
3. Homework assignments
4. Performance tests
5. Pencil-and-paper tests, both objective and essay
6. Performance on live work (repairs on autos, radios, etc., or in the service areas, such as cosmetology or food service.)
7. Observations of student work habits (However, it must be noted that this tends to be subjective rather than objective. Use care if you use this in the evaluation system.)

After the teacher determines the course requirements, it then becomes a matter of determining how much any item will count in the final evaluation process. If you use number grades, you will need some basic information about statistics.

STATISTICS FOR TEACHERS

This section reviews some of the most common statistical terms a teacher should be familiar with. It is designed as an aid for shop and laboratory teachers in the grading and evaluation of students.

ITEM.   An item is a single question or exercise or part in a test.

ITEM WEIGHT.   Item weight is the raw score point value assigned to an item. You should show the credit for each item on the test. This will tell students which questions are of the most value and which are of lesser value. Many people believe that each test should have a value of 100 per cent, which means that if you give a ten-item test, each item should count 10 points. However, each item could count just 1 point and the total test equal 10 points. What is more important is to show the student the value of each item. For example:

> 5.   The ignition is part of the _____ system of an automobile. (2)
> (The number in brackets after each item refers to the number of points given for a correct answer.)

ITEM ANALYSIS.   An item analysis is a basic operation that all published tests go through. It means that an analysis of the responses to each item on a test is made, plotting both correct and incorrect responses. This analysis can help the teacher improve the test. The teacher can do the analysis, or it can be done by a show of hands. As the teacher is reviewing the test with the class, he can ask the students how many selected items a, b, c, or d for a multiple-choice item and come up with an analysis such as follows:

> Item #15.   a)   4
> b)   10 (correct answer)
> c)   1
> d)   0

On completion of an analysis, the teacher would look for items that no one had wrong, which may be a tip off for a poor question with little or no discrimination. On the other hand, an item that no one had correct could indicate a poorly worded question and perhaps tell the teacher that the subject matter was not covered clearly in class. Figure 14-2 presents an item analysis based on a test that contained twenty items.

RAW SCORES.   This is the first quantitative result obtained in scoring a test, usually the number of right answers. If a test has a value of 10 points, the

SUBJECT: _____ DATE OF TEST _____

NUMBER OF STUDENTS _____

ITEM ANALYSIS FOR TWENTY-ITEM TEST

Item #   (Items 1–10 are true/false questions.)

	F	T
1.	10	12
2.	22	0
3.	0	22
4.	15	7
5.	18	4
6.	4	18
7.	20	2
8.	22	0
9.	11	11
10.	9	13

(Items 11–20 are four-choice multiple-choice questions.)

	A	B	C	D
11.	10	2	3	6
12.	0	0	22	0
13.	20	1	0	1
14.	0	0	20	2
15.	18	3	0	0
16.	8	8	6	0
17.	22	0	0	0
18.	11	11	0	0
19.	0	22	0	0
20.	4	4	4	10

FIGURE 14-2.   *Item Analysis*

raw score values could vary from 0 to 10. This could be based on a system of either correct or wrong answers. Five could stand for 5 correct or 5 incorrect answers. Most people score in terms of the number of correct answers. If a test has a total point value of 100 points, a range of raw scores from 0 to 100 would be possible. Based on a total of 100 points a student who scored 90 points would have a score of 90 per cent. This can also be applied to a test based on 10 points. A student who scores a 9 would also have 90 per cent correct based on a 10 point system.

EVALUATION

A teacher can keep a raw score total for a total marking period of five weeks. The total number of points possible over a five-week marking period may number 500 or more. With a raw score total of, say, 700, students could vary from 0 to 700 points. This when plotted gives a frequency distribution on the raw scores that then would have to be converted to some form of marking system to report grades. This is where a basic knowledge of statistics comes in handy.

FREQUENCY DISTRIBUTION. A frequency distribution shows how scores are distributed over a range. It also shows the number of times the various scores occur within the distribution. The material presented in Figure 14-3 is an example of a frequency distribution. The data presented is based on a test with a high value of 100 points. Twenty-two scores are reported with a range of 64–95. One student scored a high score of 95 and at the low end there was one score of 64.

RANGE. The range consists of the difference between the lowest and highest scores on a test.

N. This is the symbol commonly used to represent the number of cases in a distribution. N, standing for number, will be used to stand for the total number in a distribution or the total number taking a test. The N used in the example in Figure 14-3 is 22 and would be displayed as $N = 22$. This notation will be used in the remaining portion of the chapter.

MEAN. This is the sum of a set of scores divided by the number of scores. This can also be described as the arithmetic mean or the average. The mean can be determined by adding the scores and dividing the total by the number of scores. If six students scored 80, 85, 93, 67, and 91, the total of the five scores would be 416. This total would be divided by the N of 5, which gives a mean of 83.2. The mean or the simple average of the five scores is then 83.2. The example presented in Figure 14-4 will show a simple procedure for determining the mean when 25 is the N. This procedure is suitable for the shop or laboratory teacher.

MEDIAN. The median is the fiftieth percentile. It is the value which separates the scores into two equal parts, half of which will fall above the median value and the other half below. Generally, for the classroom teacher, a determination of an approximate median is all that is needed. With scores of 100, 90, 80, 70, it would be safe to say that the median would be approximately 85. Fifty per cent of the scores are above 85, 50 per cent are below, and 85 is midway between 80 and 70. In this illustration, 85 would also be the mean score. Figure 14-5 illustrates the plotting of a median within a distribution.

DATA:

Possible high score — 100

Number of scores — 22

Range — 64–95

Scores	Frequencies
95	1
94	0
93	1
92	0
91	0
90	0
89	0
88	2
87	2
86	1
85	0
84	0
83	0
82	0
81	2
80	1
79	1
78	0
77	0
76	3
75	0
74	0
73	0
72	1
71	1
70	0
69	0
68	3
67	0
66	2
65	0
64	1

Total scores 22

FIGURE 14-3. Frequency Distribution

This basic knowledge of statistics should be adequate for the shop or laboratory teacher in most situations. The teacher who is able to compute a mean and median score for a test or evaluation will be better prepared to explain test results to student, parents, and administration if the need arises.

After a test is given or an evaluation system of some type is used, some feedback should be given to the students. If the raw scores are listed with the highest score first and the lowest score last, it is easy to determine

EVALUATION

DATA:

Possible high score — 50

Number — N = 25

Range — 10–48

STEP I		*STEP II*	*STEP III*
Plot actual scores with tally		Multiply scores times frequency	Add sum of scores
48	//	48 x 2 = 96	96
47	///	47 x 3 = 141	141
45	///	45 x 3 = 135	135
41	/	41	41
35	/	35	35
32	///	32 x 3 = 96	96
29	//	29 x 2 = 58	58
23	////	23 x 4 = 92	92
19	//	19 x 2 = 38	38
15	//	15 x 2 = 30	30
10	//	10 x 2 = 20	20
	N = 25		782

STEP IV

Divide total of scores by the N.

782 ÷ 25 = 31.28

31.28 is the mean score.

FIGURE 14-4. *Calculation of Mean*

the range, mean, and median. This gives students a clear idea of how well each did on the evaluation compared to others in the class. This procedure does not take into account the individual differences between members of the class.

Example A		Example C	
Scores	Frequencies	Scores	Frequencies
10	/	95	/////
8	/	91	/////
6	/	89	/
----------------------Median-5		Median-87-------------------------	
4	/	85	/
2	/	78	///
1	/	76	/////
		70	//

Example B		Example D	
Scores	Frequencies	Scores	Frequencies
99	//	90	///
97	///	88	/////
90	//	78	///
----------------------Median-89.5		Median-77--77----------------- //	
89	//	76	/////
85	///	69	/
80	//	65	/////

FIGURE 14-5. *Approximation of Median*

ASSIGNMENT OF GRADES

After the test and evaluation process have been completed, the assignment of grades still remains. This is where the teacher has to make professional decisions about each student and should take individual abilities and differences into consideration. It is also at this point that the performance criteria

EVALUATION

established for the course and student must be considered. All of this must be related to the marking or evaluation system that the school is using to report grades.

If a student's final grade averaged to a 64, with an established passing average of 65, would you fail the student? Would you be able to defend your failing a student by 1 point? Is your evaluation system so good that the difference of one point means the difference between passing and failure? This kind of situation becomes a moment of truth for the teacher and honest objective consideration must be given to such a case.

In vocational subjects, what does a grade of 80 per cent or B really mean to the employer? Does it mean that a student can do 80 per cent of the work expected of him by the school? Can a student receive an 80 per cent in automotive mechanics and not be able to do a brake overhaul job on a foreign car? Vocational teachers should report grades, but should also be able to report what kinds of practical work a student has done and is able to do. This could be much like the reporting system shown in Figure 12-3.

There is no one easy answer to the assignment of grades. It is an important consideration for each and every teacher. In a class of thirty, it is not one decision but thirty. Each of these thirty decisions is a serious matter to the student.

SUMMARY

The content in this chapter applies to all areas of instruction and the basic statistics used are suitable to all areas of evaluation. The techniques suggested should prove helpful to experienced as well as inexperienced teachers.

Evaluation is that process that a teacher goes through to arrive at some form of grade for a student. The grade in many cases is a negative reinforcement for those not passing the course, program, or test. Everyone has a right to fail, and sometimes failure will result in a greater effort on that person's part. As a teacher, remember that you make the decision about who fails and who passes. Never make the statement that "I failed a student" or "I passed a student." It is much better to say that the student passed or failed.

The basic statistics presented demonstrate how to find the mean and median score within a distribution of scores. This type of information can then be presented to the students so that they understand the method of evaluation being used. The evaluation and grading system should be explained to each class at the beginning of the course; it is criminal to change the system or modify it in the middle of the course. Students like this type of treatment and it does work.

244

SOURCE MATERIALS

Glasser, William. *Schools Without Failure*. New York: Harper & Row, 1969.

Holt, John. *How Children Fail*. New York: Dell, 1971.

Katz, Martin, ed. *Short Cut Statistics for Teacher Made Tests*. Princeton: Educational Testing Service, 1964.

Ross, C. C. and Stanley, Julian C. *Measurement in Today's Schools*. New York: Prentice-Hall, 1954.

VanDalen, Deobold B. *Understanding Educational Research*. New York: McGraw-Hill, 1962.

APPENDIX

SCHOOL FORMS AND PAPER WORK

A school is a large operation and, as such, a certain amount of control and organization is necessary to keep things moving along as smoothly as possible. This operation depends on the cooperation of teachers and students.

When the central office puts a due date on a certain form, please try to comply with the request. Your organizational system and personal work schedule will have to be adjusted to keep up with the necessary paper work. Good organization on your part will cut down on the time needed for paper work and other details associated with being a teacher.

Each school system has its own records and school forms. It would be almost impossible to show and list all the forms that a teacher might be requested to use. A few examples of the more common forms will be presented along with a brief description of their use.

The emergency information card (Figure A-1) is one of the most important records a school is required to have. It is used by school personnel in the event of sickness or accident befalling a student. It indicates a phone number where either parent can be contacted in an emergency. It also indicates the family physician and dentist.

The classroom or homeroom teacher who is responsible for having students take the cards home for parents to sign should impress the impor-

Middlesex County Vocational and Technical High Schools

☐ East Brunswick ☐ New Brunswick ☐ Perth Amboy ☐ Woodbridge

EMERGENCY CARD

Name of Student _____ Grade _____
                      Last   First

Home Address _____ Phone _____
                  Street   City

Father's Name_____Place of Employment_____
                                        Phone _____

Mother's Name_____Place of Employment_____
                                        Phone_____

Physician's Name_____Address_____
                                        Phone_____

Dentist's Name_____Address_____
                                        Phone_____

Responsible adult who will care for child if parent or guardian cannot be contacted

Name_____Address_____Phone_____

Name_____Address_____Phone_____

see reverse side

Does student have any allergies?_____
                                        explain

Date of last tetanus_____

We urge you to avail yourself of the protection afforded your son-daughter
through school accident insurance.

In the event of extreme emergency, permission is hereby granted to transport
my child to the nearest hospital. I will assume responsibility for payment of emergency care.
Permission is hereby granted to call family physician.

_____   Signature _____
        Date   Parent or Guardian

FIGURE A-1. Emergency Card

PUPIL'S DAILY PROGRAM

Name_____   Class or Grade_____

Time	Pe-riod	MONDAY		TUESDAY		WEDNESDAY		THURSDAY		FRIDAY	
		Class	Rm.	Class	Rm.	Class	Rm.	Class	Rm.	Class	Rm.
	1										
	2										
	3										
	4										
	5										
	6										
	7										
	8										
Home Study											

Locker No._____   Home Room_____

FIGURE A-2. *Pupil's Daily Program*

tance of this card on the students. The teacher should check the cards as they are returned for accuracy and completeness.

The pupil's daily schedule is recorded on the Pupil's Daily Program card (Figure A-2), and it has two main purposes. First, in the event a student has to be contacted by someone on the school staff, the program card can be used to determine where a student should be at any given time. Secondly, in the event of some emergency or problem at home, a parent might request an early release for the student. The office staff can check the program and locate the student in the best and quickest manner. Teachers and students must be aware of the importance of this card. The student should take care in filling out the program, and the teacher should check for completeness.

Attendance laws and regulations vary from state to state. The attendance card shown in Figure A-3 is but one type used in one school district. School attendance is usually taken during an administrative period known in most schools as homeroom period.

The teachers assigned as homeroom teachers are responsible for keeping and recording an accurate listing of students' attendance. Some states require a state attendance register to be maintained. It is a very important document since state aid in terms of dollars usually depends on student attendance at school.

The concerned teacher will try to impress on his students the importance of good attendance. Attendance can be related to getting to work on

	1	2	3	4	5	6	7	8	9	10	11	12	13	14	15	16	17	18	19	20	21	22	23	24	25	26	27	28	29	30	31	Pres.	Abs.	Tardy
Sept.																																		
Oct.																																		
Nov.																																		
Dec.																																		
Jan.																																		
Feb.																																		
Mar.																																		
Apr.																																		
May																																		
June																																		

Register No._____   Birth Date_____

Name   District   Class

FIGURE A-3.   Attendance Card

time and not missing work any more than really necessary. Many employers will want to know and see the attendance records of first-time employees while they were in a training program. The teacher by his own work habits will be an example to the students in his classes.

The attendance card (Figure A-3) has spaces for daily attendance and monthly totals at the end of each month. The information from this card is then placed on the official district attendance record.

You will have to consult your school's *Teacher's Manual* to see how to handle attendance procedures. Use care and be accurate in taking attendance if you are assigned as a homeroom teacher.

School policies vary a great deal concerning payment of student fees and requiring students to pay for materials and supplies. If schools require teachers to handle student fees and money in general, receipts should be used. In some cases, as seen in Figure A-4, the money is paid directly to the main office. If you need to handle student fees, use care and the necessary receipt forms.

Student control is essential to the operation of a school. It requires the cooperation of both students and faculty. If a teacher is careless about

Date _____

Received from _____

_____ $ _____

for _____

Middlesex County
Vocational and Technical High School
Date _____

Received from _____

_____ $ _____

for _____

_____
Principal

FIGURE A-4. Student Receipt

student control, students will catch on and usually make the situation a bad one.

The tardy admission slip (Figure A-5) is usually issued by a person in the office to students who come to school late. The student takes the form and goes to his scheduled class. He presents the slip to the shop or classroom teacher and should be admitted to class. The teacher should indicate in his class book how late the student entered the classroom. Students who attempt to enter late and do not have a slip should be told to report to the office for

Middlesex County Vocational and Technical High School

Tardy Admission Slip

Date _____

Please Admit _____

to _____

_____ Time _____

Note Due:

FIGURE A-5. Tardy Admission Slip

Class _____   Date _____

The following pupils were absent this
☐ A. M.   ☐ P. M.

_____ | _____

_____ | _____

_____ | _____

_____ | _____

_____ | _____

_____ | _____

Tardy
_____

_____

_____

_____

Instructor_____

FIGURE A-6.   *Shop Attendance Report*

one, It informs the school attendance officer that the student has arrived at school.

The attendance card in Figure A-3 is for use by the homeroom teacher. The shop attendance report (Figure A-6) is used by the shop or laboratory teacher to report absent and tardy students to the office. It is used as a control device. For example, if a student reports to homeroom but skips his morning shop period, his absence is reported by the shop teacher. The report is usually sent to the office at the end of the normal school day. Whoever handles cases of this type would notice the fact that the student was in homeroom but skipped his morning shop. The student should be called to the office and asked to explain where he was during the morning. This is a student control device and requires the support of all faculty members to make the system work.

APPENDIX

Time Lost Sheet

Class.................   Date.......................

NAME	TIME OUT	TIME IN	TOTAL MINUTES
Sign legibly	Time limit three (3) minutes		

FIGURE A-7.   Time Lost Sheet

Permission to Visit the Guidance Counselor

STUDENT'S NAME_____ CLASS_____

DATE_____ TIME_____

INSTRUCTOR_____

APPROVED BY

_____
PRINCIPAL

FIGURE A-8. *Permission to Visit the Guidance Counselor*

The time lost sheet (Figure A-7) is another student control device. If a student, during the course of the shop period, has to leave the shop, he is required to sign out on the time lost sheet. Likewise, when he returns, he should sign back in. It must be pointed out that the student requests permission of the instructor before signing himself out. The instructor should know where every student is at all times. In the event a student is needed in an emergency, a teacher could be in an embarrassing situation if he did not know where one of his students was at that moment.

Some schools require a special type of form for students who wish to see their guidance counselor. Figure A-8 is a form which can be made out by the instructor giving the student permission to see his counselor. Since many counselors see students on a schedule basis, it is possible the student will return to the shop and be instructed to report back to the counselor at another time.

A counselor who wants to see a student would make out the permission slip and have it given to the student during homeroom period. At the correct time, the student would show the slip to his classroom teacher and be excused from class. When the student leaves the counselor, the time should be indicated on the slip, which is returned to the classroom teacher.

The exact procedure used in your school may vary somewhat from that indicated above. The important thing to remember is that this is another control device to insure the smooth operation of the school.

State laws vary concerning the control of visitors in schools. Most

VISITOR'S PASS

This Pass will admit the bearer

TO _____ *Dept.*

GOOD ON THIS DATE ONLY

Date _____

_____ **Principal**

To be taken up by instructor and returned to office.

FIGURE A-9. Visitor's Pass

schools have a sign on the door or wall instructing all visitors to report to the office. In some states, failure to do so is a legal violation, and the person is subject to fine.

After reporting to the office, the person, if need be, is issued a visitor's pass (Figure A-9) and allowed to carry on his business. Upon completion of the visit, the pass is returned to the office.

This is a control device to keep undesirable people out of school. A teacher, seeing a school-age youngster he does not recognize, should check into the situation. Likewise, adults not associated with the school should have a visitor's pass with them while in the school building.

Vocational educators have long recognized the value of industrial visits, commonly called field trips. Students are taken by bus from the school to the plant or location at which the visit is to be made. The purpose is to acquaint the students with the actual industry being studied in the school shop.

Most schools use some type of permission slip which must be signed by a parent before the student is allowed to go on the field trip. The basic purpose is to inform the parents that the student will be out of the school building on a field trip. The school, of course, is still responsible for the safety and well-being of the student while he is on the trip.

The shop teacher making plans for the trip should make sure the necessary forms are completed by the students. A typical example of a form used is shown in Figure A-10. The teacher should collect the forms and make sure he has one for each student going on the field trip.

Student control and proper behavior is the concern of every administrator and teacher in any school. Shop teachers, just as any teacher, should

FIELD TRIP PERMIT

Date_____19____

Name_____

has my permission to go with the_____grade

pupils of the_____

school on a field trip to_____

_____

on_____19____
　　　　　　Date

_____
　　　　　　　　　　　　　　　　　　　Parent's Signature

Approximate time of return will be_____

FIGURE A-10.　Field Trip Permit

try to handle behavior problems by themselves and not refer every problem case to the office. However, most teachers will at some time have a problem which has to be referred to the administrator in charge of discipline. Some form of office referral or report of misconduct (Figure A-11) is used in most school systems. The teacher writes out the report and sends it with the student to the office. It is a good idea for the teacher to go to the office as soon as possible to check on the outcome. However, never leave your shop or

REPORT OF MISCONDUCT

Name......................Room...........Date..............

Nature of Offense ....

....

....

Disposition of Case..

....

....
Teacher's Signature

FIGURE A-11. Report of Misconduct

laboratory class unsupervised for even a minute to take a student to the office.

Whenever you use an office referral, make sure you follow up on the outcome of the case. Use office referrals only as a last resort. Handle as many problems as possible yourself. But remember to always be firm, fair, and consistent when dealing with your students.

Close contact between the school and home is essential to insure the best educational system possible. At times, it may be necessary for the teacher to request a conference with the parents of certain students. The interview request form shown in Figure A-12 is one way to inform parents of the need for such a conference. Such a form may be signed by the teacher or principal, depending on the nature of the conference.

If the shop teacher wants to set up such a conference, it would be wise to make a carbon copy of the request and leave it with the student's guidance counselor. This way, if the parent fails to come in or call, the carbon copy can remain in the student's folder as an indication that the request was made.

School policy varies concerning production work in the shops. Many shop teachers are glad to take on production work if it is applicable to the types of learning experiences taking place at that time. However it is hard to justify work which does not fit into your teaching schedule, so do not be afraid to say no to such requests.

One type of production work form is shown in Figure A-13. Most forms require the approval of the principal or department chairman. Check

INTERVIEW REQUEST

Date_____ 19___

To the Parent or Guardian of:

_____ Room_____
Name of Pupil

_____
Address of Pupil

For the best interests of your son-daughter we ask that you call at the school personally, as soon as possible, to confer with the undersigned.

It is our aim to stimulate and direct the growth of each pupil physically, mentally, and socially; and to help the home in building and securing desirable character habits of study and attitudes in the pupil. Only by working together can we secure the right conditions essential to proper growth and development of your son or daughter.

If a pupil's progress is below the desired standard, a conference is requested. The most convenient time for such a conference is

_____

Kindly bring this slip with you

Yours respectfully,

_____ School

_____ Principal
Teacher

_____

Date of interview_____ 19___

With whom_____

Remarks _____

_____

_____

FIGURE A-12. *Interview Request*

Middlesex County Vocational and Technical High Schools

PRODUCTION WORK

New Brunswick____   Woodbridge____   Perth Amboy____

Month_____19____   Department_____

SHOP ORDER NO.	QUANTITY	DESCRIPTION	ACTUAL CHARGE	APPROXIMATE VALUE
MR-8				

FIGURE A-13.   Production Work

your local school policy and procedure before undertaking any production work.

Another type of production work form is shown in Figure A-14, which is used as a sales slip for a product, in this case, baked goods. Please note the statement near the bottom of the form, "Note To Our Customers."

APPENDIX

MIDDLESEX COUNTY
VOCATIONAL AND TECHNICAL HIGH SCHOOL
BAKE SHOP 955

Wanted _____

      (day)   (date)

Name _____

No.	Item	@	Ext.
	Total		

		Amt.	Date
Taken by			
Put up by			
Given out by			

─Note To Our Customers─

We appreciate your orders because they give our students a chance to practice the skills they are here to learn. Products are priced accordingly.

Orders that do not fit into our LEARNING PROGRAM cannot be accepted or filled in some cases.

ALL orders must be paid for when placed unless authorized by instructor.

FIGURE A-14. Production Work Form

259

There are many other types of forms which may be used in your school. Obtain a copy of any form that is available and that you may have need of in your own work situation. You may want to get requisition, budget, equipment, and equipment repair forms as a start. Forms vary a great deal from school to school and it is important that you be familiar with those used in your own school.

Try to keep up with all the necessary paperwork so that you don't fall behind in your day-to-day activities. At times, you may feel that 50 per cent of your time is spent doing paperwork and this can happen if you let it. Good organization and use of your time and student assistance can help relieve some of the burden.

INDEX